Ron
Pyle

Critiques of Contemporary Rhetoric

Critiques of Contemporary Rhetoric

Karlyn Kohrs Campbell

State University of New York at Binghamton

Wadsworth Publishing Company, Inc., Belmont, California

ISBN–0–534–00135–1

L. C. Cat. Card No. 76–179424

Printed in the United States of America

1 2 3 4 5 6 7 8 9 10—76 75 74 73 72

To
Paul

who makes my a life a metaphor

Preface

The last decade has produced a renaissance of interest in rhetoric. The national debate over the Indochinese War, the issue of campus dissent, the rhetoric of Black Protest, and the mushrooming public concern for "Spaceship Earth" have all contributed to an increased interest in persuasive discourse and its consequences for our society and for mankind. Never has man's persuasive power been more evident or appeared more ominous. Never has the need for persuasion seemed greater or its potential for increasing public awareness and mobilizing public action seemed more essential. Never has the need to understand the nature of persuasive discourse and to develop techniques and standards by which to analyze and evaluate them been more crucial.

Critiques of Contemporary Rhetoric is addressed to those of you who feel deep concern for national and international issues, who recognize the significant role that public persuasion has played and will play in creating, exacerbating, and resolving conflicts, and who wish to become informed and effective critics of contemporary persuasion. The chapters that follow attempt to define the characteristics of rhetorical discourse, to explain man's capacity to influence and be influenced, and to describe both the processes and the purposes of rhetorical criticism. I have compiled this book in the belief that the powerful resources of persuasion can be mobilized for the public good only if consumers of rhetoric become sophisticated critics of the persuasion that daily bombards them. I have also written it because of my deep commitment to the value of rhetorical criticism.

Chapter 1 examines two basic questions: What are the distinctive characteristics of the discourses—speeches, essays, articles, even reports—called "rhetoric"? What are the characteristics of language that make men capable of and subject to influence? Chapter 2 defines the essential characteristics of rhetorical criticism and describes the stages in the process of criticism. Chapter 3 explores the different standards and systems a critic may use in describing, interpreting, and evaluating rhetoric. Chapters 4 through 8 contain the texts of contemporary persuasive discourses followed by criticisms that illustrate and apply the concepts in the first three chapters. I have added critiques to illuminate these concepts and to provide fertile ground for discussion of the nature of rhetoric and criticism and of the merits of the particular evaluations I have made. The final chapters contain the texts of four discourses on other contemporary issues. At that point you may try your hand at rhetorical criticism, struggle with its problems, discover the excitement of revealing how a discourse works, and find the critical concepts to interpret and judge such criticism. (Of course, I encourage you to construct your own critiques of the discourses I have evaluated.)

Interestingly Spiro Agnew has said, "no nation depends more on the intelligent judgment of its citizens." If we are to thresh out our difficult problems in a democratic fashion, if we are to find the means to make necessary social changes, we shall have to find ways to tolerate dissent, and we shall have to protect our right to evaluate and analyze public persuasion as jealously as we have ever guarded any basic freedom. In short we shall have to become working rhetorical critics.

This book would never have been written had it not been for KPFK, Pacifica Radio, Los Angeles, its listeners, its staff, and in particular, Larry Moss, the station's director of news programming. I was invited by Larry Moss to do a rhetorical criticism as part of KPFK's news commentary and encouraged to continue with a series of such broadcasts. The scripts for those broadcasts formed the materials from which this book developed. I am deeply grateful to Larry Moss and the staff of KPFK not only for the opportunity to function as a rhetorical critic outside the academic world but for the complete freedom in which I was allowed to work. I am equally grateful to the KPFK listeners whose numerous responses were warm, stimulating, and insightful.

Acknowledgment is also due to the various readers of all or part of this manuscript whose comments have been encouraging and valuable. I want to express particular gratitude to Michael Prosser of Indiana University and to Wayne Brockriede of the University of Colorado. Professor Prosser's positive comments and suggestions for changes were most helpful, and Professor Brockriede's lengthy critique included an attention to detail and a comprehension of and respect for fundamental concepts that were far beyond anything I had expected or experienced.

K.K.C.

Contents

One

Rhetoric, Language, and Criticism

Any aspiring critic struggles with temptations in his criticism of the rhetoric that surrounds him. A speaker or a writer treats issues that deeply involve many people and directly affect their lives. Because of this personal involvement one of the most important motives of a critic is to expose and debunk rhetoricians who advocate positions and policies that he disagrees with and to strengthen and support the arguments of rhetoricians who reflect his points of view. The motive is not a dishonorable one, for criticism is always partially persuasion. The critic asks his reader to see a discourse as he sees it, to understand and judge it as he does. In other words criticism is never wholly impartial and objective. In all cases it is to some extent evaluative, judgmental, and subjective. The temptation is to make criticism simply and wholly persuasion—a subtle and dangerous persuasion—that masks advocacy behind the appearance of objectivity and technical analysis. The ethical problem reflected in the tension between the essential persuasiveness of rhetorical criticism itself and the temptation to become a subtle but powerful advocate for the rhetoricians with whom the critic agrees is central to the evaluation of contemporary persuasive discourse. The solution to the problem requires familiarity with the nature of rhetorical discourse and the nature of rhetorical criticism.

Although the study of the principles and practice of rhetoric is perhaps the most ancient academic discipline, the term *rhetoric* is ambiguous and difficult to define because it is used in three ways: It is often employed to refer to public statements that are abstract, empty, bombastic—"full of sound and fury, signifying nothing"; such state-

1

ments are "mere rhetoric." It is frequently used to refer to written or oral discourses that intentionally or unintentionally alter attitudes and mobilize action. Finally it is sometimes used to refer to academic disciplines that study the techniques, principles, and practices of persons who deliberate, argue, and advocate in order to alter attitudes and behavior. As used in these pages and in the title of this book, *rhetoric* refers to persuasive discourses, written and oral, that alter attitudes and actions.

At times the term can and should be used in a much broader sense. That usage includes functions other than persuasion such as interpersonal identification, confrontation, self-identification, alienation, negotiation; and it includes forms other than written and oral discourse such as gestural communication, the use of space, and certain dimensions of music, dance, painting. In this book *rhetoric* is used in the narrower sense, not because the broader usage is in any way illegitimate but because the main intent of the book is to focus attention on rhetorical works that are formed and planned. The works most fully formed, most carefully planned, the works that display rhetorical characteristics most clearly, indeed, the paradigm cases of rhetoric are almost invariably written and oral discourses.

Rhetorical discourse has five typical characteristics. First, such discourse is *propositional*—that is, formed from complete thoughts, with the sentence as its basic unit. Rhetorical discourse is designed, created, and formed in contrast to nonartistic discourse, such as casual conversation, which consists mainly of sentence fragments joined by association. Rhetorical discourse is prose discourse, planned and structured in such a consistent and coherent fashion as to justify and announce certain conclusions.[1] In this sense it is most proper to speak of an "art" of rhetoric or persuasion.

Second, rhetorical discourse is *problem solving*. What constitutes a problem may be described loosely as the difference between what is wanted and what exists, or more formally as the discrepancy between one's personal goals, or values, and the existing structures, procedures, and conditions. This characteristic focuses attention on the evaluative, subjective, and personal dimension essential to rhetoric. The substance of rhetoric is not information but the evaluation of information. For example, one student may be happy with a C grade; his goal is to "get the ticket," a college degree. Another student may be upset with a C; his goal is graduate school, and such a grade may prevent him from reaching it. Although the situations are identical, the evaluations are different.

Rhetorical discourse is concerned with the values that individuals and societies should adopt, with the implications of those values, and

[1] For further discussion of rhetoric as prose discourse, see Northrop Frye, *The Well-Tempered Critic* (Bloomington: Indiana University Press, 1963), pp. 1–51.

with the means to express or attain those values. In this sense rhetoric is properly termed *advisory*,[2] for directly or indirectly it always gives advice, takes a position, evaluates, and judges. Rhetoric is never simply the transmission of information; rather it is an interpretation of information. It gives an evaluation and asks the listener or reader to see or feel as the rhetorician does.

Third, rhetorical discourse is *public*, addressed to others. Although clearly some of the most important rhetoric is intrapersonal deliberation or self-persuasive argument,[3] for the most part rhetoric is public because it deals with circumstances and conditions that require concerted action. That is, although an individual seeks to convince himself of the rightness of his actions or motives through internal dialogue, rhetoric deals primarily with problems that the individual cannot solve himself; he requires others who share his attitudes, his way of looking at things, and who are willing to commit themselves to similar cooperative action. For this reason rhetorical discourse is usually concerned with social questions: What does it mean to be a citizen? How are conflicts between citizens to be decided? What should a society be and do? In short, rhetoric deals with issues that require shared attitudes and cooperative action for their resolution.

Fourth, rhetorical discourse is *practical*. It seeks to alter symbolic behavior, attitude, and/or action. Rhetoric is not simply an expression of feelings or a sharing of information for its own sake. Instead it is designed to communicate feelings and information for a purpose, to evoke a concrete and relevant response from an audience to the rhetorical situation. Rhetoric, then, is characterized by its instrumentality, its intent to produce further behavior.

Finally, in what seems to be a contradiction, rhetorical discourse is *poetic*.[4] The term *poetic* refers here to the degree to which a discourse displays ritualistic, aesthetic, dramatic, and emotive qualities. For ancient theorists rhetorical and poetic qualities were two elements of a unified art of composition. Even today we refer to great rhetoricians as "eloquent" and to great rhetoric as "eloquence." Such references indicate that the poetic qualities of rhetorical discourse are often an important basis for evaluation. We expect rhetoric to be part of public rituals and to celebrate and reinforce cultural values. We expect rhetorical discourses to be pleasing to the ear, and we treasure those that move us deeply, such as Martin Luther King, Jr.'s "I Have a Dream,"

[2] The essential concepts of and sources for "advisory rhetoric" are discussed in Walter Fisher, "Advisory Rhetoric: Implications for Forensic Debate," *Western Speech*, Vol. 29 (Spring 1965), pp. 114–119.

[3] The intrapersonal dimension of rhetoric is discussed in Don M. Burks, "Persuasion, Self-Persuasion, and Rhetorical Discourse," *Philosophy and Rhetoric*, Vol. 3 (Spring 1970), pp. 109–119.

[4] The intrapersonal and poetic elements in all language are discussed in Paul N. Campbell, "Language as Intrapersonal and Poetic Process," *Philosophy and Rhetoric*, Vol. 2 (Fall 1969), pp. 200–214.

John Kennedy's Inaugural Address, and William Faulkner's Nobel Prize Speech. We expect rhetoric to build to a climax, to heighten conflict, to leave us with a sense of closure, and to move us by speaking to our experiences and feelings. Although the poetic dimension in rhetorical discourses is usually less prominent than in those works we term "literature," rhetoric that ignores the poetic in its language and movement is incomplete and likely to be ineffective. The degree to which a rhetorical discourse evinces poetic qualities will directly affect the size of the potential audience, now and in the future, and the nature and intensity of the response evoked. In other words, although poetic qualities are more typical of literary works, the poetic is an essential characteristic of rhetoric.

Rhetoric, then, refers to written and oral discourses that are persuasive; and rhetorical discourses are characterized as propositional, problem solving, public, practical, and poetic. Such discourses are formed and planned works dealing evaluatively with issues and information. They address themselves to issues requiring shared attitudes and cooperation for their resolution. For this reason, they seek concrete changes in language, attitude, and action. Finally their power to move arises from poetic qualities of language and structure.

The Bases of Rhetoric

One of the most puzzling and interesting aspects of rhetorical theory is the search for explanations of how and why man is capable of and subject to persuasion. How and why is it that he can influence others and be influenced by them? Unless one believes that each man is totally isolated from all other men, one must assume that man can influence and be influenced to some degree. Based on this assumption there are three predominant explanations for human persuadability.

The first, and most familiar explanation is that man is persuadable because he is a rational being capable of conceptualizing alternatives and of spelling out the implications and consequences of those alternatives.[5] Through persuasive discourse man can discover available options framed in language and examine them for coherence and consistency, and by deliberation select one alternative rather than another. The rationalistic explanation emphasizes the importance of choice in any theory of human influence and stresses the lack of empirically verifiable answers to the questions central to rhetoric. *Thus rhetoric treats issues about which honest and informed men may disagree.*

The second explanation is that man is persuadable because he has certain psychophysiological drives and needs that can easily be stim-

[5] Traditional, rationalistic theory and criticism are described in Lester Thonssen and A. Craig Baird, *Speech Criticism* (New York: The Ronald Press Company, 1948).

ulated and directed by outside forces and must be satisfied.[6] As an animal, man has basic survival requirements, including food and water, shelter and sex; as a social being, he requires group membership and a sense of belongingness. Within human cultures and societies, group values emerge, such as courage and honesty, which are bases for the individual to attain esteem and status within the group.

Not only can the rhetorician activate man's basic animal drives, but he can direct these drives so that their satisfaction is consistent with cultural values. The psychophysiological explanation emphasizes the importance of "attention" and "motivation" in rhetoric. It calls the critic's attention to the rhetorician's appeals to individual needs and social values as important elements in the process by which he seeks to motivate his audience. Although it has certain manipulative overtones, this explanation focuses attention on the important physiological and psychological components of persuasion and encourages research into physiological and psychological bases for human behavior.

The third explanation of human persuadability is that man is a symbol-creating, using, and misusing animal.[7] Man is rhetorical because he detects, identifies, and interprets stimuli surrounding him in order to assign meaning and then uses these meanings to determine his future behavior. Hence persuasion is a result of the interaction between man and his language; man is capable of persuasion because of his ability to respond linguistically and semantically.

When used symbolically, a stimulus, such as a word, represents the user's concept of an object, event, person, condition, or relationship; and that concept indicates an attitude or meaning that another person can perceive, identify, and interpret. In turn the stimulus and its attendant concept can influence the other person's attitude toward the object, event, condition, person, or relationship. Supporters of this explanation believe that the individual creates and develops his own sense of identity, his concepts of others, and his images of the world in symbolic interactions. In addition they believe that motivation of a human is distinct from that of other animals because the interaction between man and language transforms physical, biological, and animal needs and drives into peculiarly human motives.

The human individual, as he engages in the rhetorical process, is an inseparable compound of animality and symbolicity. The process of becoming human, of being socialized and acculturated, is essentially a symbolic one; that is, basic drives are linguistically transformed into

[6] The psychophysiological approach to rhetoric is exemplified by Wallace Fotheringham, *Perspectives on Persuasion* (Boston: Allyn and Bacon, 1966). The author's discussion of "choice" on pp. 75–104 serves to contrast this approach to traditional rationalism. See pp. 155–173 for the role of language in persuasion as seen from this point of view.

[7] The definition of man as a symbol-using animal is developed and explained by Kenneth Burke, *Language as Symbolic Action* (Berkeley: University of California Press, 1968), pp. 1–24.

socially and culturally acceptable motives that can never be divorced from their symbolic origins. Through language and interaction with other individuals, man transforms his basic needs into socially accepted forms and chooses culturally acceptable means for their satisfaction.

This explanation of human persuadability focuses attention on the significant role of language in rhetorical transactions. It suggests that the rhetorician's language provides important clues to his attitudes and values, and it encourages the critic to be concerned with how the speaker or the writer uses particular terms to describe or classify.

The criticisms in this book reflect this point of view. This is not to suggest that the other explanations are of no value or should be ignored. In fact the three explanations are interrelated; the thorough critic is concerned with the argumentation, the psychological appeals, and the language and symbolic strategies of a rhetorical discourse.[8]

The Rhetorical
Dimension of Language

In its ordinary sense the term *language* refers to verbal symbol systems such as English or French. However, language includes a wide variety of verbal and nonverbal symbol systems, constituted not only of words but also of space, movement, sound, pitch, time, color, and so on. In their most developed forms these symbol systems are called dance, music, sculpture, architecture, painting, poetry, and so forth. Through the use of many different symbol systems, man can order his sensations and assign them meaning so they become identifiable experiences and perceptions that he can remember. Instead of being bombarded with the "blooming, buzzing confusion" of myriads of totally different and unfamiliar stimuli, language enables man to make order of this chaos and to deal with a structured world of recognizable objects, events, and conditions. Because verbal symbol systems are of greatest concern here, the analysis that follows centers primarily upon the characteristics of verbal language.[9]

The first dimension of language is naming—the process by which an individual notices, recognizes, and labels certain elements or qualities in himself and in the world around him. Names permit the individual to recognize and select relevant or significant events and phenomena from the multitudes of surrounding stimuli. The vocabulary of an individual or group is a rough index of what is and has been important to that

---

[8] For a more extensive discussion of these three explanations of human persuadability, see Karlyn Kohrs Campbell, "The Ontological Foundations of Rhetorical Theory," *Philosophy and Rhetoric*, Vol. 3 (Spring 1970), pp. 97–108.

[9] An excellent discussion of the capacities of language is provided in John Condon, *Semantics and Communication* (New York: The Macmillan Company, 1966).

person or group, an assumption reflected in the "verbal ability" sections of many college entrance examinations.

Naming becomes a process of ordering the world and of focusing an individual's attention. A name is not a label for one thing but rather for a group or category of relatively similar objects or events with certain similar qualities or characteristics. Nouns, verbs, adjectives, and adverbs are labels for categories of objects, actions, events, feelings, qualities, and characteristics found or noticed under many different conditions at many different times by many different persons. Even conjunctions and prepositions label certain kinds of recurring relationships. As labels referring to categories, names permit a person to ignore the differences among individual objects and events and to lump them together into manageable units to which he can respond in relatively similar ways. For example, if I identify an object as a "chair," I respond to it as, and predict that it will be, a man-made object with arms or a back, intended for the category of actions labeled "sitting," and I ignore the unique characteristics of the particular chair. However, if this process is to work, a set of criteria must exist to determine whether a particular object, person, or event may be included in a particular category, that is, whether it may be labeled with a particular name. Such sets of criteria are called *definitions*.

A definition specifies the essential attributes or characteristics that something must have to be labeled in a particular way by a particular linguistic community. For example, if I am to decide whether a creature should be called a "heifer," I must know whether it is bovine, female, and has never calved. In relation to this particular name category, I need not be concerned with characteristics of size, color, breed, or the presence or lack of horns. These "accidental" characteristics simply distinguish one heifer from other heifers and do not determine whether the creature falls into the larger category.

A definition of the common and essential characteristics that place something in a category and give it a label is usually called a denotative definition. For all terms there are specifiable, commonly understood bases for application or definitions. But people do not learn meanings from dictionaries where such definitions are collected. They learn them in particular situations, by having experiences with the use of labels and with members of the categories to which they refer. In the specific contexts in which meanings are learned, individuals have feelings about the situations, categories, and labels. Consequently names are not simply factual or descriptive; they are labels for an individual's experiences with and for his feelings about the acts, events, objects, persons, conditions, and relationships to which they refer. As a result names are evaluative because they stand for experiences and feelings; hence meaning includes subjective qualities.

At a minimum, names are evaluative because they indicate interest and relevance. For example, if you knew the meaning of the word *heifer*, this knowledge indicates some past experience in which that term had some importance. If you grew up on a farm, as I did, you learned the word because it represented particular problems, financial values, and special functions. Or if you heard the Biblical story of Samson and his riddle, you may have learned the meaning of the word to understand the metaphorical use of it (Judges 14:18). Or if your only contact with the word has been in reading this discussion you may remember it and associate it with this book or with rhetoric.

The evaluative capacity of symbols is great. When we speak of "loaded" or "emotional" language, we refer to words that produce strong feelings; the person who hears or reads them has vivid, intense associations because of his experiences with the terms. No matter how limited the degree of emotionality, no term understood by or meaningful to a person is simply neutral or factual. It is always bound up with his experiences and will always contain evaluative associations resulting from those experiences.

The letter of Eldridge Cleaver and the criticism following it illustrate this process. For Black Protest speakers, *Negro* is not a neutral term referring to a category defined by certain "racial" characteristics. Instead the term is filled with all the negative evaluations these people have experienced. *Black* is also an evaluative term, but it is positive in this case with its sense of pride, beauty, and power. The words used to label acts, persons, objects, events, qualities, and relationships indicate an attitudinal bias in an individual's perception of the world, based on his experiences. In addition the words he uses influence the attitudinal biases of others because the situations in which the words are used become new or additional experiences for both the user and the audience. By labeling or relabeling a particular phenomenon, a rhetorician places it in a category and thereby associates it, for the reader or listener, with other members of that category. Or he attempts to change the associations of a label by providing the audience with new experiences designed to alter their feelings about the category and hence their evaluation of it. Much rhetoric is directed toward changing labels, a first step in altering attitudes and behavior.

The critic must carefully examine a rhetorician's attempts to structure or restructure the perceptions and attitudes of his audience through his use of language. In other words one reason why persuasion is possible is that language has the capacity to name, categorize, define, and evaluate; and among the most important rhetorical stratagems are the techniques the rhetorician uses to change the verbal behavior of his audience.[10]

This concept of language is closely related to the defining character-

---

[10] For further discussion of the role of "images" in rhetoric, see Kenneth Boulding, *The Image* (Ann Arbor: University of Michigan Press, 1956).

istics of rhetorical discourse. Rhetoric, in a narrow sense, may be thought of as an explicit, highly articulated version of the suasory dimension of language itself. As an art of prose, rhetoric is discourse that makes complete statements, draws conclusions, points out implications, and suggests evaluations. Just as language is never neutral or impersonal, so rhetoric, no matter how expository or informative it may seem, is always designed to gain acceptance for certain ways of evaluating and labeling things. Similarly, as the naming process includes feelings and attitudes toward what is named, so rhetoric, because it is concerned with problems, seeks to label and evaluate what is in ways that make present conditions unsatisfactory, even intolerable, for the audience.

Rhetorical discourse is rooted in the essential characteristics of language and in the capacities of humans as symbol-using creatures. Unless the language of a writer or speaker pleases and moves other people, unless it arouses feelings and associations, such language will be meaningless and irrelevant; it will remain outside experience, outside the associations that give significance and importance to concepts and terms.

Rhetoric as
Conflict and Process

Numerous attempts have been made to describe the process of communication, and many models have been developed to diagram the stages, elements, and factors in a communicative transaction.[11] However, many of these models describe communication and rhetoric in rather static, linear terms. Some of the analyses are valuable and may be found in supplementary readings, but here the concern is to locate and explore the conflicting forces and tensions that are inherent in the persuasive situation. These tensions and conflicts are not fixed and static; they are the core of the rhetorical *process*.

Rhetoric arises out of conflict—within an individual, between individuals, or between groups. The basic conflict involves the perception of a problem—a gap between existing conditions and desired change, or between current policies and practices and proposed goals. Often the conflict involves values: psychological and financial rewards of racism versus equality; technological development versus preservation of the environment; military defense versus human survival; desire for peace versus fear of defeat. The conflict becomes public controversy when an

[11] Essays that develop and explain a variety of communication models may be found in Joseph DeVito, ed., *Communication: Concepts and Processes* (Englewood Cliffs, N. J.: Prentice-Hall, 1970).

individual assumes that other people will feel or recognize the conflict as he perceives it.

In the process the rhetorician risks rejection by his audience, attacks from others, and forced changes in his attitudes and perceptions.[12] Public reaction to Spiro Agnew's speeches about the mass media and to Eldridge Cleaver's statements on Black Power are familiar illustrations.

In broad terms the rhetorician induces discussion, choice, and action.[13] Although he seeks agreement, that is rarely an adequate description of the rhetorician. Richard Nixon seeks to alienate the "doves" from the moderates; Agnew seeks to threaten newsmen and alienate them from their audience; Cleaver and other Black Protest speakers challenge and threaten white audiences; Edgar Friedenberg states explicitly the values that, if held, will eliminate certain persons from his audience. In other words, much contemporary public rhetoric, rather than being conciliatory, provokes argument and dissent. It seeks to stimulate disagreement and to polarize individuals into conflicting groups.[14] The critic must recognize that a rhetorician *selects* his audience or audiences and may seek different responses from different groups. In all cases the rhetorician sifts out from his potential audience those persons he wishes to reach and believes he can influence and induce to join him in his purpose.[15]

A critic is faced with difficult evaluations. For example, I condemn the divisiveness of Nixon in his Vietnam speech but praise the divisiveness of Black Power speakers. Similarly I condemn the address of George Wald for its failure to speak to the general audience but approve of Friedenberg's selective alienation on the grounds of honesty and argumentative consistency. Another critic might disagree for just reason. Still, conflict is a frequent and perhaps desirable outcome of persuasive discourse. Good rhetoric must stir up public discussion and controversy; it must speak to basic human conflicts if it is to fulfill its functions as rhetoric. The selections in this book are a reflection of that belief.

Some conflict arises in rhetorical situations because the intent of the speaker may be different from the purposes of the audience. Regardless of the rhetorician's purpose or message the audience may seek confirmation of prior beliefs and attitudes. For instance, white audiences

[12] The concept of risk in argumentation is developed in Maurice Natanson and Henry W. Johnstone, Jr., eds., *Philosophy, Rhetoric and Argumentation* (University Park: Pennsylvania State University Press, 1965), pp. 1–20.

[13] The notion that the end of rhetoric is choice and action is developed in Thomas Olbricht, "The Self as a Philosophical Ground of Rhetoric," *Pennsylvania Speech Annual*, Vol. 21 (September 1964), pp. 28–36.

[14] The characteristics of confrontative rhetoric are described in Robert L. Scott and Donald K. Smith, "The Rhetoric of Confrontation," *Quarterly Journal of Speech*, Vol. 55 (February 1969), pp. 1–8.

[15] The ways in which rhetoricians select audiences are discussed in Edwin Black, "The Second Persona," *Quarterly Journal of Speech*, Vol. 56 (April 1970), pp. 109–119, and Craig R. Smith, "Actuality and Potentiality: The Essence of Criticism," *Philosophy and Rhetoric*, Vol. 3 (Summer 1970), pp. 133–140.

listening to Black Protest speakers or to excerpts from such rhetoric in the media may seek confirmation of a prior belief that such advocates are "black racists," and this message is what they "hear." Similarly the criticism of Agnew's addresses suggests that the audience's wish to express, confirm, and legitimize their resentments of "Eastern, elitist, liberal" newsmen resulted in some positive response toward Agnew. The critic should be aware that he is an active participant in the rhetorical process and has personal beliefs he wants confirmed, regardless of the purpose of the rhetorician whose discourse he is examining.

The rhetorician, in this view, initiates a continuous process that arises out of conflict, and as a result he is open to risks of attack and rejection, especially when his purposes differ from those of his audience. The process places great emphasis on change, which both rhetorician and audience resist; as a result a variety of responses from different audiences may lead to confrontation and polarization. The medium of this process is language, which allows the rhetorician to label and relabel, structure and restructure his own reality and that of the audience to induce changes in thought, attitude, and action. The discourses in this book are part of cultural dialogues not yet completed. The issues are unresolved, and policy questions are still unanswered. Any rhetorician is not likely to induce major change through a single discourse. At best he might stir up an internal dialogue in the audience, causing them to rethink and reconsider and leaving them open to future persuasive messages on the issue.

Rhetoric as a Discipline

The discipline of rhetoric is the study of man's symbolic attempts to make order of his world, to discover who he is, and to interact with others in ways that make his life more satisfying. In this sense rhetoric includes the study of the persuasive dimension of all language. More specifically, it examines those discourses that are distinctively suasory. As a theoretical discipline it explores three interrelated questions: (1) How and why is man capable of and subject to influence, and what is the nature of human motivation? This question explores the intrapersonal dimension of rhetoric, the relation between man and his language. (2) What is the relationship between rhetoric and reality? This question focuses on the symbolic relationships between man and the world around him.[16] (3) What is the relationship between rhetoric and history, and as a consequence what are the ethical standards that may be used to evaluate persuasive discourse? This question is concerned

[16] An excellent discussion of the relationship between rhetoric and reality may be found in Robert L. Scott, "On Viewing Rhetoric as Epistemic," *Central States Speech Journal*, Vol. 18 (February 1967), pp. 9–17.

with the relationships between man and man.[17] All rhetorical theorizing attempts to answer one or more of these questions.

Rhetorical Criticism

Rhetorical criticism is the description, analysis, interpretation, and evaluation of persuasive uses of language. These stages in the critical process have three general purposes: (1) to describe discourses accurately and perceptively so that the unique qualities of individual discourses or genres of discourse become clear to the reader; (2) to analyze internal elements and stratagems of discourses, and to describe the relationship between discourses and their cultural contexts and the persuasive forces impinging on them; (3) to make evaluative judgments of discourses based on explicit criteria so that the grounds for evaluation are apparent to the reader. Well-done, thorough criticism increases the reader's capacity to appreciate rhetorical discourses and enables the general audience to make informed and deliberate judgments based on persuasive discourse. In addition such criticism improves the quality of persuasive discourse in society, and tests and modifies both theories of rhetoric and critical systems.[18] Unfortunately there is far too little criticism of contemporary persuasion; and when it appears, such criticism is available only to limited, usually academic, audiences. It is even more tragic that powerful political figures, such as the President and Vice President, attack critical efforts despite the essential part that careful criticism plays in the decision-making process of a democratic society.

[17] Some of the essays exploring ethical standards may be found in Richard L. Johannesen, ed., *Ethics and Persuasion* (New York: Random House, 1967).
[18] An innovative statement of the nature of rhetorical criticism may be found in Lawrence Rosenfield, "The Anatomy of Critical Discourse," *Speech Monographs*, Vol. 25 (March 1968), pp. 50–69.

Two

The Process of Rhetorical Criticism

In its final form rhetorical criticism is the result of a three-stage process: The critic locates the unique characteristics of a discourse or group of discourses; he analyzes the internal workings of the discourse and its relation to its milieu; and he selects or creates a system of criticism to make evaluative judgments of its quality and effects. The three stages are not distinguishable in a written criticism; the critic must go through these stages in *preparation* of his critique. *In the final criticism each process is integrated into a coherently developed structure.* There is no guarantee that performing these steps will make a "great" critic, but the chance of producing insightful and creative criticism is greatly increased.

The critical approach used in this book rests on a strong personal commitment to organic or situational criticism in contrast to formulary or prescriptive criticism. The prescriptive approach to criticism applies a formula or set of prescriptions to all discourses. For example, such criticism frequently examines discourses in terms of the classical canons of invention, disposition, style, and delivery and the classical modes of proof—*logos*, *pathos*, and *ethos*. The critic of contemporary rhetorical discourse must make a conscious decision about the system of criticism he intends to use. For some discourses traditional precepts constitute an ideal and workable critical system. For many others, especially in the contemporary American milieu, they are inappropriate. Traditional, rationalistic theory, in keeping with its classical origins, is committed to the values of reason, order, and law. These values are being challenged today in rhetorical acts which argue that power holders use such values to rationalize injustice and oppression. The contemporary critic must examine and develop critical systems to interpret and understand such rhetoric in ways that do not inevitably force him to censure its purposes and stratagems.[1]

The organic approach to criticism is concerned with the specific goals of particular persuaders in specific contexts; it views rhetorical acts as patterns of argument and interaction that grow out of particular conditions. In such an approach the critic applies critical categories that grow out of the nature of the discourse, and he adapts the critical system to reveal and respond to the peculiarities of the discourse.

Conflict between the two approaches need not be irreconcilable. Good criticism is often the result of selection and application of the formula most suitable to the discourse under consideration. Three broad critical systems are outlined in Chapter 3. In one sense these are formulas or prescriptions that represent options for the critic. But for many discourses the critic must invent a critical approach adapted to the discourse or genre he intends to evaluate. The critiques of the Paul Ehrlich essay, Black Protest rhetoric, and, to some extent, the Nixon, Agnew, and Wald addresses illustrate such invention.

Descriptive Analysis:
The First Stage of Criticism

Through descriptive analysis, the first stage in the critical process, the critic attempts to discover the unique and defining characteristics that make a discourse or genre distinctive. At the completion of this stage, the critic will be familiar with the nuances of the discourse and will be aware of the rhetorician's selections of language, structure, arguments, and evidence. He will have excellent grounds for determining the rhetorician's purpose and the responses that rhetorician seeks from his audience. The critic will also have extracted information to determine the role the speaker or writer has chosen to play, the ways he perceives and selects his audience, and his choice of persuasive strategies.

The stage of descriptive analysis is entirely intrinsic; that is, the critic makes descriptive statements solely on the basis of the content *of the discourse itself*. He uses outside materials only to determine the authenticity of the text. At this stage the critic ignores information about the context, the audience, the author, and the occasion. Rather he is concerned with the elements of tone, purpose, structure, and strategy; he concentrates on the supportive materials and the relationship between rhetorician and audience implied in the text itself.

---

[1] For discussion of the conflict between traditional rhetorical theory and contemporary rhetoric, see Robert L. Scott and Donald K. Smith, "The Rhetoric of Confrontation," *Quarterly Journal of Speech*, Vol. 55 (February 1969), pp. 1–8.

Tone

The term *tone* refers to those elements (primarily language elements) that suggest the rhetorician's attitude toward his audience and his subject matter. Statements about tone are inferences drawn from stylistic qualities. The critic may describe tone in an infinite number of ways: as personal, direct, ironic, satirical, sympathetic, angry, bitter, intense, scholarly, dogmatic, distant, condescending, "tough" or realistic, "sweet" or euphemistic, incisive, elegant, and so on. Each such label should reflect, as accurately as possible, whether the language is abstract or concrete, socially acceptable or unacceptable, technical or colloquial; it should reflect sentence length and complexity. The critic should also be prepared to support each label with evidence from the discourse that shows most clearly the general attitudes of the rhetorician toward the audience and the subject. For example, the tone of "The Generation Gap" is generally incisive and cutting, often satirical, quite personal (giving information about the author), and very direct. The section of criticism discussing stratagems and uses of language in the Agnew speeches is based on a descriptive analysis of the tone of those discourses.

Purpose

The term *purpose* refers to the argumentative conclusions, particularly the major conclusion, or thesis, of the discourse and the reasons and explanations that justify it. Analysis of purpose usually requires an outline of the argumentative structure which states the major ideas and diagrams their relationships. In many discourses the argumentative conclusion, or thesis, is explicitly stated, as in Nixon's Vietnam address. In others, such as in Agnew's speeches, there is an apparent purpose—to question whether the concentration of the mass media represents a threat to the dissemination of information and decision making in this society—and an implicit purpose—to alienate large segments of the population from media outlets critical of administrative policy. The implicit purpose is closely allied to the tone of the discourse.

In an analytical description of the implicit purpose the critic attempts to determine the kinds of responses that the author seeks from his audience or from different parts of his audience. Such purposes may include the traditional goals of acceptance and understanding or such "radical" goals as shame, confrontation, polarization, and alienation. For example, confrontation of Anglo-Americans and evocation of shame and guilt are essential parts of the purpose of "A Letter to the World from Jerusalem." The rhetorician's implicit purposes are related to his perceptions of the audiences he addresses. Eldridge Cleaver has different purposes for black audiences and white audiences; Ben Yisrael has different purposes for Jewish audiences and non-Jewish audiences. For instance, although he confronts and shames Anglo-Americans, Ben Yisrael provides many bases for identification between this audience and himself.

Structure

The term *structure* refers to the form of the discourse, the method of its development, and the nature of its movement. The critic should describe how and why the discourse develops, how it creates expectations in the audience, whether it promotes a sense of inevitability, and how the speaker or writer constructs a context for materials that follow. The kinds of structure in rhetorical discourses are numerous, and a rhetorical act usually employs more than one form. The method of development may be narrative–dramatic, historical–chronological, logical or pragmatic (problem–solution, cause–effect, or effect–cause), topical (analysis by a number of facets or perspectives), or taxonomical (division of a process into its relevant parts). These forms are not mutually exclusive; the discourses in this book all use a combination of them.

The structure of the discourse is important because it represents the rhetorician's choice of the most significant perspective on the subject, issue, or section of reality he wishes to examine. A historical–chronological form emphasizes development over time. A narrative–dramatic form reflects an organic view of reality and assumes that vicarious sharing of integrally related experiences is essential to the understanding of a concept or situation. A problem–solution form emphasizes the need to discover a concrete policy in order to resolve a troublesome situation. A cause–effect form stresses the prediction of consequences. A topical form selects certain facets of the subject and suggests that others are relatively unimportant. A taxonomical form focuses on the interrelationships between the parts of a process or between the parts and the whole. Each structural form represents a choice of perspective that emphasizes certain elements of the material over others. The writer or speaker uses the structural form to develop the discourse in order to support his point of view and lead most directly to his desired goal. For example, an understanding of the structural form and method of development of Wald's address is probably the most important factor in discovering the unique qualities of that discourse.

With the exception of addresses using a narrative or historical structure, an outline of the major ideas and arguments of the discourse is a helpful critical technique for determining structural form. An outline may also serve as a basis for testing the coherence and validity of the rhetorician's arguments. Because the critic is concerned with ideas and conclusions rather than topics a full-sentence outline is best to use. At this stage of analysis the chronological order in which ideas appear in the discourse is not important; the critic reorders concepts so that reasons and conclusions appear in logical relationships. At times the critic may need to experiment with alternate forms to discover which one, or ones, most accurately and completely reflect the patterns of development.

Supporting Materials

The supporting materials of a discourse are the explanations, illustrations, statistics, analogies, and testimony from lay and expert persons used to clarify ideas, to verify statements, and to make concepts vivid and memorable. In descriptive analysis the critic is not concerned with testing the validity, reliability, and credibility of support materials because such processes require the use of extrinsic sources. At this stage he is concerned with *describing* the support materials and analyzing their *functions* in the discourse.

Each form of evidence serves different proof functions. To the degree that an audience can identify with the persons or events, a detailed example is a vivid, personal, dramatic method of illustrating a principle, concept, or condition. Its primary function is psychological identification, for one example has only limited demonstrative value. In most instances a single case of anything is not adequate grounds for drawing a conclusion; it may turn out to be an atypical situation, even a remarkable coincidence or accident. Illustrations, like dramas, serve to "clothe ideas in living flesh," and their greatest strength is in their concrete impact on individuals. Extended examples also serve to introduce narrative–dramatic form into a discourse.

Analogies, or comparisons, function primarily for the purposes of prediction; they connect what exists and is known with what is in the future and is unknown. Figurative analogies (comparisons between things unlike in detail but similar in principle) operate the same way to connect the known, familiar, and simple with the unknown, unfamiliar, and complex.

Expert testimony or authoritative evidence provides criteria, standards, or principles to interpret data. Such evidence increases the interpretative capacities of an audience inexpert in the area being discussed. In addition authoritative evidence demonstrates that experts share the rhetorician's perspective or attitudes. Instances of lay testimony generally serve the same functions as examples.

Statistical evidence demonstrates the frequency of occurrence of phenomena. Used in conjunction with examples, statistics provide evidence of the typicality of the examples and the size or scope of a problem. Statistical evidence is strengthened by cultural preference for the quantified and scientific; but because statistics are often dull, the audience may have difficulty absorbing or retaining such data.

In descriptive analysis the critic describes the support materials used in the discourse and their functions. He also considers how the supporting evidence is related to the tone, purpose, and structure of the discourse. Different structural forms require different kinds of supporting materials, and the rhetorician may select a structure to avoid certain evidential requirements. For example, Nixon's speech on Vietnam is so structured that it requires moral or ethical justification rather than demonstrations of feasibility and practicality. The selection of a structural form to emphasize certain kinds of evidential questions is closely related to the descriptive analysis of strategies.

Strategies

The description of strategies determines how the rhetorician shapes his material in terms of the audience and his purposes. Strategies include selection of structural form, arguments, and supporting materials. They also include choice of language, use of definitions, and repetition of key words and phrases. The critic might consider certain questions to determine the rhetorician's strategies: What elements in the discourse create common grounds between the rhetorician and his intended audience? What attempts does the rhetorician make to label or relabel, define or redefine, structure or restructure the experienced reality of the audience? How does the speaker or writer attempt to provide new experiences for the audience? What changes in evaluation or association does he seek? In this book the critiques of Black Protest rhetoric and Agnew's speeches best illustrate use of the concept of strategies.

Audience

The speaker or writer constructs his discourse for particular individuals or groups. In descriptive analysis the critic concentrates on the ways the rhetorician's discourses "select" an audience or audiences. The critic locates statements that indicate the rhetorician is aware of more than one audience. He decides who will compose the actual audience and what part of that audience will be alienated by the discourse. He also determines the sorts of people the arguments are constructed for and examines the supporting materials.

Rhetorician

At this stage the critic is concerned with the relationship between the discourse and the identity the rhetorician creates for himself through the discourse.[2] What is the function of the discourse for its author? How does it serve to create an identity for him? To what degree does the discourse serve as self-expression or self-persuasion? If the discourse were the only piece of evidence available from which to determine the

[2] A major work concerning the identity the author creates in his discourse is Wayne C. Booth, *The Rhetoric of Fiction* (Chicago: University of Chicago Press, 1961). See also Richard B. Gregg, "The Ego-Function of the Rhetoric of Protest," *Philosophy and Rhetoric*, Vol. 4 (Spring 1971), pp. 71-91.

character of the author, what inferences could be made about him? Discourses serve to reveal the attitudes and beliefs of their authors. The rhetorician's views of man, truth, and society may reveal the philosophic position or perspective from which he speaks.[3]

Descriptive analysis, the first stage in the critical process, is almost entirely intrinsic and organic. As textual analysis it is designed to focus attention on the *discourse*. At this basic stage in the critical process the critic gathers the data that will provide the basis for subsequent analysis and interpretation. Therefore care and thoroughness at this stage is extremely important. In the criticism of *rhetoric* information and commentary about rhetoricians, contexts, and audiences are relevant and appropriate only insofar as they shed light upon the rhetorical discourse.

Historical–Contextual Analysis:
The Second Stage of Criticism

Unlike the stage of descriptive analysis, which is almost entirely intrinsic and organic, the second stage of criticism examines the extrinsic elements of discourse. This stage requires further research. The critic first acquires information about the historical–cultural context, the rhetorician, the audience, and the persuasive forces operating in the scene and then determines why the rhetorician made the choices of tone, purpose, structure, and strategies analyzed in the descriptive stage of the critical process.

The extrinsic elements—the external limitations, constraints, or influences on the rhetorician's choices—affect "the rhetorical problem," [4] which emphasizes rhetoric as goal-directed behavior intended to produce certain responses. A discourse is the rhetorician's solution to a problem he perceives in a particular context, that is, the rhetorician's attempt to "encompass a situation." The elements of the rhetorical problem represent the obstacles that prevent the author from accomplishing his purpose immediately and easily. These elements include the audience, the historical–cultural context, other persuasive forces, and the rhetorician himself.

Audience

At this stage the critic is concerned with discovering as much information as possible about the persons actually exposed to the discourse. The

[3] Two excellent discussions of the critical process of examining philosophic positions may be found in Thomas Nilsen, "Interpretative Function of the Critic," and Joseph Blau, "Public Address as Intellectual Revelation," *Western Speech*, Vol. 21 (Spring 1957), pp. 70–83.

[4] For further discussion of the rhetorical problem, see Robert Cathcart, *Post-Communication* (New York: Bobbs-Merrill, 1966), pp. 36–39.

medium (television, radio, print, live presentation, and so on) through which the audience participated in the rhetorical situation is important in determining the characteristics of the actual audience. Whether a given audience was exposed to the entire discourse, to excerpts, or to an edited version is also an important point. The attitudes and beliefs of the audience—discovered through research information about age, occupation, political affiliation, cultural experience, education, interests, economic status, and social class—affect their attitudes toward the rhetorician and the issue and provide insights into the rhetorician's choice of persuasive strategies. The audience's degree of involvement with the issue and their feelings (apathy, ignorance, hostility) toward the issue, the rhetorician, and the purpose of the discourse are also particularly relevant.

Historical-Cultural Context

To interpret a rhetorical act, the critic needs information about the immediate social context in which the act occurred, the particular occasion, and the place of the discourse in the ongoing dialogue of the culture. What events served to focus public attention on the issue discussed? What is the relationship between the discourse and the occasion? What events preceded and followed the discourse? What are the social, political, and economic pressures on the rhetorician and the audience? What is the social or cultural attitude toward this issue? How is the issue related to the ongoing American dialogue about liberty, equality, freedom, brotherhood, free enterprise, and so on?

Persuasive Forces

Closely related to the historical–cultural context are competing persuaders and alternative policies and positions. The thorough critic determines what information about the issue was generally disseminated through influential media and considers whether and how the rhetorician dealt with alternative policies. He also discovers what groups are in conflict with the rhetorician's position and what groups are associated with it. In addition the critic considers whether the rhetorician attempts to associate (or disassociate) himself and his position with (or from) other groups or causes and tries to discover possible reasons.

Rhetorician

Extrinsic analysis allows the critic to discover information about the rhetorician's experience, knowledge, and prior rhetorical actions. Is the rhetorician generally recognized as an expert on this subject? What statements has he made in the past that limit his choices in this case?

What associations or interests influence the rhetorician's choices (financial interests, constituency, ideology, ambitions)? With what other issues and causes is the rhetorician associated? To what extent is the discourse the work of ghost writers?

Supporting Materials

In the second stage of criticism the critic should test the validity, reliability, and credibility of the supporting evidence: How accurate are the citations? What sources does the rhetorician use? Are the supporting materials adequate and typical evidence? During this stage of the critical process the critic should consider all the tests applicable for the particular types of evidence.[5] However, if a critic were to apply these criteria strictly, most discourses in this book would appear seriously flawed. In this respect the least flawed would be the discourses of Paul Ehrlich and Jo Freeman. Other discourses, particularly those of Black Protest rhetoric and of Ben Yisrael, should be examined differently because of their use of dramatic form, allusion, and definition.

Interpretative Analysis:
The Third Stage of Criticism

In the third stage of critical analysis the critic selects or creates a system of criticism and determines criteria for interpreting, evaluating, and making his final judgments on the rhetoric. He bases his decisions on his *intrinsic descriptive analysis and extrinsic analysis of the historical–cultural context.*

While the first stage of criticism focuses on the discourse and the second stage focuses on the context and scene, the third stage focuses on the critic, reflecting his interests and biases. George Bernard Shaw once wrote that "all criticism is autobiography," and other theorists have recognized that criticism is persuasive discourse. (In a sense rhetorical criticism is entirely reflexive; all critical processes used to evaluate a discourse should also be used to evaluate the criticisms of that discourse.)

Although the discussion of the first two stages of the critical process indicates strongly that the critic must test his judgments against the discourse and against research from other sources, "good" criticism is not objective and impersonal; it is evaluative. It makes clear and unmistakable judgments about the quality, worth, and consequences of

[5] For an examination of the tests of evidence in the second stage of the critical process, see Robert P. Newman and Dale R. Newman, *Evidence* (Boston: Houghton Mifflin Company, 1969).

the discourse.[6] However, "good" criticism can be distinguished from "poor" criticism in several ways. First, whether it makes positive or negative judgments, "good" criticism increases the reader's understanding and appreciation of the discourse it criticizes. Second, in "good" criticism the reader can clearly identify the criteria the critic uses as a basis for his evaluations. In short good critics identify the system and standards they use, and their criticism is coherent and consistent so that the reader recognizes the grounds for critical judgments. Third, "good" criticism makes a contribution to the ongoing dialogue about the role of persuasive discourse in a humane society. It deals with ethical and moral questions and gives the reader a glimpse of an "ideal" rhetoric.

In light of his descriptive and historical–contextual analyses, the critic should consider the following questions as a general guide in selecting a critical system for interpretation and in choosing critical standards.

First, what distinctive characteristics of this rhetorical act should be emphasized and high-lighted in a critique? The purpose of criticism is to help the reader become a more appreciative, insightful audience for persuasive discourse. This question is crucial if criticism is to reveal the discourse, explore its peculiarities, and expose its internal workings. It focuses critical attention on artistic elements in the rhetoric and encourages the critic to produce innovative and creative criticism. This question was extremely influential in the choice of the critical techniques applied to Ehrlich's essay and was somewhat influential in the selection of techniques used in the criticism of Black Protest rhetoric and the addresses of Wald and Agnew.

Second, does the rhetorician suggest criteria for judging his work? Frequently the authors of persuasive discourses suggest standards for evaluation, which are inherent in statements of their beliefs about the proper analysis of an issue and the purposes of their discourses. This question suggests that the critic should take the rhetorician "on his own terms." The influence of the question is particularly evident in the critique of Nixon's address.

Third, what critical system will allow the critic to focus on the criterion or criteria that seem most significant in responding to this discourse or genre? This question assumes that in some cases the critic will decide that certain judgments or evaluations of the discourse need to be made. Perhaps he deems the work highly unethical, a significant

---

[6] The necessity for judgment and evaluation in rhetorical criticism is cogently stated by Lawrence W. Rosenfield, "The Anatomy of Critical Discourse," *Speech Monographs*, Vol. 35 (March 1968), pp. 50–69. The notion that rhetorical criticism need not be judgmental is suggested in Jerry Hendrix, "Rhetorical Criticism: Prognoses for the Seventies—A Symposium," *Southern Speech Journal*, Vol. 36 (Winter 1970), p. 104. Mark Klyn, "Toward a Pluralistic Rhetorical Criticism," in Thomas R. Nilsen, ed., *Essays on Rhetorical Criticism* (New York: Random House, 1968), pp. 143–157, objects to the narrow evaluative limits prescribed by neo-Aristotelian criticism.

violation of the truth criterion, a unique approach to a complex ethical problem, a distinctively aesthetic work, or a major reinterpretation of an issue or value system. In each case he should seek a critical system that will allow him to explicate and justify his conclusions most intelligently and cogently. The critique of Black Protest rhetoric shows the influence of this question as does the use of Northrop Frye's concept of "genuine speech" in the criticism of Agnew's addresses.

Fourth, what critical system would be most antagonistic in its judgment of the rhetoric or most sympathetic in its assessments? The question is designed to make the critic self-aware and self-conscious, to force him to consider alternative critical conclusions that might be reached on different grounds. The two criticisms of Richard Nixon's "Checkers Speech" by Barnet Baskerville and Henry E. McGuckin, Jr. illustrate contrasting critical systems and evaluations.* This question focuses the critic's attention on what the discourse is and is not, to induce him to pause and question the fairness of his standards. It also makes him aware of both positive and negative grounds for rating the discourse. The two critical approaches used on Wald's address, and the divergent judgments reached, illustrate the influence of this question.

These four questions underlie the three stages of the critical process. They represent the bases for selecting critical systems and criteria. The three stages of the process culminate in the act of formulating and writing a piece of rhetorical criticism. The finished written document is itself a rhetorical act that can and must be criticized. I have suggested the purpose of criticism and indicated that these purposes function as criteria for distinguishing "good" criticism. Test your criticisms, my criticisms, and the criticisms of others by these purposes, and develop other standards for judgment.

* See page 57.

Three

The Systems of Rhetorical Criticism

This book cannot possibly specify all the available modes of criticism. In a significant sense criticism is a creative activity; the critic has the option of creating his own system of criticism in response to a particular discourse or genre. This chapter describes three broad critical systems, outlines a general method for the application of each, and explains the criterion or criteria for evaluation emphasized in each system.

System I:
Traditional Rationalism

Traditional rationalism has dominated the scholarly analysis of public discourse in the field of speech. This critical approach rests on the assumptions that men are persuadable because they are rational beings, that the function of rhetorical discourse is to make truth effective, and that ethical rhetoric seeks rational judgments from audiences because these are the "best" decisions a society can make. Edwin Black has sharply criticized this system, labeling it "neo-Aristotelian criticism."[1] This system usually involves a formulary application of the classical canons and an analysis of the discourse in terms of the classical modes of proof. It emphasizes the examination of the presuppositions underlying arguments; the validity of argumentative structure; and the credi-

---

[1] Edwin Black's critique of the "neo-Aristotelian" system of criticism is found in *Rhetorical Criticism: A Study in Method* (New York: The Macmillan Company, 1965).

bility, relevance, and sufficiency of evidence. It stresses the adequacy of the speaker's or writer's analysis of the issue; his ability to respond to counterarguments; and his capacity to adapt the materials of his discourse to the expectations, experiences, and interests of his audience.

Because traditional rationalism rests on the assumption that rhetorical discourse is reasoned discourse or argumentation, this critical system is best adapted to highly discursive or argumentative discourses that make extensive use of supporting materials, are structurally developed in a "logical" fashion, and clearly present reasoned conclusions. Because it assumes that through rhetorical acts truths may be realized in thought, attitude, and action, traditional rationalism inevitably forces the critic to place primary emphasis upon the truth criterion as a basis for making evaluations. It also emphasizes the effects of a discourse on the immediate audience, assuming that rhetoric of quality will induce men to *make* rational judgments and to *take* the actions that such judgments imply.

The truth criterion is a basic standard for rhetorical evaluation. Using this criterion, the critic assesses the accuracy and adequacy of the rhetorician's supporting materials and evaluates the validity of the rhetorician's arguments, that is, how effectively both his reasons and his evidence justify his conclusions. In addition on the basis of this criterion the critic extracts the argumentative structure of the discourse and examines it carefully, testing the coherence of the argumentative development. He also evaluates the credibility of the rhetorician's sources and the sufficiency of the supporting data, testing the rhetorician's evidence against evidence from other sources. Although such considerations are an important part of criticism, as illustrated particularly in my critiques of Nixon's and Agnew's addresses, problems arise from the application of this criterion.

First, a discourse is never long enough to tell the whole truth. Of necessity discourses require the selection of evidence, arguments, and explanations. The rhetorical act is an incomplete analysis of an issue and a partial presentation of relevant data. In addition on many issues informed persons disagree and arrive at different conclusions; in fact rhetorical acts result from such disagreement. The images, values, and goals of an individual influence what he sees as "true"; consequently simple assessments of the "truth" of a discourse are usually quite difficult. Even when applied strictly, the truth criterion is a comparison of one symbolic reality (the rhetorical discourse) with other symbolic realities (the views of experts, research findings, and so forth). Finally some discourses are accurate, complete, and thorough (particularly those of highly expert persons) but are effective for only a small body of other experts. If the truth criterion alone were applied, such discourses, however limited in their effectiveness, would have to be adjudged excellent. Hence, in isolation, this criterion has serious limitations.

A larger philosophical question also arises. In analysis of the rhetoric of Black Protest, for the most part the critique ignores traditional applications of the truth criterion and emphasizes "truths" situationally created by the interaction of the rhetorician and the audience. These "truths" are symbolic—redefinitions and reinterpretations of the experiences of a group—and are not verifiable in any traditional fashion. The critic can test their acceptability by whether members of a group see such restructurings as accurate interpretations of their experience. If "truths" are symbolic, situationally created out of audience–rhetorician interaction, then the truth criterion, as understood in the traditional, rationalistic system of criticism, becomes inapplicable. (The proponents of this system point out the dangers of such a reinterpretation of the truth criterion. If this concept were carried to its logical extreme, "truth" would become merely group acceptance. What is true becomes what is believed to be true, and truth considerations are indistinguishable from the measurement of positive audience response.)

In addition to the truth criterion rationalistic criticism emphasizes the effectiveness of discourses in achieving desired responses. The discussion of the second system of criticism deals with the effects criterion, which is the primary standard of evaluation in this system, and the problems involved in its application.

Traditional, rationalistic criticism makes minimal aesthetic demands. It requires only that discourses evince qualities of unity, coherence, and emphasis in their structure and that the language of rhetorical acts be clear, correct, and appropriate. It presumes that ethical rhetoric is valid argumentation sustained by adequate and credible evidence that seeks a reasoned judgment from the audience. The discussion of the third system of criticism deals at length with aesthetic and ethical criteria, which are the primary evaluative standards in that system.

The methodology of traditional rationalism illustrates the theoretical concepts of this system and emphasizes the truth criterion. It is governed by the classical canons and modes of proof.

Invention

This canon explores the rhetorician's ability to create and select arguments and supporting materials adapted to the issue, the occasion, and the audience. Of primary interest is the *logos* of the discourse, a term that refers to the logical or rational elements of the discourse and to the ways such elements effect persuasion. The critic should examine the issue in dispute to determine the *locus* of the controversy. Is the issue a question of fact (What really occurred?), of value (Did the situation cause harm or injury? What criteria should be used to evaluate available data?), or of policy (What is the best course of action?)? The critic should discover whether the rhetorician understands the issue and the points in dispute; in this light the critic should assess the appropriateness and effectiveness of the analysis and the refutation of any opponents' counterarguments. He should also consider the *topoi*, or lines of argument developed in the discourse, and evaluate the selection of arguments in terms of the belief structure of the audience and the particular context of the rhetorical act. Finally he should examine the evidence and assess its validity, reliability, and credibility, paying special attention to how it is adapted to the rhetorician's role, to the occasion, and to the audience.

Another critical concern of invention is *pathos*, the rhetorician's use of nonlogical appeals to put the audience into a frame of mind that will make them less hostile to his arguments. The critic should describe and analyze psychological appeals to the audience's needs, drives, and desires and emotional appeals directed toward their experiences and condition. Of primary interest is the rhetorician's adaptation of logical materials to the audience and occasion, the selection of arguments and supporting materials most likely to interest and move the audience. The critic should determine how the rhetorician's use of language served to produce strong emotional responses. Because of its strongly rationalistic bias, this system of criticism views psychological and emotional appeals as legitimate only when they enhance and support a rhetorical act that is primarily a reasoned discourse.

A third concern in invention is an assessment of *ethos*, a term referring to the influence of the rhetorician's character, intelligence, integrity, and reputation on the audience. The critic should attempt to describe how the rhetorician demonstrates his involvement with the issue and his expertise in the subject area. The critic should also consider how the speaker or writer attempts to establish his credibility as a source of information and his concern for the welfare of the audience. And the critic should note if the rhetorician attempts to discredit the character and credibility of his opponents and the means for such attempts.

Disposition

This canon calls for an assessment of the selection, orderly arrangement, and proportion of the parts of a discourse. It requires a determination of how parts of the discourse perform their respective functions; a description of the structural form; and a judgment of the unity, coherence, and emphasis created by the method of development. The elements discussed in the section on "structure" in the first stage of criticism are also relevant at this point.

Style

This canon of traditional rationalism examines the language of rhetorical discourse to determine whether it is clear and simple, correct and precise, and appropriate to the issue, speaker, and audience. It sometimes describes how the rhetorician uses language to make the discourse aesthetically pleasing to the audience (although it rarely includes judgments of the aesthetic worth of particular elements).[2]

Delivery

For oral rhetorical discourses, with data known about the mode of presentation, this canon evaluates the influence of delivery on the success of the address.

As presented, this methodology of traditional rationalism is an abbreviated formula for the application of this system to rhetorical discourse.

System II:
Psychological Criticism

Theories and concepts associated with psychology led to the development of the second general system of criticism. Theorists who describe the rhetorical act from this perspective define *persuasion* as "that body of effects in receivers, relevant and instrumental to source-desired goals, brought about by a process in which messages have been a major determinant of those effects,"[3] or as the "conscious attempt to modify thought and action by manipulating the motives of men toward predetermined ends."[4] William N. Brigance has argued that "persuasion takes place not on an intellectual, but on a motor level."[5] These statements indicate that the theoretical base for this critical system emphasizes the criterion of effects and the role that psychophysiological factors play in determining behavior. Consequently this critical system focuses on analysis of the audience, the speaker, and the ways in which the rhetorician uses his message to activate and direct the needs and motives of the audience. Psychological criticism is keyed to the rhetorician's effectiveness in achieving his goals. The critic's primary concern is to analyze and explain how and why these effects were produced.

The effects criterion is another basic standard applicable to dis-

[2] Although the possibility of assessing the effect of a use of *logos* or of uses of language for the audience is an option open to the critic who takes a traditional, rationalistic approach, such evaluations are not characteristic of the criticisms made by critics who follow this system. See Edwin Black, *op. cit.*, pp. 27–78.

[3] Wallace Fotheringham, *Perspectives on Persuasion* (Boston: Allyn and Bacon, 1966), p. 7.

[4] Winston L. Brembeck and William Smiley Howell, *Persuasion: Means of Social Control* (Englewood Cliffs, N. J.: Prentice-Hall, 1952), p. 24.

[5] William Norwood Brigance, "Can We Re-Define the James-Winans Theory of Persuasion?" *Quarterly Journal of Speech*, Vol. 21 (February 1935), p. 21.

courses for evaluation. It judges the rhetorician's success in inducing responses from his audience, particularly his effectiveness in convincing the audience to accept his conclusions and commit themselves to the actions he desires. Because rhetoric is goal-directed communicative behavior, the rhetorician's success or failure in eliciting desired responses is an important consideration in evaluating a rhetorical act.

This criterion creates some problems for the critic, not the least of which is the difficulty in determining just what is reliable evidence of the effects of a rhetorical act. When the rhetorician orally addresses an immediate audience, clapping may be a polite social convention, a response to the occasion, or a reflection of the audience's feelings about the speaker. Scales measuring shifts of opinion are open to serious challenge because they tend to measure what individuals "say" has occurred. When the rhetorician presents a written address, effects are difficult to ascertain, and validity and reliability may be questioned if the critic tries to surmount this difficulty by counting the number of references to or citations from a discourse. In such cases the nature of the publication in which the discourse appears and whether the discourse is edited or excerpted may distort the effects.

A more serious challenge to the measurement of effects is the difficulty in isolating the effects of a single rhetorical act from related persuasive efforts. Persuasive discourses rarely occur in isolation; they are part of a variety of persuasive forces operating in a particular context, and audience reactions are likely to be a response to a group of rhetorical situations. A related difficulty is the problem of assessing the long-range effects of a discourse, which are exceedingly difficult to measure. The variations in response to Agnew's rhetoric are illustrative. Response to his addresses, as measured by the Gallup poll, for instance, was quite positive in the fall of 1969 but was far less so during the congressional campaigns of the fall of 1970. Some discourses, on the other hand, may have little immediate effect, but their long-range influence may be considerable. Again, the critic is faced with the difficult problem of deciding whether immediate or long-range effects are more significant and how such effects can validly be measured. He might make a rhetorical judgment on the kinds of effects the discourse is *capable* of producing and could reasonably be expected from the effort put forth. Such judgment is, of course, a way of predicting long-range effects, of gauging the durability a discourse may be expected to have. However, despite these problems the critic should take into account all available evidence of the responses to rhetorical acts.

When applied in isolation, this criterion generates a major philosophical problem. Many persuasive attempts are highly successful, but they have appalling social and ethical consequences. The advertisements of tobacco companies and the rhetoric of Nazi Germany serve as illustrations. In isolation the effects criterion implies that what works is good regardless of its social consequences, a totally destructive and inhumane position. When it is expanded to include an evaluation of long-range effects on the society, the effects criterion is usually infused with ethical considerations. Thus a simple assessment of the immediate effects on an audience is, by itself, an inadequate basis for critical conclusions; consequently it is never used alone in the critiques in the subsequent chapters.

The methodology of psychological criticism illustrates the theoretical concepts of this system and emphasizes the effects criterion. The elements of this methodology explain how and why the rhetorician produced certain effects in the audience. The methodology involves analysis of the rhetorician's psychological impact, factors in the audience that affect persuasive success, and characteristics of the message that activate or direct needs and motives.

The Rhetorician's *Ethos*

Psychological criticism attempts to analyze the effects of the rhetorician's character, intelligence, and sincerity as perceived by the audience. Some theorists suggest a variety of questions as a method of analysis: (1) How does the rhetorician associate himself with what is virtuous and elevated? (2) How does the rhetorician bestow praise on himself and his cause and blame on his opponents and their cause? (3) How does the rhetorician create an impression of sincerity? (4) How does the rhetorician identify himself with the experiences, values, and attitudes of his audience? (5) How does the rhetorician discount personal biases and interests?[6] These questions, of course, assume that successful rhetoricians must do these things and that an understanding of their occurrence will account for persuasive success. Conversely insofar as they are not done, or are done ineptly, the lack of accomplishment is a clue to the persuasive failure.

A second approach to analysis of the rhetorician's psychological impact assumes that audiences grant or withhold prestige to rhetoricians because of certain needs. Thus the *ethos* of the speaker might originate in a need or deficiency felt by the audience. In the process of granting a certain role to the rhetorician the audience attempts to satisfy, conceal, or lessen this deficiency. Three general deficiencies generally result in three patterns of *ethos*.[7]

In the "hero" pattern the audience feels deficient in its capacity to make intelligent choices about complex issues. It wishes to escape from

[6] These questions are developed from Brembeck and Howell, *op. cit.*, p. 387, and Lester Thonssen and A. Craig Baird, *Speech Criticism* (New York: The Ronald Press Company, 1948), p. 378.
[7] The hero, agent, and identification patterns are developed from an unpublished paper by Otis M. Walter.

the pain and responsibility for such decisions. Consequently it confers a "heroic" role on the rhetorician and designates him as an authority delegated with decision-making power. Rhetoricians who seek such a role wish to enhance their power and position and emphasize their willingness to "lead." In turn they tend to argue authoritatively because of their special expertise or their knowledge of generally unavailable information. The final section of the Nixon speech illustrates discourse in this pattern.

In the "identification" pattern each member of the audience has an idealized image of himself—what he would like to be but despairs of reaching. However, he may reach this goal by granting prestige to a person he perceives as possessing qualities similar to his idealized image. For example, the relationship between the two main characters in the movie "Joe" results from Joe's conferring prestige upon the father, who has behaved as Joe wishes he had the courage to behave. Agnew's success might be, in part, a result of his being granted prestige by "forgotten Americans," who view him as representing an idealized image of themselves.

In the "agent" pattern the specialization of a modern technological society requires a person to delegate to others the power and responsibility for helping him achieve his goals. Consequently he grants prestige to other persons who can function as agents or instruments. The prestige bestowed on physicians, who are essential agents in maintaining health, illustrates such *ethos*. The rhetorician who seeks this kind of prestige argues that he can do for others what they cannot do themselves or that he has been instrumental in the achievement of goals, as a politician who "runs on his record." The prestige people grant or withhold from elected representatives is generally related to this pattern. In his Vietnam address Nixon appeals for this kind of *ethos* when he refers to the letters he has sent through special channels to Ho Chi Minh.

Audience Analysis

An important part of this critical system is the analysis of an individual's basic needs and the culturally and socially acquired behaviors the individual learns to satisfy those needs. The study of learned behaviors or motives may be an analysis of the shared cultural values dominant in a particular society at a particular time, or it may be an analysis of the values, attitudes, and beliefs of persons in particular segments of the society. Such analyses function as typologies for explaining the success or failure of a particular rhetorical act or campaign, or as bases from which the rhetorician or critic may predict the sorts of arguments or appeals most likely to be successful for a particular audience. Henry E. McGuckin, Jr., analyzes the American value system to explain the success of Nixon's "Checkers Speech" and to describe the frequency and types of appeals made by the speaker.[8] Similar analyses of Nixon's and Agnew's speeches in this book might produce insights into the reasons for their immediate success.

Motive Appeals

A third area of concern in this critical system is an analysis of the rhetorician's appeals to the needs and motives of his audience. In such analysis the critic classifies and describes the rhetorician's arguments and evidence in terms of appeals to basic needs (survival, security, love and belongingness, status or esteem, and self-actualization, for example[9]), to cultural values, and to beliefs and attitudes of people in certain segments of society. In his descriptions the critic analyzes how language functions to arouse and direct needs and motives. (The worth of the psychological treatment of motive appeals is sharply limited because that treatment explains but does not evaluate.)

As presented, the methodology of psychological criticism is an abbreviated formula for the application of this system to rhetorical discourse.

System III:
Dramatistic Criticism

Theories of symbolic interaction, particularly from the works of Kenneth Burke, led to the development of the third general system of criticism.[10] Dramatistic criticism analyzes language and thought as modes of action rather than as means of conveying information. This system rests on the assumption that man is a symbol-using creature and that the most crucial element determining changes in attitude and action is the creation and identification of meaning. Kenneth Burke states this assumption most succinctly: "Where there is persuasion, there is rhetoric. And where there is meaning, there is persuasion."[11] Consequently the critic is primarily interested in the rhetorician's language and is concerned with examining the rhetorician's strategies for changing his own symbolic behavior and that of his audience.

In such a view the "receiver" is an active participant in the persuasive

---

[8] The analysis of American cultural values that underlies McGuckin's criticism may be found in Edward D. Steele and Charles W. Redding, "The American Value System: Premises for Persuasion," *Western Speech*, Vol. 26 (Spring 1962), pp. 83–91.

[9] The examples of basic needs are taken from Abraham Maslow, *Motivation and Personality* (New York: Harper & Row, 1954).

[10] The dramatistic system of criticism is developed most clearly in Kenneth Burke, *A Grammar of Motives and A Rhetoric of Motives* (New York: Meridian Books, 1962).

[11] *Ibid.*, p. 696.

process: He detects, identifies, and interprets the symbolic stimuli composing the message; he cooperates in creating the meaning of the message which becomes the most significant element in his future behavior. Such theory presumes that each man is unique, divided from other men because his experiences, his "meanings," his values and opinions are peculiar to him. The misunderstandings and misinterpretations that inevitably result from this uniqueness require rhetorical acts proclaiming common interests and calling for concerted action. Men have common interests because of their experiences as members of groups. But if they are to function as grounds for identification, these interests must be recognized and announced symbolically for unification of attitude or action to occur. Rhetoric, says Burke, is "rooted in an essential function of language itself, . . . the use of language as a symbolic means of inducing cooperation in beings that by nature respond to symbols." [12]

The critic who selects this rhetorical system analyzes and describes the rhetorician's strategies in his attempts to create identifications between himself and the audience and among members of the audience. Both the rhetorician and the audience create the "truths" that emerge from rhetorical interaction in a particular situation or cultural context. Consequently the critic tends toward the criticism of genres because in this system discourses are part of an ongoing dialogue influenced by persuasive forces that include other discourses, persistent social conflicts, and cultural values. Such genres tend to share both stylistic and philosophical similarities.

This critical approach has a strong commitment to ethical criteria. Because the system assumes that human division and hostility as well as human cooperation and identification depend on symbolic behavior, and because it assumes that a major function of rhetoric is to promote such cooperation and identification, the critic must be a careful student of the constructive and destructive capacities of symbolic behavior. From this point of view ethical rhetoric is *"the discovery of the means of symbolism which lead to the greatest mutual understanding and mutual influence."* [13] Even more strongly such a view suggests that humane uses of language structure reality in ways that allow men to see themselves as capable of making choices and acting to transcend existing conditions.

The emphasis on ethical and aesthetic criteria in this system should be evident from the foregoing statements. As applied in this critical system, the two criteria are interrelated and interdependent.

The aesthetic criterion describes the artistic quality of the rhetorical act, deepens awareness, and heightens appreciation of the rhetorical act as an art form. Critical assessment on aesthetic grounds ideally recalls "a sense of the finer discriminations and precisions of which language is

[12] *Ibid.,* p. 567.
[13] Otis M. Walter and Robert L. Scott, *Thinking and Speaking,* 2nd ed. (New York: The Macmillan Company, 1968), p. 231.

capable." [14] Aesthetic evaluation is concerned with form on the assumption that an individual can increase his understanding of content through an understanding of form. The aesthetic criterion evaluates such formal elements as narrative development, dramatic conflict, the *persona* of the speaker, and the use of precise, elegant, and metaphorical language—all of which are important elements determining the universality and durability of a rhetorical work. In this light rhetoric involves drama —the enactment of ideas as well as their discursive demonstration. A high aesthetic judgment of a work implies that the work is a unique artistic event with the capacity to speak to many audiences and to endure as an interpretative insight into the human condition. Great rhetorical works have been so judged: the ideal examples of the art, the touchstones to which a critic may turn for standards of quality and beauty. Because of their formal qualities, many works require an aesthetic evaluation, particularly those works that celebrate important public rituals—inaugural addresses, eulogies, Nobel Prize addresses, and so forth. This criterion is essential for the analysis of the "poetic" dimensions of rhetorical acts and is central to the rhetorical analysis of literary works.[15] The application of this criterion is illustrated in the critique of Cleaver's essay.

The ethical criterion determines the social worth of the rhetorical act and defines standards for the humane use of persuasive discourse. In using this criterion, the critic selects the values or ideas he believes rhetoric should exemplify and support. As one might easily imagine, theorists have differed about the ethical principles that should guide such judgments.

There are two general areas in which ethical appraisals seem to be essential in criticism: in judging the consequences of a discourse or a genre on society and in judging the consequences of the formal elements of a discourse or a genre on future rhetorical activity. First, the critic should consider how the discourse influences the decision-making processes in that society: the values it upholds, the image it presents as ideal. The issues here are closely related to the concept of "freedom of speech," the preservation of the fundamental values underlying a democratic society, and the ways such values should be reflected in rhetor-

[14] John Rathbun, "The Problem of Judgment and Effect in Historical Criticism: A Proposed Solution," *Western Speech*, Vol. 33 (Summer 1969), p. 150. This article provides an excellent discussion of the aesthetic criterion in rhetorical criticism.
[15] The rhetorical analysis of literary works is explored in Wayne C. Booth, *The Rhetoric of Fiction* (Chicago: University of Chicago Press, 1961), and in G. M. A. Grube, "Rhetoric and Literary Criticism," *Quarterly Journal of Speech*, Vol. 42 (December 1956), pp. 339–344; S. John Macksoud and Ross Altman, "Voices in Opposition: A Burkeian Rhetoric of *Saint Joan*," *Quarterly Journal of Speech*, Vol. 57 (April 1971), pp. 140–146; S. John Macksoud, "Kenneth Burke on Perspective and Rhetoric," *Western Speech*, Vol. 33 (Summer 1969), pp. 167–174; Thomas O. Sloan, "Argument and Character in Wyatt's 'They Flee from Me,'" *Western Speech*, Vol. 28 (Summer 1964), pp. 145–153; Thomas O. Sloan, "A Rhetorical Analysis of John Donne's 'The Prohibition,'" *Quarterly Journal of Speech*, Vol. 48 (February 1962), pp. 38–45.

ical discourse.[16] Some theorists have argued for a "free and open market-place" of ideas, contending that with some minimal limitations all points of view should be freely and equally presented for public discussion.[17] This view assumes that such a marketplace would be self-corrective, revealing the inadequacies of arguments and policies and correcting misinformation in the process of open debate. It also assumes that the best arguments and the most accurate interpretations would triumph in such an exchange. Obviously such a view is open to serious criticism. Not all points of view have access to the marketplace; those with greater economic resources, social status, and political influence are "more equal" than others. Further there is some reason to doubt that the public would examine all points of view fairly and completely and make conscious, reasoned decisions on the basis of such deliberations. None-theless some of the commentary in the criticisms of addresses by Agnew, Nixon, and Wald and some of the statements about the responsibilities of white audiences in relation to the rhetoric of Black Protest convey my personal commitment to a "free and open market of ideas."

The second area of ethical judgment is an intrinsic one. Edwin Black argues that "some techniques of argument can have an effect independ-ent of the substance of the argument," that rhetorical discourses work "to make certain techniques conventional, to shape an audience's expecta-tions for discourses that they will later hear or read, to mold an au-dience's sensibilities to language." [18] The central concept here is that the critic can make judgments of rhetorical strategies in terms of the rhe-torical conventions they establish and the rhetorical expectations they create in an audience. The rhetoric of any period sets up ethical norms for what is acceptable, appropriate, and "good" rhetoric, and this proc-ess is amenable to critical evaluation. The Agnew critique is illustrative. Regardless of the position he might advocate, Agnew's rhetorical strat-agems are unethical and undesirable because they establish conventions of argumentation and persuasion that diminish the ability of the society to make good decisions. Barnet Baskerville's analysis of Richard Nixon's "Checkers Speech" also illustrates that certain rhetorical stratagems may prevent audiences from reaching socially or ethically justifiable decisions. Similarly my and Robert Newman's critiques of Nixon's Viet-nam War speech make this argument about the nature of the analysis of policy alternatives in that address. Such ethical judgments appraise argumentative analysis and rhetorical stratagems because these can be, in and of themselves, ethical or unethical.

The methodology of dramatistic criticism illustrates the theoretical

---

[16] An ethical system for rhetoric developed from the fundamental values of a free society is discussed in Karl Wallace, "An Ethical Basis of Communication," *Speech Teacher*, Vol. 4 (January 1955), pp. 1–9.

[17] The free and open marketplace view was advocated by John Stuart Mill, *On Liberty* (New York: Appleton-Century-Crofts, 1947), pp. 15–54.

[18] Black, *op. cit.*, p. 56.

concepts of this system and emphasizes aesthetic and ethical criteria. Because it is the most organic of the three systems, dramatistic criticism is difficult to outline. Five general areas for critical scrutiny direct attention to the role of language in persuasive acts and lay the foundation for aesthetic and ethical judgments.

Verbal Behavior

The critic can best describe the rhetorician's purpose by specifying the changes that the rhetorician seeks in his verbal behavior and that of the audience—in the naming, defining, structuring, and interpreting of persons, acts, events, relationships, conditions, and issues. The critic must attempt to recreate the "universe of discourse" or the system of thought that the rhetorician tries to create through his action.

Symbolic Strategies

The critic locates and describes the rhetorician's language techniques that alter verbal behavior. For example, he considers the rhetorician's use of argument, narrative, allusions, associations, definitions, repetitions of words and phrases, method of development, and expectations created by form. However, the critic cannot rely on a prescriptive formulation for analysis because he must respond to and describe the peculiar characteristics of each discourse and genre. For instance, the symbolic strategies used by Agnew, Ehrlich, Black Protest speakers, and Wald differ widely because each strategy is a distinctive response to a particular rhetorical problem, issue, or situation.

Situational Truths

If he assumes that the "truths" created in rhetorical discourses are a result of the interaction of the rhetorician and the audience in a particular context, the critic must attempt to discover how audience characteristics, cultural conditions, the role of the rhetorician, and the language of the discourse interact to create and justify certain perceptions of reality. For such analysis the critic relies on information from a synthesis of materials he prepared and researched in the first two stages of criticism. For example, the conditions of blacks in America, the conflict between those conditions and the values of this society, the roles played by Black Protest speakers, society's treatment of these speakers, and the messages they produce have fused together to create a method of analysis and an ideology reflected in Eldridge Cleaver's essay. The critic must explain the fusion of elements that creates acceptance for a way of perceiving and structuring reality.

Genre

Because this system of criticism assumes that any given discourse is a fragment of an ongoing cultural dialogue (rather than assuming that discourses are discrete events—the normal procedure of the other two systems of criticism), the critic must discover what discourses share basic stylistic and philosophical judgments that unify them in a rhetorical genre. He must make some attempt to delineate the defining characteristics of the genre and to locate other discourses that might be included. This element in the methodology transfers critical vistas from isolated discourses to types or genres of discourse. For example, I treat the addresses of Richard Nixon and George Wald as single events; I discuss Agnew's two addresses as though they were one, and I include his general conflict with mass media coverage; I talk about Paul Ehrlich's essay in terms of the general problems of ecological rhetoric; and I analyze Black Protest rhetoric as an entire class or genre of discourse. Thus the criticisms are arranged in this book in a progression from examinations of single discourses to criticisms of ever-larger rhetorical genres.

Ethics

An essential part of the methodology of this critical system is an assessment of the consequences of rhetorical acts for society and for future discourses. The critic is involved in difficult appraisals as he evaluates to what extent discourses give evidence of mutual understanding and increase the audience's capacity to choose, to act, and to unify into groups so that identification and cooperation become possible. In so doing, he should recognize, however, that all unity is achieved at the cost of division, that an inherent tension exists between the desire for unity and the toleration of dissent which is essential in a democratic society. Finally he must weigh these contradictory elements within an ethical framework to discover uses of language that fully protect the "selfhood" of the participants.[19]

As presented, the methodology of dramatistic criticism is an abbreviated formula for the application of this system to rhetorical discourse. As the following critiques make evident, I prefer the system of dramatistic criticism. However, I have described the three systems not only because all three systems suggest the different directions a critic may take but also because they provide valuable insights into the analysis and evaluation of rhetorical discourse. The following critiques

---

[19] The concept of selfhood as a basis for ethical judgments is discussed in Thomas Olbricht, "The Self as a Philosophical Ground of Rhetoric," *Pennsylvania Speech Annual*, Vol. 21 (September 1964), pp. 28–36.

are, I hope, creatively eclectic in using concepts from all three systems, especially when such concepts aid in analysis and interpretation.

In the bibliography that is found at the end of this chapter, I have listed works to which you may turn to expand your critical options and to examine the application of a wide variety of critical techniques and methodologies. I highly recommend them. They include some of the finest rhetorical criticism ever written and some of the most insightful and provocative statements ever made about criticism itself.

For Further Reading

Ray Lynn Anderson, "Rhetoric and Science Journalism," *Quarterly Journal of Speech,* Vol. 41 (December 1970), pp. 358–368.

Lloyd Bitzer, "The Rhetorical Situation," *Philosophy and Rhetoric,* Vol. 1 (January 1968), pp. 1–14.

Edwin Black, *Rhetorical Criticism: A Study in Method* (New York: The Macmillan Company, 1965), pp. 79–90.

Parke Burgess, "The Rhetoric of Moral Conflict: Two Critical Dimensions," *Quarterly Journal of Speech,* Vol. 56 (April 1970), pp. 120–130.

Kenneth Burke, "The Rhetoric of Hitler's Battle," *Philosophy of Literary Form* (New York: Vintage Books, 1941), pp. 164–189.

Richard Gregg, "A Phenomenologically Oriented Approach to Rhetorical Criticism," *Central States Speech Journal,* Vol. 17 (May 1966), pp. 83–90.

D. Ray Heisey, "The Rhetoric of the Arab–Israeli Conflict," *Quarterly Journal of Speech,* vol. 56 (February 1970), pp. 12–21.

Richard Hofstadter, *The American Political Tradition* (New York: Vintage Books), pp. 68–92, 137–163.

Richard Hofstadter, "The Paranoid Style of American Politics," *Harper's,* Vol. 86 (November 1964), pp. 77–86.

Richard L. Johannesen, Rennard Strickland, and Ralph T. Eubanks, eds., *Language Is Sermonic: Richard M. Weaver on the Nature of Rhetoric* (Baton Rouge: Louisiana State University Press, 1970).

Perry Miller, "The Rhetoric of Sensation," *Errand into the Wilderness* (New York: Harper Torchbooks, 1956), pp. 167–183.

Richard Weaver, *The Ethics of Rhetoric* (Chicago: Henry Regnery Company, 1953).

Edmund Wilson, "Abraham Lincoln: The Union as Religious Mysticism," *Eight Essays* (Garden City, N. Y.: Doubleday & Company, 1954), pp. 181–202.

Theodore O. Windt, Jr., "The Rhetoric of Peaceful Coexistence: Khrushchev in America, 1959," *Quarterly Journal of Speech,* Vol. 57 (February 1971), pp. 11–22.

Four

Richard M. Nixon

The following address is a major policy statement delivered by Richard M. Nixon almost precisely one year after he was elected to the Presidency. Announcement of the address was made weeks in advance, on October 13, and was preceded by an extraordinary amount of publicity. Various administrative sources described the forthcoming address in terms that made it possible for liberals and "doves" to hope that the address would announce an important change in United States policy for Vietnam. The address was delivered over nationwide television on November 3, 1969. On October 15, 1969, the first organized, nationwide Vietnam moratorium protests occurred; on November 15, 1969, a second, larger national protest was staged. Prior to the first moratorium, Nixon said that he would not be affected by such protests and that American foreign policy would not be formulated in the streets. Thus this address was delivered at a time of intense national unrest, was bracketed by two major protests, and occurred in a rhetorical situation in which most Americans had vested and vital interests.

Vietnamization:
The President's Address on War

1 Tonight I want to talk to you on a subject that deeply concerns every American and other people throughout the world—the war in Vietnam.

From *Congressional Record*, Vol. 115, Part 24, pp. 32784–32786.

2 I believe that one of the reasons for the deep division in this nation about Vietnam is that many Americans have lost confidence in what their government has told them about our policy. The American people cannot and should not be asked to support a policy which involves the overriding issues of war and peace unless they know the truth about that policy.

3 Tonight I would like to answer some of the questions that I know are on the minds of many of you listening to me.

—How and why did America get involved in Vietnam in the first place?

—How has this Administration changed the policy of the previous Administration?

—What has really happened in the negotiations in Paris and on the battlefront in Vietnam?

—What choices do we have if we are to end the war?

—What are the prospects for peace?

4 Let me begin by describing the situation I found when I was inaugurated on January 20.

—The war had been going on for four years.

—31,000 Americans had been killed in action.

—The training program for the South Vietnamese armed forces was behind schedule.

—540,000 Americans were in Vietnam with no plans to reduce the number.

—No progress had been made at the negotiations in Paris, and the United States had not put forth a comprehensive peace proposal.

—The war was causing deep division at home and criticism from many of our friends as well as our enemies abroad.

5 In view of these circumstances there were some who urged I end the war at once by ordering the immediate withdrawal of all American forces. From a political standpoint this would have been a popular and easy course to follow. After all, we became involved in the war while my predecessor was in office. I could blame the defeat which would be the result of my action on him and come out as the peacemaker. Some put it quite bluntly: This was the only way to avoid allowing Johnson's war to become Nixon's war.

6 But I had a greater obligation than to think only of the years of my Administration and the next election. I had to think of the effect of my decision on the next generation and the future of peace and freedom in America and the world.

7   Let us all understand that the question before us is not whether some Americans are for peace and some Americans against it. The great question at issue is not whether Johnson's war becomes Nixon's war. The question is: How can we win America's peace?

8   Let us turn now to the fundamental issue. Why and how did the the United States become involved in Vietnam in the first place? Fifteen years ago North Vietnam, with the logistical support of Communist China and the Soviet Union, launched a campaign to impose a Communist government on South Vietnam by instigating and supporting a revolution. In response to the request of the government of South Vietnam, President Eisenhower sent economic aid and military equipment to assist the people of South Vietnam in their efforts to prevent a Communist takeover. Seven years ago, President Kennedy sent 16,000 military personnel to Vietnam as combat advisors. Four years ago, President Johnson sent American combat forces to South Vietnam.

9   Many believe that President Johnson's decision to send American combat forces to South Vietnam was wrong. Many others—I among them—have been strongly critical of the way the war has been conducted.

10   But the question facing us today is—now that we are in the war, what is the best way to end it? In January I could only conclude that the precipitate withdrawal of all American forces from Vietnam would be a disaster not only for South Vietnam but for the United States and for the cause of peace.

11   For the South Vietnamese, our precipitate withdrawal would inevitably allow the Communists to repeat the massacres which followed their takeover of the North fifteen years ago.
  —They then murdered more than fifty thousand people and hundreds of thousands more died in slave labor camps.
  —We saw a prelude of what would happen in South Vietnam when the Communists entered the city of Hue last year. During their brief rule there, there was a bloody reign of terror in which some 3,000 civilians were clubbed, shot to death and buried in mass graves.
  —With the sudden collapse of our support, these atrocities of Hue would become the nightmare of the entire nation—and particularly for the million and a half Catholic refugees who fled to South Vietnam when the Communists took over the North in 1954.

12   For the United States, this first defeat in our nation's history would result in a collapse of confidence in American leadership, not only in Asia but throughout the world.

13   Three American Presidents have recognized the great stakes involved in Vietnam and understood what had to be done.

>   —In 1963, President Kennedy said with his characteristic eloquence
>   and clarity, "We want to see a stable government there carrying on
>   the struggle to maintain its national independence. We believe
>   strongly in that. We're not going to withdraw from that effort. In
>   my opinion for us to withdraw from that effort would mean a
>   collapse not only of South Vietnam, but Southeast Asia, so we're
>   going to stay there."

>   —President Eisenhower and President Johnson expressed the same
>   conclusion during their terms of office.

14   For the future of peace, precipitate withdrawal would thus be a
disaster of immense magnitude.

>   —A nation cannot remain great if it betrays its allies and lets down
>   its friends.

>   —Our defeat and humiliation in South Vietnam would without ques-
>   tion promote recklessness in the councils of those great powers
>   who have not yet abandoned their goals of world conquest.

>   —This would spark violence wherever our commitments help main-
>   tain peace—in the Middle East, in Berlin, eventually even in the
>   Western Hemisphere.

15   Ultimately, this would cost more lives. It would not bring peace.
It would bring more war.

16   For these reasons, I rejected the recommendation that I should
end the war by immediately withdrawing all our forces. I chose instead
to change American policy on both the negotiating front and the battlefront. In order to end a war fought on many fronts, I initiated a pursuit
for peace on many fronts. In a television speech on May 14, in a speech
before the United Nations, and on a number of other occasions I set
forth our peace proposals in great detail.

>   —We have offered the complete withdrawal of all outside forces within
>   one year.

>   —We have proposed a ceasefire under international supervision.

>   —We have offered free elections under international supervision with
>   the Communists participating in the organization and conduct of
>   the elections as an organized political force. The Saigon government
>   has pledged to accept the result of the elections.

17   We have not put forth our proposals on a take-it-or-leave-it basis.
We have indicated that we are willing to discuss the proposals that have
been put forth by the other side. We have declared that anything is

negotiable except the right of the people of South Vietnam to determine their own future. At the Paris peace conference, Ambassador Lodge has demonstrated our flexibility and good faith in 40 public meetings. Hanoi has refused even to discuss our proposals. They demand our unconditional acceptance of their terms; that we withdraw all American forces immediately and unconditionally and that we overthrow the government of South Vietnam as we leave.

18 We have not limited our peace initiatives to public forums and public statements. I recognized that a long and bitter war like this usually cannot be settled in a public forum. That is why in addition to the public statements and negotiations I have explored every possible private avenue that might lead to a settlement.

19 Therefore, tonight I am taking the unprecedented step of disclosing some of our other initiatives for peace—initiatives we undertook privately and secretly because we thought that we thereby might open a door which publicly would be closed.

20 I did not wait for my inauguration to begin my quest for peace.

—Soon after my election, through an individual who is directly in contact on a personal basis with the leaders of North Vietnam, I made two private offers for a rapid, comprehensive settlement. Hanoi's replies called in effect for our surrender before negotiations.

—Since the Soviet Union furnishes most of the military equipment for North Vietnam, Secretary of State Rogers, my assistant for National Security Affairs, Dr. Kissinger, Ambassador Lodge, and I personally, have met on a number of occasions with representatives of the Soviet government to enlist their assistance in getting meaningful negotiations started.

21 In addition we have had extended discussions directed toward that same end with representatives of other governments which have diplomatic relations with North Vietnam. None of these initiatives have to date produced results.

—In mid-July, I became convinced that it was necessary to make a major move to break the deadlock in the Paris talks. I spoke directly, in this office, where I'm now sitting, with an individual who had known Ho Chi Minh on a personal basis for 25 years. Through him I sent a letter to Ho Chi Minh. I did this outside of the usual diplomatic channels with the hope that with the necessity of making statements for propaganda removed, there might be constructive progress toward bringing the war to an end. Let me read from that letter:

Dear Mr. President:
I realize that it is difficult to communicate meaningfully across the
gulf of four years of war. But precisely because of this gulf, I wanted to
take this opportunity to reaffirm in all solemnity my desire to work for
a just peace. I deeply believe that the war in Vietnam has gone on too
long and delay in bringing it to an end can benefit no one—least of all
the people of Vietnam.

The time has come to move forward at the conference table toward an
early resolution of this tragic war. You will find us forthcoming and
open-minded in a common effort to bring the blessings of peace to the
brave people of Vietnam. Let history record that at this critical juncture,
both sides turned their face toward peace rather than toward conflict
and war.

I received Ho Chi Minh's reply on August 30, three days before his
death. It simply reiterated the public position North Vietnam had
taken in the Paris talks and flatly rejected my initiative. The full
text of both letters is being released to the press.

—In addition to the public meetings I have referred to, Ambassador
Lodge has met with Vietnam's chief negotiator in Paris in 11 private
meetings.

—We have taken other significant initiatives which must remain
secret to keep open some channels of communication which may
still prove to be productive.

22   The effect of all the public, private, and secret negotiations which
have been undertaken since the bombing halt a year ago, and since this
Administration came into office on January 20, can be summed up in
one sentence—no progress whatever has been made except agreement on
the shape of the bargaining table.

23   Well now, who's at fault? It has become clear that the obstacle in
negotiating an end to the war is not the President of the United States.
And it is not the South Vietnamese government. The obstacle is the other
side's absolute refusal to show the least willingness to join us in seeking
a just peace. It will not do so while it is convinced that all it has to do is
to wait for our next concession, and our next concession after that one,
until it gets everything it wants. There can be now no longer any doubt
that progress in negotiation depends above all on Hanoi's deciding to
negotiate—to negotiate seriously.

24   I realize that this report on our efforts on the diplomatic front is
discouraging to the American people. But the American people are entitled to know the truth—the bad news as well as the good news where
the lives of our young men are involved.

25   Let me now turn, however, to a more encouraging report on another front. At the time we launched our search for peace, I recognized

that we might not succeed in bringing an end to the war through negotiation. I therefore put into effect another plan to bring peace—a plan which will bring the war to an end regardless of what happens on the negotiating front. It is in line with a major shift in U. S. foreign policy which I described in my press conference at Guam on July 25. Let me briefly explain what has been described as the Nixon Doctrine—a policy which not only will help end the war in Vietnam but which is an essential element of our program to prevent future Vietnams.

26   We Americans are a do-it-yourself people—an impatient people. Instead of teaching someone else to do a job, we like to do it ourselves. This trait has been carried over into our foreign policy. In Korea and again in Vietnam, the United States furnished most of the money, most of the arms, and most of the men to help the people of those countries defend their freedom against Communist aggression. Before any American troops were committed to Vietnam, a leader of another Asian country expressed this opinion to me when I was traveling in Asia as a private citizen. "When you are trying to assist another nation defend its freedom, U. S. policy should be to help them fight the war but not to fight the war for them."

27   Well, in accordance with this wise counsel, I laid down in Guam these three principles as guidelines for future American policy toward Asia:

1. The United States will keep all of our treaty commitments.
2. We shall provide a shield if a nuclear power threatens the freedom of a nation allied with us or of a nation whose survival we consider vital to our security.
3. In cases involving other types of aggression, we shall furnish military and economic assistance when requested in accordance with our treaty commitments. But we shall look to the nation directly threatened to assume the primary responsibility of providing the manpower for its defense.

28   After I announced this policy, I found that the leaders of the Philippines, Thailand, Vietnam, South Korea, and other nations which might be threatened by Communist aggression welcomed this new direction in American foreign policy.

29   The defense of freedom is everybody's business—not just America's business. And it is particularly the responsibility of the people whose freedom is threatened. In the previous Administration we Americanized the war in Vietnam. In this Administration we are Vietnamizing the search for peace. The policy of the previous Administration not only resulted in our assuming the primary responsibility for fighting the war

but even more significantly it did not adequately stress the goal of
strengthening the South Vietnamese so that they could defend themselves when we left.

30   The Vietnamization Plan was launched following Secretary Laird's
visit to Vietnam in March. Under the plan, I ordered a substantial increase in the training and equipment of South Vietnamese forces. In
July, on my visit to Vietnam, I changed General Abram's orders so that
they were consistent with the objectives of our new policy. Under the
new orders the primary mission of our troops is to enable the South
Vietnamese forces to assume the full responsibility for the security of
South Vietnam. Our air operations have been reduced by over 20 percent.

31   We have now begun to see the results of this long overdue change
in American policy in Vietnam.
   —After five years of Americans going into Vietnam, we are finally
      bringing American men home. By December 15, over 60,000 men will
      have been withdrawn from South Vietnam—including 20 percent of
      all of our combat troops.
   —The South Vietnamese have continued to gain in strength. As a re-
      sult they have been able to take over combat responsibilities from
      our American forces.

32   Two other significant developments have occurred since this Ad-
ministration took office in January.
   —Enemy infiltration, infiltration which is essential if they are to
      launch an attack, over the last three months is less than 20 percent
      of what it was over the similar period last year.
   —Most important—United States casualties have declined during the
      last two months to the lowest point in three years.

33   Let me turn now to our program for the future. We have adopted
a plan which we have worked out in cooperation with the South Vietnamese for the complete withdrawal of all U. S. ground combat forces
and their replacement by South Vietnamese forces on an orderly scheduled timetable. This withdrawal will be made from strength and not from
weakness. As South Vietnamese forces become stronger, the rate of
American withdrawal can become greater.

34   I have not and do not intend to announce the timetable for our
program. There are obvious reasons for this decision which I am sure
you will understand. As I have indicated on several occasions, the rate of
withdrawal will depend on developments on three fronts:
   —One is the progress which may be made at the Paris talks. An
      announcement of a fixed timetable for our withdrawal would com-

pletely remove any incentive for the enemy to negotiate an agreement.

—They would simply wait until our forces had withdrawn and then move in.

35   The other two factors on which we will base our withdrawal decisions are the level of enemy activity and the progress of the training program of the South Vietnamese forces. And I am glad to be able to repeat tonight progress on both these fronts has been greater than we anticipated when we started the withdrawal program in June. As a result, our timetable for withdrawal is more optimistic now than when we made our first estimates in June. This clearly demonstrates why it is not wise to be frozen in on a fixed timetable. We must retain the flexibility to base each withdrawal decision on the situation as it is at that time rather than on estimates that are no longer valid.

36   Along with this optimistic estimate, I must—in all candor—leave one note of caution. If the level of enemy activity significantly increases, we might have to adjust our timetable accordingly. However, I want the record to be completely clear on one point. At the time of the bombing halt last November, there was some confusion as to whether there was an understanding on the part of the enemy that if we stopped the bombing they would stop shelling cities of South Vietnam. I want to be sure there is no misunderstanding on the part of the enemy with regard to our withdrawal program.

37   We have noted the reduced level of infiltration and the reduction of our casualties and are basing our withdrawal decisions partially on those factors. If the level of infiltration or our casualties increase while we are trying to scale down the fighting, it will be the result of a conscious decision by the enemy. Hanoi could make no greater mistake than to assume that an increase in violence will be to its own advantage. If I conclude that increased enemy action jeopardizes our remaining forces in Vietnam, I shall not hesitate to take strong and effective measures to deal with that situation.

38   This is not a threat. This is a statement of policy which as Commander-in-Chief of our Armed Forces I am making in meeting my responsibility for the protection of American fighting men wherever they may be. I am sure that you can recognize from what I have said that we have only two choices open to us if we want to end the war.

—I can order an immediate, precipitate withdrawal of all Americans from Vietnam without regard to the effects of that action.

—Or we can persist in our search for a just peace through a negotiated settlement if possible, or through continued implementation of our plan for Vietnamization if necessary—a plan in which we will withdraw all of our forces from Vietnam on a schedule in accordance with our program, as the South Vietnamese become strong enough to defend their own freedom.

39   I have chosen the second course. It is not the easy way. It is the right way. It is a plan which will end the war and serve the cause of peace—not just in Vietnam but in the Pacific and in the world.

40   In speaking of the consequences of a precipitate withdrawal, I mentioned that our allies would lose confidence in America. Far more dangerous, we would lose confidence in ourselves. The immediate reaction would be a sense of relief as our men came home. But as we saw the consequences of what we had done, inevitable remorse and divisive recrimination would scar our spirit as a people.

41   We have faced other crises in our history and have become stronger by rejecting the easy way out and taking the right way in meeting our challenges. Our greatness as a nation has been our capacity to do what had to be done when we knew our course was right.

42   I recognize that some of my fellow citizens disagree with the plan for peace I have chosen. Honest and patriotic Americans have reached different conclusions as to how peace should be achieved. In San Francisco a few weeks ago, I saw demonstrators carrying signs reading: "Lose in Vietnam, bring the boys home."

43   One of the strengths of our free society is that any American has a right to reach that conclusion and to advocate that point of view. But as President of the United States, I would be untrue to my oath of office if I allowed the policy of this nation to be dictated by the minority who hold that view and who attempt to impose it on the nation by mounting demonstrations in the street.

44   For almost two hundred years, the policy of this nation has been made under our Constitution by those leaders in the Congress and in the White House who were elected by all the people. If a vocal minority, however fervent its cause, prevails over reason and the will of the majority, this nation has no future as a free society.

45   And now I would like to address a word, if I may, to the young people of this nation who are particularly concerned—and I understand why they are concerned—about the war.

—I respect your idealism.

—I share your concern for peace.

—I want peace as much as you do.

46   There are powerful personal reasons I want to end this war. This week I will have to sign 83 letters to mothers, fathers, wives, and loved ones of men who had given their lives for America in Vietnam. It is very little satisfaction to me that this was only one-third as many as I signed during my first week in office. There is nothing I want more than to see the day come when I no longer must write any of these letters. I want to end the war to save the lives of those brave young men in Vietnam.

—I want to end it in a way which will increase the chance that their younger brothers and their sons will not have to fight in some future Vietnam someplace in the world.

—I want to end the war so that the energy and dedication of our young people, now too often directed into bitter hatred against those they think are responsible for the war, can be turned to the great challenges of peace, a better life for all Americans and for people throughout the world.

47   I have chosen a plan for peace. I believe it will succeed. If it does not succeed, what the critics say now won't matter. Or if it does succeed, what the critics say now won't matter. If it does not succeed, anything I say then won't matter.

48   I know it may not be fashionable to speak of patriotism or national destiny these days. But I feel it is appropriate to do so on this occasion. Two hundred years ago this nation was weak and poor. But even then, America was the hope of millions in the world. Today we have become the strongest and richest nation in the world. The wheel of destiny has turned so that any hope the world has for the survival of peace and freedom in the last third of this century will be determined by whether the American people have the moral stamina and the courage to meet the challenge of free world leadership.

49   Let historians not record that when America was the most powerful nation in the world we passed on the other side of the road and allowed the last hopes for peace and freedom of millions of people on this earth to be suffocated by the forces of totalitarianism.

50   And so tonight—to you, the great silent majority of my fellow Americans—I ask for your support.

51   I pledged in my campaign for the Presidency to end the war in a way that we could win the peace. I have initiated a plan of action which will enable me to keep that pledge. The more support I can have from the American people, the sooner that pledge can be redeemed; for the more divided we are at home, the less likely the enemy is to negotiate in Paris. Let us be united for peace. Let us also be united against defeat.

Because let us understand: North Vietnam cannot defeat or humiliate the United States. Only Americans can do that.

52   Fifty years ago, in this very room and at this very desk, President Woodrow Wilson wrote words which caught the imagination of a war-weary world during World War I. He said: "This is the war to end wars." His dream for peace after that war was shattered on the hard realities of great power politics, and Wilson died a broken man.

53   Tonight I do not tell you that the war in Vietnam is the war to end wars. But I do say this: I have initiated a plan which will end this war in a way that will bring us closer to that great goal of a just and lasting peace to which Woodrow Wilson and every American President in our history has been dedicated. As President I hold the responsibility for choosing the best path to that goal and then for leading our nation along it. I pledge to you tonight that I will meet this responsibility with all the strength and wisdom I can command in accordance with your hopes, mindful of your concerns, sustained by your prayers.

Critique

An Exercise
in the Rhetoric of Mythical America

This major policy address on the Vietnam War was, in part, a response to the October moratorium demonstration, despite Nixon's assertion that he would, under no circumstances, be affected by it.[1] The address was followed by an even larger moratorium demonstration in November and by Spiro Agnew's harsh attacks on the news media for their analyses and evaluations of the President's speech.[2] This criticism is an attempt to appraise this discourse primarily in terms of criteria suggested within the address by the President himself.

At the outset the President tells us that there is deep division in the nation partly because many Americans have lost confidence in what the government has told them about the war. In the President's opinion the people of the nation should be told the truth. The three criteria the President explicitly suggests are truth, credibility, and unity, and he later implies a fourth criterion based on responsibility and ethical principles. In other words Nixon tells us that the address is intended to relate the truth, increase the credibility of Administrative statements about the war, unify the nation, and remind us of our duties as Americans.

[1] Cited in "Beyond the Moratorium," *New Republic*, Vol. 161 (October 25, 1969), p. 7.
[2] See Chapter 6.

Two serious misrepresentations cast doubt on the truthfulness of the President. First, he misrepresents his opposition by treating them as a homogeneous group who seek immediate, precipitate withdrawal epitomized by the slogan "Lose in Vietnam; bring the boys home." Hence he also misrepresents the policy options available to him. As the President recognizes, somewhat indirectly, there are four alternatives to the policy of Vietnamization: escalation, immediate and precipitate withdrawal, disengagement through negotiation, and a scheduled withdrawal with a fixed date of termination. He mentions the possibility of escalation only as a threat to Hanoi, should increased enemy activity jeopardize the process of Vietnamization. The primary focus of the President's refutation is immediate, precipitate withdrawal—a justifiable argumentative stance only if the bulk of his opposition supported this policy. Instead most of his critics supported the fourth option—a scheduled withdrawal with a fixed date of termination, such as former Senator Charles Goodell's proposed disengagement plan, which called for total withdrawal of all American troops in a year's time but continued economic and military aid to South Vietnam at the discretion of Congress and the President.[3] A few critics, such as Eugene McCarthy, advocated a negotiated settlement. But only a small minority of the peace movement supported immediate, total withdrawal. The President's characterization of his opposition is designed to make the alternatives to Vietnamization appear as extreme as possible so that the voices urging them will not be heeded. The misrepresentation of the opposition and the consequent focus on immediate, total withdrawal as the most important alternative allow the President to transform a complex policy question into a simple either–or decision:

> I am sure that you can recognize from what I have said that we have only two choices open to us if we want to end the war. I can order an immediate precipitate withdrawal of all Americans from Vietnam without regard to the effects of that action. Or we can persist in our search for a just peace through . . . Vietnamization. . .

The misrepresentation of his opposition makes the only apparent alternative to his policy as unattractive and radical as possible. This strategy may gull the audience, and it may make his speech more persuasive for some listeners, but the technique violates his earlier promise to tell the truth.

The second misrepresentation occurs in relation to what the President calls the "fundamental issue. Why and how did the United States become involved in Vietnam in the first place?" He answers this question with a dubious description of the beginning of the war:

[3] Charles E. Goodell, "Set a Deadline for Withdrawal," *New Republic*, Vol. 161 (November 22, 1969), p. 13.

Fifteen years ago North Vietnam, with the logistical support of Communist China and the Soviet Union, launched a campaign to impose a
Communist government on South Vietnam by instigating and supporting a revolution.

Now "fifteen years ago" was 1954, the year of the Geneva Agreements
that were to unify Vietnam through elections to be held in 1956. Those
elections never occurred because the United States supported Diem,
who refused elections and attempted to destroy all internal political
opposition, Communist and otherwise. The Vietcong did not persuade
Hanoi or Peking or Moscow to aid them against Diem until about 1959.
By 1965 South Vietnam was clearly losing, the point at which President
Johnson decided to send in United States combat forces.[4]

The surprising decision to give top priority to the historical question,
in a policy address that perforce must concern itself with the best means
of disengagement, merits consideration. The President's attempt to
perpetuate the now largely discredited justifications for United States
intervention serves at least two functions. First, it allows Nixon to appeal to history and historical values, to the prior decisions of Presidents
Eisenhower, Kennedy, and Johnson and to Woodrow Wilson and his
dream of a just peace. Nixon's policy becomes the logical outcome of the
decisions and values of his predecessors, and Nixon's way becomes the
American way. Second, emphasis on the origins of the war structures
the argument so that the primary justifications for the policy can be
ethical rather than pragmatic. The speech contains no information about
how the plan will work, no evidence for the consequences predicted, and
no analysis of how the Vietcong or Hanoi will view it. Instead almost
all the justifications are ethical; Vietnamization is "the right way." Although the misrepresentation of the beginning of the war may be believed because of the authority of the speaker, the evasion of the hard
questions of feasibility and costs is not consistent with the President's
promise to tell the truth.

Two major contradictions damage the President's status as a truth-
teller. Early in the speech he tells the audience that immediate withdrawal would be the popular and easy course, enhancing the prestige of
the Administration and increasing its chances of reelection. Yet at the
end of the speech it is clear that the President believes his opposition is
a "vocal minority" and that his policy represents the will of the "great,
silent majority." If so, isn't his policy the popular and easy one with the
best chance of returning him to the White House?

[4] "Nixon's Non-Plan," *New Republic*, Vol. 161 (November 15, 1969), p. 10; Tom
Wicker, "In the Nation: Mr. Nixon Twists and Turns," *New York Times*, 9 November
1969, p. E15.
   For a detailed summary of the history of United States involvement in Vietnam,
see "Historical Report on U. S. Aggression in Vietnam 1964 to 1967, Testimony by
Charles Fourniau" and "Juridical Report on Aggression in Vietnam, Testimony by
the Japanese Legal Committee," in John Duffett ed., *Against the Crime of Silence*
(New York: O'Hare Books, 1968), pp. 79–90, 105–118.

Similarly early in the speech Nixon explains that immediate and total withdrawal would be a disaster for the South Vietnamese because it would inevitably allow the Communists to repeat the massacres that followed their takeover of the North.[5] In response former Senator Goodell remarked that this argument rests on the assumption that the South Vietnamese army would be powerless to prevent a complete take-over of the South. Yet at the time of the address the South Vietnamese had over a million men under arms, while the Vietcong had about 100,000, and the North Vietnamese had about 110,000 in the South.[6] If these smaller armies could take over and massacre, then the president's proposed policy of Vietnamization is surely doomed because it assumes that the South Vietnamese army, with American equipment and training, can successfully take over the fighting of the war and defeat both the Vietcong and the North Vietnamese. The two notions seem somewhat contradictory.

The overwhelming questions concerning credibility are, of course, whether the President really had a secret plan for withdrawal and whether he really intended to end the war? The events that followed this address answered these questions for most Americans. Shortly after the address a Gallup poll reported that the Nixon Administration is facing the same crisis in public confidence on the war that confronted the Johnson administration: 69 percent of the Americans feel that the Administration is not telling the American people all they should know about the war, and 46 percent disapprove of the President's way of handling the Vietnam situation.[7] One critic, after careful analysis of the credibility issue, concludes that Nixon had a plan and sincerely intended to end the war. However, even this critic says "that his heart was not in it, that only the pressure of public opinion had caused him to em-brace what he for fifteen years rejected,"[8] and that the address seri-ously lowered his credibility with newsmen.[9]

In an immediate sense the speech may be called highly credible but, at the same time, extremely divisive. Gallup reported that 77 percent of those who heard it gave the President a vote of confidence;[10] still the divisions over the war were not healed. In fact the address played an important part in exacerbating the bitter conflict between what the President termed the "silent majority" and a "vocal minority" fervently seeking to prevail "over reason and the will of the majority." He char-acterized dissenters as a small group trying to impose their views and dictate policy "by mounting demonstrations in the streets," terms that

[5] For an analysis of the massacre issue, see Tran Van Dinh, "Fear of a Blood-bath," *New Republic*, Vol. 161 (December 6, 1969), pp. 11–14.
[6] Goodell, "Set a Deadline for Withdrawal," p. 13.
[7] *Los Angeles Times*, 7 March 1971, p. I1.
[8] Robert P. Newman, "Under the Veneer: Nixon's Vietnam Speech of November 3, 1969," *Quarterly Journal of Speech*, Vol. 56 (April 1970), pp. 170–171.
[9] *Ibid.*, p. 176.
[10] *Los Angeles Times*, 5 November 1969, p. I25.

place them outside acceptable processes for change in a democratic
society. He implied that the opposition was a partial cause for the con-
tinuation of the war when he said that "the more divided we are at
home, the less likely the enemy is to negotiate." Finally he says that
"only Americans," presumably only *dissenting* Americans, "can humiliate
and defeat the United States." These statements belie the theme of unity
and contradict his earlier assertion that "honest and patriotic Americans
have reached different conclusions as to how peace should be achieved."
In fact one critic has argued that the address was deliberately designed
to isolate dissenters from the majority of opinion.[11] If this address is to
unify Americans and fulfill the President's Inaugural promise to "bring
us together," it will do so only to the degree that the speaker has
silenced his opposition or shamed them into acquiescence.

The President also suggests a fourth criterion. The notion of responsibility or obligation appears frequently, and the President emphasizes that his policy is not the easy, but the right, way. An ethical
principle seems implicit. However, despite his numerous protestations,
the address does not call on Americans to assume responsibility. First,
the President never holds the United States responsible in any way for
its part in the war despite the role of the United States in undermining
the Geneva Agreements. Instead he places all blame for the initiation
and escalation of the war on North Vietnam, China, and Russia. Similarly he places all blame for the failure to negotiate a settlement on
Hanoi. Praise and blame on such controversial and complicated questions can be assigned so simply and clearly only if the intent is to avoid
all responsibility. Second, the President's repeated assertion of *his* responsibility, including his responsibility to choose the best path and
lead the nation along it, becomes the individual citizen's *ir*responsibility: The President will decide, the President will lead, and the President
will be responsible; while the "silent majority" of "forgotten Americans"
will follow, patriotic and undissenting, in the sure knowledge that quiet
acquiescence to his considered judgment is the path to victory, peace,
and honor.

The powerlessness and frustration felt by dissenters and demonstrators in the face of this rhetoric should be mirrored to some extent in
all of us. The President tells us, in effect, there is nothing we can do. By
definition, if we are vocal and dissenting, we are the minority whose
will must not prevail and to whom no heed will be paid. The only alternative is to join "the great, silent majority" in support of his policy.

In addition as many commentators have pointed out, the policy of
Vietnamization, viewed at its worst, is war by proxy in which the Viet-
namese supply the bodies while we supply guns, money, and advice.[12]
In this sense the policy is a means to avoid the responsibility for making

---

[11] Newman, "Under the Veneer," p. 172.
[12] "Nixon's Non-Plan," p. 10.

moral judgments about the war. Whether it is viewed as war by proxy or as a long, slow, costly process for ending American involvement, the policy of Vietnamization makes the pace of American withdrawal dependent on decisions made in Hanoi and Saigon and on factors almost wholly beyond United States control. Vietnamization may be "the right way," but it is also a way that limits United States' responsibility severely by placing the burden of decision on others. If the enemy is irresponsible, the threat, although disclaimed, is clear: Troop withdrawals will stop and military action will escalate; and it will be *their* responsibility. As a consequence Americans clearly are not asked to assume moral obligations.

From the point of view of the critic, the most intriguing statements in the speech are these:

> I have chosen a path for peace. I believe it will succeed. If it does not succeed, what the critics say now won't matter. Or, if it does succeed, what the critics say now won't matter. If it does not succeed, anything I say then won't matter.

The two statements about criticism are cryptic and more than a little mystifying. What does the President mean when he says, "If it does not succeed, what the critics say now won't matter"? Presumably he expects the critics to be negative and dissatisfied as they have often been. If they point out weaknesses in the policy, in the arguments, in the truth of what he says, if they point out contradictions and inconsistencies, and if the policy does not succeed, then what? Is the criticism of no matter? Such criticism should provide a partial explanation of why the policy did not work and what was faulty in the decision-making process. The same is true of the criticism of a rhetorical discourse. If the rhetorical act fails, the critics' comments are important because criticism should give some reasons for the failure of the rhetoric. Clearly, however, the President is giving notice that under no circumstances will he be affected by what the critics say, and such warning is precisely the tragedy, for criticism is the mechanism by which to improve the quality of rhetoric and of decision making. But Nixon has been quite bitter about criticism, as was evident in his concession speech of the 1962 gubernatorial campaign in California.[13]

What does the President intend when he says, "If it does succeed, what the critics say now won't matter"? In such a case the President would have proved the critics wrong, vindicating himself and calling the critics' methods and assumptions into serious question. In all likelihood such a moment would be gratifying for the President. However, if we take the rhetorical act as an analogy, can we consider the critical comments in-

[13] Richard Bergholz, "Nixon Admits Defeat, Indicates Intention to Give Up Politics," *Los Angeles Times*, 8 November 1962, p. 1.

consequential simply because the address was successful (at least in terms of the Gallup poll)? I think not. It may be futile to warn against the rhetorician who misrepresents, who is self-contradictory, who is divisive while asserting his desire for unity, or who disclaims responsibility while praising the idea of fulfilling moral obligations. But unless we become careful, discriminating critics, questioning and evaluating, we shall be constrained to make poor decisions and supporting policies destructive of ourselves, our society, and the world. In this respect Agnew's attacks on the concept of immediate critical analysis and evaluation are particularly ironic because his protest suggests that the policy and the address are both extremely fragile. The decision worth making and the policy deserving support, as well as the rhetorical act of quality, will withstand, even be strengthened by, critical scrutiny, and such criticism is the essence of democratic decision making.

Finally this address is an example of the perpetuation of American mythology. The President describes a mythical America whose business is the defense of freedom, whose strength has resulted from facing crises and rejecting the easy way, whose greatness has been the capacity to do what had to be done when it was known to be right. This mythical America is the last hope for the survival of peace and freedom in the world; this most powerful nation will not allow the forces of totalitarianism to suffocate the hopes of the peoples of the earth. This is a nation of destiny.

Nonmythical America presents quite a different picture. Nonmythical America supports totalitarian governments all over the world. Nonmythical America is engaged in a war in South Vietnam in which it is systematically destroying the civilian population and agricultural capacity of the country it is ostensibly defending. Nonmythical America practices a racism that makes a mockery of its mythic principles. The examples could go on and on. Concentrating so on the details of this address—whether this point or that is true or distorted—the critic can so easily forget that all these considerations rest on the speaker's assumption of a mythical America, which always seeks justice, freedom, and right despite difficulty and cost. These considerations become irrelevant and fragmented outside this mythic context. One commentator has made the point that "the only salutary aspect of Vietnam [is] the fact that it is forcing us to examine the misconceptions about ourselves and the world on which postwar American foreign policy has been based." [14]

Although this speech fails to meet the President's criteria of truth, credibility, unity, and responsibility, the most significant criticism is that this rhetorical act perpetuates the myths about America, which must be debunked and shattered if we are to find solutions to the prob-

[14] Fred Warner Neal, "Government by Myth," *The Center Magazine*, Vol. 2 (November 1969), p. 2.

lems that threaten imminently to destroy us. The "silent majority" may want to get out of Vietnam and to save face; it cannot have both—at least not quickly.

To avoid Vietnams of the future we must make a concerted effort to discover and scrutinize *non*mythical America. If in that scrutiny we pay particular attention to the rhetorical discourses that thresh out and formulate ideas of ourselves and our society, we may begin to solve the problems of the *real* America and of this shrinking world. That President Nixon is unwilling or unable to face the *real* problems is precisely the reason why this address is doomed to be so disappointing. It is, as almost every commentator has recognized, just "more of the same." [15]

[15] See, for example, Robert J. Donovan, "Verdict on President's Speech Up to 'Great Silent Majority,'" *Los Angeles Times*, 4 November 1969, p. 1; "The Legitimacy of Protest," *New York Times*, 9 November 1969, p. E14; John W. Finney, "The Critics: It Is Not a Plan to End U. S. Involvement," *New York Times*, 9 November 1969, p. E1.

For Further Discussion

1 Carefully describe the techniques used in the preceding critique and set up an alternative approach that would result in different evaluations.

2 What are the perceptible biases, if any, of the critic? Do they invalidate, wholly or in part, the critical evaluations offered? Explain.

3 To what extent does this address widen or narrow the "credibility gap" of the Nixon Administration? In this respect compare this address to the President's addresses announcing the Cambodian incursion of April 30, 1969 and justifying the policy of Vietnamization of April 7, 1971.

4 Read Richard Nixon's "Checkers Speech" and the criticisms by Barnet Baskerville and Henry E. McGuckin, Jr. Rhetorically speaking, do you think there is an "old Nixon" and a "new Nixon"?

5 Addresses that announce and advocate new policies are traditionally expected to encompass questions of practicality, feasibility, costs, and benefits. Evaluate the degree to which this speech fulfills these expectations.

For Further Reading

Barnet Baskerville, "The Illusion of Proof," *Western Speech*, Vol. 25 (Fall 1961), pp. 236–242.

Philip E. Converse and Howard Schuman, " 'Silent Majorities' and the Vietnam War," *Scientific American*, Vol. 222 (June 1970), pp. 17–25.

Henry E. McGuckin, Jr., "A Value Analysis of Richard Nixon's 1952 Campaign-Fund Speech," *Southern Speech Journal*, Vol. 33 (Summer 1968), pp. 259–269.

Robert P. Newman, "Under the Veneer: Nixon's Vietnam Speech of November 3, 1969," *Quarterly Journal of Speech*, Vol. 56 (April 1970), pp. 168–178.

Richard Nixon, "My Side of the Story," *Vital Speeches*, Vol. 19 (October 15, 1952) pp. 11–15.

Richard Nixon, *Six Crises* (Garden City, N. Y.: Doubleday & Company, 1962).

Neil Sheehan, Hedrick Smith, E. W. Kenworthy, and Fox Butterfield, *The Pentagon Papers* as published by the *New York Times* (New York: Bantam Books, 1971).

Five

George Wald

On March 4, 1969, scientists at the Massachusetts Institute of Technology, largest academic defense contractor in the nation, called a one-day work stoppage to dramatize their concern over the militarization of American science. On that date George Wald, professor of biology at Harvard University and a Nobel Laureate in physiology, made an address entitled "A Generation in Search of a Future." The immediate audience was composed of students and faculty in the sciences who shared the speaker's intense dislike for United States military policy and for the collaboration of scientists that made that policy possible.

The address still exists only because a Boston radio station reporter recorded it. Wald's message reached a larger audience because two Boston Globe reporters present at the address convinced their editors to print the complete text, a rare journalistic event. Massive public response resulted: The newspaper distributed 87,000 reprints; discussions and broadcasts of the speech occurred throughout the nation; and full or partial reprints appeared in seven foreign languages.*

---

* The process by which this address became available to the national audience is described in Ron Dorfman, "George Wald: But for the Grace of the *Boston Globe* . . . ," *Chicago Journalism Review*, Vol. 2 (May 1969), p. 4. A recording of the live presentation of this address is available from Caedmon Records (TC 1264). The address is reprinted here by permission of the author.

A Generation
In Search of a Future

1   All of you know that in the last couple of years there has been student unrest breaking at times into violence in many parts of the world: in England, Germany, Italy, Spain, Mexico, and needless to say, in many parts of this country. There has been a great deal of discussion as to what it all means. Perfectly clearly it means something different in Mexico from what it does in France, and something different in France from what it does in Tokyo, and something different in Tokyo from what it does in this country. Yet unless we are to assume that students have gone crazy all over the world, or that they have just decided that it's the thing to do, there must be some common meaning.

2   I don't need to go so far afield to look for that meaning. I am a teacher, and at Harvard, I have a class of about 350 students—men and women—most of them freshmen and sophomores. Over these past few years I have felt increasingly that something is terribly wrong—and this year ever so much more than last. Something has gone sour, in teaching and in learning. It's almost as though there were a widespread feeling that education has become irrelevant.

3   A lecture is much more of a dialogue than many of you probably appreciate. As you lecture, you keep watching the faces; and information keeps coming back to you all the time. I began to feel, particularly this year, that I was missing much of what was coming back. I tried asking the students, but they didn't or couldn't help me very much.

4   But I think I know what's the matter, even a little better than they do. I think that this whole generation of students is beset with a profound uneasiness. I don't think that they have yet quite defined its source. I think I understand the reasons for their uneasiness even better than they do. What is more, I share their uneasiness.

5   What's bothering those students? Some of them tell you it's the Vietnam War. I think the Vietnam War is the most shameful episode in the whole of American history. The concept of War Crimes is an American invention. We've committed many War Crimes in Vietnam; but I'll tell you something interesting about that. We were committing War Crimes in World War II, even before the Nuremberg trials were held and the principle of war crimes started. The saturation bombing of German cities was a War Crime. Dropping atom bombs on Hiroshima and Nagasaki was a War Crime. If we had lost the war, some of our leaders might have had to answer for those actions.

6   I've gone through all of that history lately, and I find that there's
a gimmick in it. It isn't written out, but I think we established it by
precedent. That gimmick is that if one can allege that one is repelling or
retaliating for an *aggression*—after that everything goes. And you see we
are living in a world in which all wars are wars of defense. All War Departments are now Defense Departments. This is all part of the double
talk of our time. The aggressor is always on the other side. And I suppose this is why our ex-Secretary of State, Dean Rusk—a man in whom
repetition takes the place of reason, and stubbornness takes the place
of character—went to such pains to insist, as he still insists, that in
Vietnam we are repelling an aggression. And if that's what we are doing
—so runs the doctrine—anything goes. If the concept of war crimes is
ever to mean anything, they will have to be defined as categories of acts,
regardless of alleged provocation. But that isn't so now.

7   I think we've lost that war, as a lot of other people think, too.
The Vietnamese have a secret weapon. It's their willingness to die, beyond our willingness to kill. In effect they've been saying, you can kill
us, but you'll have to kill a lot of us, you may have to kill all of us. And
thank heavens, we are not yet ready to do that.

8   Yet we have come a long way—far enough to sicken many Americans, far enough even to sicken our fighting men. Far enough so that
our national symbols have gone sour. How many of you can sing about
"the rockets' red glare, bombs bursting in air" without thinking, those
are *our* bombs and *our* rockets bursting over South Vietnamese villages?
When those words were written, we were a people struggling for freedom against oppression. Now we are supporting real or thinly disguised
military dictatorships all over the world, helping them to control and
repress peoples struggling for their freedom.

9   But that Vietnam War, shameful and terrible as it is, seems to me
only an immediate incident in a much larger and more stubborn situation.

10   Part of my trouble with students is that almost all the students I
teach were born since World War II. Just after World War II, a series
of new and abnormal procedures came into American life. We regarded
them at the time as temporary aberrations. We thought we would get
back to normal American life some day. But those procedures have
stayed with us now for more than 20 years, and those students of mine
have never known anything else. They think those things are normal.
Students think we've always had a Pentagon, that we have always had a
big army, and that we always had a draft. But those are all new things
in American life; and I think that they are incompatible with what America meant before.

11   How many of you realize that just before World War II the entire American army including the Air Force numbered 139,000 men? Then World War II started, but we weren't yet in it; and seeing that there was great trouble in the world, we doubled this army to 268,000 men. Then in World War II it got to be 8 million. And then World War II came to an end, and we prepared to go back to a peacetime army somewhat as the American army had always been before. And indeed in 1950—you think about 1950, our international commitments, the Cold War, the Truman Doctrine, and all the rest of it—in 1950 we got down to 600,000 men.

12   Now we have 3.5 million men under arms: about 600,000 in Vietnam, about 300,000 more in "support areas" elsewhere in the Pacific, about 250,000 in Germany. And there are a lot at home. Some months ago we were told that 300,000 National Guardsmen and 200,000 reservists —so half a million men—had been specially trained for riot duty in the cities.

13   I say the Vietnam War is just an immediate incident, because so long as we keep that big army, it will always find things to do. If the Vietnam War stopped tomorrow, with that big a military establishment, the chances are that we would be in another such adventure abroad or at home before you knew it.

14   As for the draft: Don't reform the draft—get rid of it.

15   A peacetime draft is the most un-American thing I know. All the time I was growing up I was told about oppressive Central European countries and Russia, where young men were forced into the army; and I was told what they did about it. They chopped off a finger, or shot off a couple of toes; or better still, if they could manage it, they came to this country. And we understood that, and sympathized, and were glad to welcome them.

16   Now by present estimates four to six thousand Americans of draft age have left this country for Canada, another two or three thousand have gone to Europe, and it looks as though many more are preparing to emigrate.

17   A few months ago I received a letter from the Harvard Alumni Bulletin posing a series of questions that students might ask a professor involving what to do about the draft. I was asked to write what I would tell those students. All I had to say to those students was this: If any of them had decided to evade the draft and asked my help, I would help him in any way I could. I would feel as I suppose members of the underground railway felt in pre–Civil War days, helping runaway slaves to get to Canada. It wasn't altogether a popular position then, but what do you think of it now?

18 A bill to stop the draft was recently introduced in the Senate (S.503), sponsored by a group of senators that ran the gamut from McGovern and Hatfield to Barry Goldwater. I hope it goes through; but any time I find that Barry Goldwater and I are in agreement, that makes me take another look.

19 And indeed there are choices in getting rid of the draft. I think that when we get rid of the draft, we must also cut back the size of the armed forces. It seems to me that in peacetime a total of one million men is surely enough. If there is an argument for American military forces of more than one million men in peacetime, I should like to hear that argument debated.

20 There is another thing being said closely connected with this: that to keep an adequate volunteer army, one would have to raise the pay considerably. That's said so positively and often that people believe it. I don't think it is true.

21 The great bulk of our present armed forces are genuine volunteers. Among first-term enlistments, 49 percent are true volunteers. Another 30 percent are so-called "reluctant volunteers," persons who volunteer under pressure of the draft. Only 21 percent are draftees. All re-enlistments, of course, are true volunteers.

22 So the great majority of our present armed forces are true volunteers. Whole services are composed entirely of volunteers: the Air Force for example, the Navy, almost all the Marines. That seems like proof to me that present pay rates are adequate. One must add that an Act of Congress in 1967 raised the base pay throughout the services in three installments, the third installment still to come, on April 1, 1969. So it is hard to understand why we are being told that to maintain adequate armed services on a volunteer basis will require large increases in pay; that they will cost an extra $17 billion per year. It seems plain to me that we can get all the armed forces we need as volunteers and at present rates of pay.

23 But there is something ever so much bigger and more important than the draft. That bigger thing, of course, is the militarization of our country. Ex-President Eisenhower warned us of what he called the military–industrial complex. I am sad to say that we must begin to think of it now as the military–industrial–labor union complex. What happened under the plea of the Cold War was not alone that we built up the first big peacetime army in our history, but we institutionalized it.

We built, I suppose, the biggest government building in our history to run it, and we institutionalized it.

24   I don't think we can live with the present military establishment and its $80–100 billion a year budget, and keep America anything like we have known it in the past. It is corrupting the life of the whole country. It is buying up everything in sight: industries, banks, investors, universities; and lately it seems also to have bought up the labor unions.

25   The Defense Department is always broke; but some of the things they do with that $80 billion a year would make Buck Rogers envious. For example: the Rocky Mountain Arsenal on the outskirts of Denver was manufacturing a deadly nerve poison on such a scale that there was a problem of waste disposal. Nothing daunted, they dug a tunnel two miles deep under Denver, into which they have injected so much poisoned water that beginning a couple of years ago Denver began to experience a series of earth tremors of increasing severity. Now there is a grave fear of a major earthquake. An interesting debate is in progress as to whether Denver will be safer if that lake of poisoned water is removed or left in place (*New York Times*, 4 July 1968; *Science*, 27 September 1968).

26   Perhaps you have read also of those 6000 sheep that suddenly died in Skull Valley, Utah, killed by another nerve poison—a strange and, I believe, still unexplained accident, since the nearest testing seems to have been 30 miles away.

27   As for Vietnam, the expenditure of fire power has been frightening. Some of you may still remember Khe Sanh, a hamlet just south of the Demilitarized Zone, where a force of U. S. Marines was beleaguered for a time. During that period we dropped on the perimeter of Khe Sanh more explosives than fell on Japan throughout World War II, and more than fell on the whole of Europe during the years 1942 and 1943.

28   One of the officers there was quoted as having said afterward, "It looks like the world caught smallpox and died" (*New York Times*, 28 March 1968).

29   The only point of government is to safeguard and foster life. Our government has become preoccupied with death, with the business of killing and being killed. So-called Defense now absorbs 60 percent of the national budget, and about 12 percent of the Gross National Product.

30   A lively debate is beginning again on whether or not we should deploy antiballistic missiles, the ABM. I don't have to talk about them, everyone else here is doing that. But I should like to mention a curious circumstance. In September, 1967, or about 1½ years ago, we had a meeting of M.I.T. and Harvard people, including experts on these matters, to talk about whether anything could be done to block the Sentinel system, the deployment of ABM's. Everyone present thought them undesirable; but a few of the most knowledgeable persons took what seemed to be the practical view, "Why fight about a dead issue? It has been decided; the funds have been appropriated. Let's go on from there."

31   Well, fortunately, it's not a dead issue.

32   An ABM is a nuclear weapon. It takes a nuclear weapon to stop a nuclear weapon. And our concern must be with the whole issue of nuclear weapons.

33   There is an entire semantics ready to deal with the sort of thing I am about to say. It involves such phrases as "those are the facts of life." No—they are the facts of death. I don't accept them, and I advise you not to accept them. We are under repeated pressure to accept things that are presented to us as settled—decisions that have been made. Always there is the thought: let's go on from there! But this time we don't see how to go on. We will have to stick with those issues.

34   We are told that the United States and Russia between them have by now stockpiled in nuclear weapons approximately the explosive power of 15 tons of TNT for every man, woman, and child on earth. And now, it is suggested that we must make more. All very regrettable, of course; but those are "the facts of life." We really would like to disarm; but our new Secretary of Defense has made the ingenious proposal that now is the time to greatly increase our nuclear armaments so that we can disarm from a position of strength.

35   I think all of you know there is no adequate defense against massive nuclear attack. It is both easier and cheaper to circumvent any known nuclear defense system than to provide it. It's all pretty crazy. At the very moment we talk of deploying ABM's, we are also building the MIRV, the weapon to circumvent ABM's.

36   So far as I know, the most conservative estimates of Americans killed in a major nuclear attack, with everything working as well as can be hoped and all foreseeable precautions taken, run to about 50 millions. We have become callous to gruesome statistics, and this seems at first to be only another gruesome statistic. You think, Bang!—and next morning, if you're still there, you read in the newspapers that 50 million people were killed.

37   But that isn't the way it happens. When we killed close to 200,000 people with those first little, old-fashioned uranium bombs that we dropped on Hiroshima and Nagasaki, about the same number of persons was maimed, blinded, burned, poisoned, and otherwise doomed. A lot of them took a long time to die.

38   That's the way it would be. Not a bang, and a certain number of corpses to bury; but a nation filled with millions of helpless, maimed, tortured, and doomed persons, and the survivors of a nuclear holocaust will be huddled with their families in shelters, with guns ready to fight off their neighbors, trying to get some uncontaminated food and water.

39   A few months ago Senator Richard Russell of Georgia ended a speech in the Senate with the words: "If we have to start over again with another Adam and Eve, I want them to be Americans; and I want them on this continent and not in Europe." That was a United States senator holding a patriotic speech. Well, here is a Nobel Laureate who thinks that those words are criminally insane.

40   How real is the threat of full-scale nuclear war? I have my own very inexpert idea, but realizing how little I know and fearful that I may be a little paranoid on this subject, I take every opportunity to ask reputed experts. I asked that question of a very distinguished professor of government at Harvard about a month ago. I asked him what sort of odds he would lay on the possibility of full-scale nuclear war within the foreseeable future. "Oh," he said comfortably, "I think I can give you a pretty good answer to that question. I estimate the probability of full-scale nuclear war, provided that the situation remains about as it is now, at 2 percent per year." Anybody can do the simple calculation that shows that 2 percent per year means that the chance of having that full-scale nuclear war by 1990 is about one in three, and by 2000, it is about 50–50.

41   I think I know what is bothering the students. I think that what we are up against is a generation that is by no means sure that it has a future.

42   I am growing old, and my future, so to speak, is already behind me. But there are those students of mine who are in my mind always; and there are my children, two of them now 7 and 9, whose future is infinitely more precious to me than my own. So it isn't just their generation; it's mine too. We're all in it together.

43   Are we to have a chance to live? We don't ask for prosperity, or security; only for a reasonable chance to live, to work out our destiny in peace and decency. Not to go down in history as the apocalyptic generation.

44   And it isn't only nuclear war. Another overwhelming threat is the population explosion. That has not yet even begun to come under control. There is every indication that the world population will double before the year 2000; and there is a widespread expectation of famine on an unprecedented scale in many parts of the world. The experts tend to differ only in the estimates of when those famines will begin. Some think by 1980, others think they can be staved off until 1990, very few expect that they will not occur by the year 2000.*

45   That is the problem. Unless we can be surer than we now are that this generation has a future, nothing else matters. It's not good enough to give it tender loving care, to supply it with breakfast foods, to buy it expensive educations. Those things don't mean anything unless this generation has a future. And we're not sure that it does.

46   I don't think that there are problems of youth, or student problems. All the real problems I know are grown-up problems.

47   Perhaps you will think me altogether absurd, or "academic," or hopelessly innocent—that is, until you think of the alternatives—if I say as I do to you now: we have to get rid of those nuclear weapons. There is nothing worth having that can be obtained by nuclear war: nothing material or ideological, no tradition that it can defend. It is utterly self-defeating. Those atom bombs represent an unusable weapon. The only use for an atom bomb is to keep somebody else from using one. It can give us no protection, but only the doubtful satisfaction of retaliation. Nuclear weapons offer us nothing but a balance of terror; and a balance of terror is still terror.

48   We have to get rid of those atomic weapons, here and everywhere. We cannot live with them.

49   I think we've reached a point of great decision, not just for our nation, not only for all humanity, but for life upon the Earth. I tell my students, with a feeling of pride that I hope they will share, that the carbon, nitrogen, and oxygen that make up 99 percent of our living substance were cooked in the deep interiors of earlier generations of dying stars. Gathered up from the ends of the universe, over billions of years, eventually they came to form in part the substance of our sun, its planets, and ourselves. Three billion years ago life arose upon the Earth. It seems to be the only life in the solar system. Many a star has since been born and died.

50   About two million years ago, man appeared. He has become the dominant species on the Earth. All other living things, animal and plant, live by his sufferance. He is the custodian of life on Earth. It's a big responsibility.

* This paragraph was added by Professor Wald in the edited version of the address; it was not included in the original presentation.

51   The thought that we're in competition with Russians or with Chinese is all a mistake, and trivial. Only mutual destruction lies that way. We are one species with a world to win. There's life all over this universe, but in all the universe we are the only men.

52   Our business is with life, not death. Our challenge is to give what account we can of what becomes of life in the solar system, this corner of the universe that is our home and, most of all, what becomes of men— all men of all nations, colors, and creeds. It has become one world, a world for all men. It is only such a world that now can offer us life and the chance to go on.

Critique

An Exercise
in the Rhetoric of Ultimate Values

"A Generation in Search of a Future" is, if not rhetorically unique, very nearly so, for this address, delivered extemporaneously to a small and select audience by a relatively unknown scientist, became a national event that ultimately reached a large and diverse national and international audience. Because of these unusual circumstances, there are two speech occasions and two audiences, each of which requires special and distinct criticism. But because the speaker could not have predicted that his address would reach the larger audience, he cannot be held responsible for whatever deficiencies the address may have for them.

As addressed to the immediate, friendly, and relatively homogeneous audience, the discourse is a masterpiece of moral and philosophical analysis; it reveals the basic principle underlying present United States military policy and offers an alternative and opposing principle to re-order the hierarchy of concerns for the audience. Rhetorical theorists have discussed such basic principles or ultimate values as *god terms*.[1] In rhetorical discourse a god term functions as an organizing principle that orders ideas into a hierarchy of relationships. The term symbolizes an ultimate value reflected in attitudes and actions or a fundamental principle unifying patterns of beliefs.

Wald rightly assumes the immediate audience shares his convictions that the Vietnamese War is morally wrong and should be ended, that the draft is undemocratic and unnecessary, that the military–industrial complex is the dominant force in the present United States foreign policy, and that all nuclear weapons should be eliminated. The address

[1] See Kenneth Burke, *A Rhetoric of Motives* (Berkeley: University of California Press, 1969), pp. 183–189; Richard Weaver, *The Ethics of Rhetoric* (Chicago: Henry Regnery Company, 1953), pp. 211–232.

attempts to strengthen or reinforce each of these preexisting attitudes. However, based on this description the discourse would not have received a standing ovation or have reached a larger audience. The address is creative, insightful, and eloquent because it explains the "profound uneasiness" of "this whole generation of students" by revealing that all the problems disturbing this generation are outgrowths of the fear of *death*, the ultimate value, or god term, of United States policy. Wald sets up a new hierarchy of dissent and concern in terms of an alternate value, *life*. The structure and movement of the entire rhetorical act reveal that all these contemporary sources of dissatisfaction form a hierarchy ordered by the god terms "life" and "death."

There are, then, two arguments in the address: (1) Their real and appropriate concern that they may have no future is the cause for the deep uneasiness of this generation of students. (2) The primary concern of those persons who wish to preserve "life" is the elimination of nuclear weapons. Each section of the discourse deals with military and foreign policy and, in terms of the values "life" and "death," points to these conclusions.

The first major section of the address deals with the Vietnam War, which some people believe is the major cause of student unrest. Although he believes this war "is the most shameful episode in the whole of American history," Wald concludes that the "Vietnam War, shameful and terrible as it is, seems to me only an immediate incident in a much larger and more stubborn situation." Even in regard to the Vietnam War, however, he introduces the god terms "life" and "death." He argues that we have lost the war, at least in part, because:

> . . . the Vietnamese have a secret weapon. It's their willingness to die, beyond our willingness to kill. . . . Yet we have come a long way—far enough to sicken many Americans, far enough even to sicken our fighting men. Far enough so that our national symbols have gone sour.

The implication is that the central moral evil of the war has to do with its preoccupation with killing and that this preoccupation has produced a deep *malaise* in the American spirit.

The second section of the address deals with the Pentagon, a big army, and the draft. Wald points out that although these "new and abnormal procedures" were instituted after World War II, students born since then assume these institutions have always existed and are normal. He also explains the relative insignificance of the war in Vietnam in relation to the size of our armed forces: ". . . the Vietnam War is just an immediate incident, because so long as we keep that big army, it will always find things to do." In other words as long as we have a large standing army, we will continue to be involved in death-dealing enterprises at home or abroad. Integral to maintaining a large standing army is a peacetime draft, which, according to Wald, is "the most un-American thing I know." A peacetime draft contradicts not only mere survival but a quality of life, the democratic way of life. Wald recalls this value by referring to American sympathy in the past for those individuals who tried to evade a peacetime draft in "oppressive Central European countries and Russia." Although Wald believes the draft should be eliminated, like the Vietnam War, it is of relative insignificance: ". . . there is something ever so much bigger and more important than the draft. . . . the militarization of our country." Wald argues that the present military establishment, particularly the Pentagon, "is corrupting the life of the whole country." His supporting examples—deadly nerve poison injected into a tunnel under Denver causing earth tremors, nerve gas killing thousands of sheep in Utah, and incredible amounts of firepower used at Khe Sanh—are all concerned with "life" and "death" and with irresponsible and inhumane behavior. At the end of this section he explicitly contrasts the two ultimate values: "The only point of government is to safeguard and foster life. Our government has become preoccupied with death, with the business of killing and being killed."

The third section of the discourse discusses nuclear weapons, a "dead" issue for experts who take a practical view and who consider such weapons "facts of life" that we are expected to accept. Wald is in violent disagreement; for him nuclear weapons are facts of "death" and the issue is "life." They cannot and must not be accepted as givens. "We will have to stick with those issues." Why? Because the issues of atomic weaponry *are* the issues of "life" and "death." Wald refers to the amount of nuclear armaments stockpiled in the United States and the Soviet Union and gives a vivid picture of what would happen if those weapons were used, a picture based on what happened when they were used in the past. Wald is trying to force us to understand what the god term "death" really means: "Not a bang, and a certain number of corpses to bury; but a nation filled with millions of helpless, maimed, tortured, and doomed persons."

The most dramatic moments occur near the end of the discourse. Wald creates a vivid, personal contrast between a world view based on "death" and one based on "life":

> A few months ago Senator Richard Russell of Georgia ended a speech in the Senate with the words: "If we have to start over again with another Adam and Eve, I want them to be Americans; and I want them on this continent and not in Europe." That was a United States senator holding a patriotic speech. Well, here is a Nobel Laureate who thinks that those words are criminally insane.

The intensity of the conflict between the two values could not be made more dramatic or explicit. The four concluding points of the address are personal statements by a biologist and humanist, who bases his world view on the god term "life." Wald marvels at the miracle of life itself and of human life on the planet Earth. He insists on man's responsibility for all life and emphasizes that man, despite national boundaries, cultural differences, and ideological conflict, is one species. He calls us to account for what happens to life, for we are its custodians. He reminds us that our Earth is one world and that mankind will have a chance to survive and endure only if we live by that belief.

In effect Wald contends that each person must choose between "life" and "death" for the human species and for all others. Choice of the god term "death" inevitably leads to the nuclear arms race, the ever-increasing possibility of nuclear annihilation, the militarization of American life, and involvement in perpetual violence and murder. If we choose "life," we stand in awe before the miracle of its development, see mankind as one species, and take responsibility for its preservation. Hence by working to eliminate nuclear weapons, the Pentagon, a large standing army, and the peacetime draft we will, in turn, eliminate their symptoms, such as the war in Vietnam.

For the immediate audience and other individuals sharing the speaker's beliefs the discourse is a masterpiece of moral and philosophical analysis; it illuminates a basic conflict in values and organizes what were formerly only loosely related problems—student dissent, the Vietnam War, the draft, the power of the Pentagon, and disarmament—into a coherent and consistent hierarchical structure. For this audience the discourse is a moment of insight in which the reader or listener suddenly glimpses the meaning of the uneasiness he feels. His uneasiness now makes sense, for by ordering these problems into a coherent structure in terms of ultimate values, the rhetorical act validates his discontent as appropriate, justified, and intelligible.

The discourse is far less satisfactory for the large, diverse audience that developed so unexpectedly. Although I personally agree with the conclusions of the author and admire his insight, commitment, and recognition of the responsibility of science for this state of affairs,[2] I believe that, for the most part, the discourse is a failure for the larger audience because it speaks primarily, if not solely, to those already in agreement, asserting rather than justifying its conclusions.

Wald begins by discussing the Vietnam War with which he clearly disagrees. Although opinion in the United States has moved steadily toward support of an early withdrawal, it is doubtful that a majority of Americans, now or at the time that he spoke, share his view that the United States has been committing war crimes in Vietnam [3] and com-

---

[2] Wald deleted several paragraphs in the edited version of the address reprinted here. In the live presentation, Wald directly implicates the American Institute of Biological Sciences and the National Academy of Sciences for their work with the Department of Defense. The illustrations leave no doubt of the active cooperation of these and other scientific groups in programs for the development of chemical and biological weaponry.

[3] Research on American reactions to evidence about the My Lai massacre is briefly summarized in Edward M. Opton, Jr., and Robert Duckles, "Mental Gymnastics on My Lai," *New Republic*, Vol. 162 (February 21, 1970), pp. 14–16.

mitted them in World War II, even before the essential principles of such crimes were defined at Nuremberg. Wald's proof of this statement is that he has studied the history of the World War II period and that the saturation bombing of German cities might have been used to indict some military leaders had the United States lost the war. Wald does not present evidence of United States war crimes in Vietnam, nor are his statements about such crimes in World War II likely to be convincing to the national audience. The now documented massacres in Vietnam, the subsequent trials of military personnel,[4] and the testimony of Vietnam veterans[5] have made these assertions more credible; but the speaker simply presumes that the audience agrees, and his statements are acceptable only to those persons already sharing his beliefs.

Similarly Wald attacks the double-talk that renames "War Departments," "Defense Departments," and he expounds against the justification of any means to repel aggression so that war crimes become impossible, a notion he attributes to ex-Secretary of State Dean Rusk. He presumes the audience believes, as he does, that we are not repelling aggression in Vietnam and that we cannot use "defense" as a justification for the terrible acts we have committed. But he does not explain; he does not argue; he does not demonstrate. He asserts and assumes. For those persons in agreement, his statement that we have gone so far in Vietnam that "our national symbols have gone sour" is deeply moving, and his question, "How many of you can sing about 'the rockets' red glare, bombs bursting in air' without thinking, those are *our* bombs and *our* rockets bursting over South Vietnamese villages?" requires no answer. But for a hostile audience, the appeal is ineffective.

The second issue Wald discusses—the Pentagon, a big army, and the draft—is the most effective for the larger audience. He attacks these institutions historically, reminding his audience that before World War II, all United States forces numbered only 139,000 men. He recalls that although the number rose to 8 million men during the war, it was only 600,000 in 1950 despite the cold war, the Truman Doctrine, and other commitments. Now, he tells us, we have 3.5 million men under arms including 200,000 reservists specially trained for riot duty in our cities. Such comparisons provide a perspective emphasizing the enormity of present "peacetime" forces, but his conclusion that "so long as we keep that big army, it will always find things to do" is highly controversial.

He argues that the draft must end and that a peacetime draft is un-American. Surely many people in the larger audience will recall a predraft America and will reminisce with Wald about stories of young men who tried to avoid impressment, in some cases by flight to the

---

[4] Ted Sell, "2 Generals, 12 Other Officers Cited for My Lai Dereliction," *Los Angeles Times*, 18 March 1970, p. 1.

[5] See, for example, Philip Scribner Balboni, "What Every Vietnam Veteran Knows," *New Republic*, Vol. 163 (December 19, 1970), pp. 13–15.

United States where they were welcomed. Wald immediately notes the estimated numbers of draft-age Americans who have emigrated to Canada and Europe, a jarring comparison even though many Americans, among them Vice President Agnew, would view such men as traitors.[6]

Wald believes that the size of our armed forces must be cut back, asserting that "a total of one million men is surely enough." Instead of defending that figure, he shifts the burden of proof from himself, stating, "If there is an argument for American military forces of more than one million men in peacetime, I should like to hear that argument debated." The argument to which he refers, whatever its merits, involves the complicated issues of American military presence in Europe and Asia.[7] Wald does not make a convincing case himself; he merely asserts his position and implies that no legitimate opposing arguments exist. For individuals in agreement the assertion is enough; for a larger audience it is not convincing. A similar problem exists with the speaker's analysis of the feasibility of a volunteer army. The processes by which he arrives at the conclusions that nearly half of our present armed forces are "true volunteers" and that present rates of pay are adequate to maintain an all-volunteer army are open to serious question.[8] Again, Wald speaks only to persons who already share his position.

Wald begins his discussion of the military–industrial complex by reminding the audience of former President Eisenhower's warning, a reference that is generally appealing. But he relabels it, with regret, the "military–industrial–labor union complex" without any explanation of the nature of alleged labor union complicity. The speaker uses three examples to document the monstrous effects of this complex. The first two were relatively unknown outside scientific and/or radical circles at the time of the address: the tunnel dug under Denver for disposal of nerve gas [9] and the thousands of sheep killed in Utah by a nerve gas, ostensibly because of a "testing error." [10] These illustrations are disturbing, and Wald's authority as a scientist may be sufficient to establish their credibility. To Wald and other persons sharing his view the third example that more explosives fell on Khe Sanh during the siege than fell on Japan in World War II or on Europe in 1942 and 1943 is an incredible, inhuman madness. However, to those persons supporting the war this

[6] See Chapter 6, p. 92.
[7] Alfred B. Fitt, discussing these issues, says that "over the last 20 years . . . we have had 2.5 million or more men on active duty. It seems likely that such a large force will be 'required' for years to come, so the feasibility question should be discussed in light of a 2.5-million man target." ("All-Volunteer Army: The Price Is Too High," Los Angeles Times, 31 January 1971, p. F1).
[8] Ibid. See also Jonathan Bingham, "Replacing the Draft," New Republic, Vol. 164 (January 16, 1971), pp. 17–21.
[9] Walter Sullivan, "Denver Gets a 'Shrinkage' Test as Quake-Area Well Is Tapped," New York Times, 4 July 1968, p. 42; J. H. Healy et al., "The Denver Earthquakes," Science, Vol. 161 (September 27, 1968), pp. 1301–1310.
[10] Seymour Hersh, "On Uncovering the Great Nerve Gas Coverup," Ramparts, Vol. 7 (June 1969), pp. 13–18.

example will not deter their hope that we can "win" although they may be surprised at such graphic evidence of the unbelievable resilience of the Vietnamese.

The last and most important idea of the address is the discussion of nuclear weapons. Wald argues that we cannot accept these weapons as necessary givens because the *fundamental* wrong in the world is their existence and their potential to annihilate all life. Wald explains that these weapons do not protect their owners because "there is no adequate defense against massive nuclear attack. It is both easier and cheaper to circumvent any known nuclear defense system than to provide for it." For the immediate, scientific audience simply stating that such weapons systems are self-defeating may be sufficient, but additional explanations and information is necessary for a larger, more general audience. However, the Hiroshima and Nagasaki models are clear and frightening to anyone. Wald gives a vivid, horrifying picture of the aftermath of nuclear attack, which results from the madness of developing nuclear weapons and the belief in a viable defense against them. He dramatizes this "criminal insanity" by quoting the statement of Senator Richard Russell, a poignant illustration of the chauvinism that has led to this dreadful predicament. This insanity is real to Wald, to his immediate audience, to me. But how many individuals in the larger audience share the sentiments of the Senator from Georgia rather than those of the Nobel Laureate?

How real is the threat of annihilation? Wald takes an expert estimate that if the present situation persists, the probability is 2 percent per year and calculates that the odds of full-scale war will be one in three by 1990 and 50–50 by the year 2000. I do not understand his calculations, and I do not believe the general audience will understand or accept his figures either. Yet he must convince them that the threat is real, imminent, and increasing.

The conclusion to all his arguments is put simply and clearly: "I think I know what is bothering the students. I think that what we are up against is a generation that is by no means sure that it has a future." He extends this conclusion to the larger audience by stating that this problem is indeed a real one for adults too, not just a problem for youth or students. As a biologist he pleads that men recognize they must fulfill their responsibilities as custodians of life on Earth: "The thought that we're in competition with Russians or with Chinese is all a mistake and trivial. . . . We are one species with a world to win. . . . Our business is with life, not death." And I agree. But I agreed before. And if you too believe that the Vietnam War is a shame and a horror, that we must end the draft and reduce our armed forces, that we must remove the stranglehold of the military–industrial complex on American life, and that we must eliminate nuclear weapons if we are to survive, then you will be deeply moved by this address. If you doubt those conclusions, then this discourse will not be convincing, and that is a tragedy of major proportions. The problem of nuclear weapons has become more complicated, and the odds of nuclear war have increased since the date of this address. Faced with such problems, we can ill afford the luxury of talking only to persons who already share our beliefs. Never was effective rhetoric needed more to rouse the unconcerned and the unknowing to the danger of nuclear warfare and to refute the death-dealing assumptions of persons who support further nuclear arms development. Unquestionably we require moral and philosophical analyses of the god terms underlying our policies, and we need such analyses from men like George Wald, who are both noted scientists and deeply committed humanists. But we also need basic information. In this confused, shrinking and expanding world, seeing simple facts simply is enormously difficult, and this problem is particularly true of nuclear weaponry. We must present facts to the uninformed and the undecided, and we must repeat these statements over and over again.

In response to 70 defensive antiballistic missiles (ABMs) deployed around Moscow by the Soviet Union, the United States has developed multiple independent reentry vehicles (MIRVs)—missiles capable of carrying many nuclear warheads, each of which may be aimed independently. There are now 41 American nuclear submarines, each of which carries 16 missiles—a total of 656. After MIRV, with each missile carrying 10 separately targetable warheads, American nuclear submarines will carry a total of 6,560 warheads, each missile about three times as powerful as the bomb that destroyed Hiroshima. These warheads became operational in January 1971. The first landbased MIRVs—Minutemen IIIs, each with three warheads—were deployed in June 1970. When these weapons become operational, our landbased warheads will increase from 1,000 to 3,000. In other words, in response to 70 defensive Soviet ABMs we are deploying about 8,000 additional offensive nuclear warheads— possibly the most overreactive offensive move in military history.[11] Now because of our deployment the Soviets are "MIRVing" their missiles, a move "Defense" Secretary Laird used to justify expansion of American ABMs.[12] The Nixon Administration decided recently that continued progress in deploying the MIRV is necessary both to national security and to negotiate from a position of strength at the Strategic Arms Limitation Talks,[13] an example of the sort of reasoning Wald describes

[11] These data are presented in two articles, "U. S. Will Deploy 1st MIRV's in June," *Los Angeles Times*, 11 March 1970, p. 1, and Irving S. Bengelsdorf, "Action . . . and Over-reaction . . . and Over-re-reaction . . . and . . . ," *Los Angeles Times*, 12 March 1970, p. II7.

[12] *Ibid.* For a more detailed discussion of Laird's arguments, see "U. S. Weighs Soviet Nuclear Intentions," *Los Angeles Times*, 24 May 1970, p. H4.

[13] D. J. R. Bruckner, "Arms Race Halt Hopes Dimming," *Los Angeles Times*, 10 April 1970, p. II6; Hubert Humphrey, "It's Nuclear Arms Curbs Now—or Perhaps Never," *Los Angeles Times*, 13 April 1970, p. II7; Ralph Lapp, "Correcting Our Posture," *New Republic*, Vol. 162 (March 28, 1970), pp. 12–15.

as part of world nuclear madness. And Wald is by no means alone in condemning present nuclear policy, for on March 4, 1970, one year after Wald's address, scientists throughout the nation met again to protest the misuse of scientific knowledge. Harold Brown, president of the California Institute of Technology and United States delegate to the first round of the Strategic Arms Limitation Talks at Helsinki, made the following statement:

> Past history has shown that the arms race consists of actions and re-actions. Most informed observers who have examined the array of nuclear and thermonuclear warheads, aircraft and anti-aircraft weapons, missiles and anti-missiles, have concluded that new cycles, like past ones, are unlikely to improve the security of either side, in the sense of making it less subject in case of a thermonuclear war to nearly complete destruction of its urban population and industry.[14]

In effect I have considered Wald's address as two distinct rhetorical events, and such treatment is something of a critical oddity. Usually when he intends a discourse for a select group, the speaker or writer can easily predict the second audience, or larger segment of the general public. Wald's discourse is one of the rare cases in which no such prediction was possible. Thus I must repeat that no rhetorical blame attaches to the speaker. However, we must view the philosophical and moral issues that Wald raised in this address in relation to the attitudes of the American people. If the beliefs of Wald, many of his fellow scientists, steadily increasing numbers of leading figures in all walks of American life, and myself are well-grounded, precisely these philosophical and moral issues must effectively be presented to the general public if we wish to ensure our survival.

---

[14] Bengelsdorf, "Action . . . and over-reaction. . . ." For a scientific estimate of the effect of MIRV's on the nuclear situation, see Leo Sartori, "The Myth of MIRV," *Saturday Review,* Vol. 52 (August 30, 1969), pp. 10 ff.

For Further Discussion

1   Carefully describe the techniques used in the preceding critique to arrive at both evaluations and set up alternative approaches that would result in different conclusions.

2   What are the perceptible biases, if any, of the critic? Do they invalidate, wholly or in part, the critical evaluations offered? Explain.

3   Compare and contrast the poetic and dramatic dimensions of this address with the poetic and dramatic dimensions of Paul Ehrlich's essay. To what extent are these dimensions significant for the success of this discourse as a rhetorical act?

4   Describe the ways in which this address is not a discrete rhetorical unit

but is an integral part of the continuing American dialogue concerning disarmament, the abuses of science, and the use of nuclear weapons.

For Further Reading

Edgar Bottome, *The Balance of Terror: A Guide to the Arms Race* (Boston: Beacon Press, 1971).

Matthew S. Meselson, "Chemical and Biological Weapons," *Scientific American*, Vol. 222 (May 1970), pp. 15–25.

G. W. Rathjens and G. B. Kistiakowsky, "The Limitation of Strategic Arms," *Scientific American*, Vol. 222 (January 1970), pp. 19–29.

Herbert Scoville, Jr., "The Limitation of Offensive Weapons," *Scientific American*, Vol. 224 (January 1971), pp. 15–25.

Six

Spiro T. Agnew

In 1969 Spiro T. Agnew achieved fame as a political figure by delivering addresses that savagely attacked various persons and processes with which the Vice President disagreed. The following two discourses are the most notorious of Agnew's rhetorical efforts and resulted in numerous articles, newspaper columns, and commentaries discussing Agnew's rhetoric and Agnew the man.

The spectacle of a Vice President attacking the intellectual community and the communications industry, with apparent Presidential approval, was a sobering one. Many persons argued that Agnew's discourses exerted divisive and dangerous pressures on the American political system. Other individuals applauded vigorously. Of all the major figures on the contemporary American political scene, Agnew seems most fairly described as a rhetorical "extremist."

The Vice President delivered the first of the following two addresses to the Mid-West Regional Republican Committee at Des Moines, Iowa, on November 13, 1969; the address was broadcast over national television.

Criticizing
Television on Its Coverage of the News

1   Tonight I want to discuss the importance of the television news medium to the American people. No nation depends more on the intelligent judgment of its citizens. No medium has a more profound influence over public opinion. Nowhere in our system are there fewer checks on vast power. So, nowhere should there be more conscientious responsibility exercised than by the news media. The question is are we demanding enough of our television news presentations? And are the men of this medium demanding enough of themselves?

2   Monday night a week ago, President Nixon delivered the most important address of his Administration, one of the most important of our decade. His subject was Vietnam. His hope was to rally the American people to see the conflict through to a lasting and just peace in the Pacific. For 32 minutes, he reasoned with a nation that has suffered almost a third of a million casualties in the longest war in its history.

3   When the President completed his address—an address, incidentally, that he spent weeks in the preparation of—his words and policies were subjected to instant analysis and querulous criticism. The audience of 70 million Americans gathered to hear the President of the United States was inherited by a small band of network commentators and self-appointed analysts, the majority of whom expressed in one way or another their hostility to what he had to say.

4   It was obvious that their minds were made up in advance. Those who recall the fumbling and groping that followed President Johnson's dramatic disclosure of his intention not to seek another term have seen these men in a genuine state of non-preparedness. This was not it.

5   One commentator twice contradicted the President's statement about the exchange of correspondence with Ho Chi Minh. Another challenged the President's abilities as a politician. A third asserted that the President was following a Pentagon line. Others, by the expression on their faces, the tone of their questions and the sarcasm of their responses made clear their sharp disapproval.

6   To guarantee in advance that the President's plea for national unity would be challenged, one network trotted out Averell Harriman

From *Congressional Record*, Vol. 115, Part 25, pp. 34257–34259.

for the occasion. Throughout the President's message, he waited in the wings. When the President concluded, Mr. Harriman recited perfectly. He attacked the Thieu Government as unrepresentative; he criticized the President's speech for various deficiencies; he twice issued a call to the Senate Foreign Relations Committee to debate Vietnam once again; he stated his belief that the Vietcong or North Vietnamese did not really want a military takeover of South Vietnam; and he told a little anecdote about a "very, very responsible" fellow he had met in the North Vietnamese delegation.   .

7   All in all, Mr. Harriman offered a broad range of gratuitous advice —challenging and contradicting the policies outlined by the President of the United States. Where the President had issued a call for unity, Mr. Harriman was encouraging the country not to listen to him.

8   A word about Mr. Harriman. For 10 months he was America's chief negotiator at the Paris peace talks—a period in which the United States swapped some of the greatest military concessions in the history of warfare for an enemy agreement on the shape of the bargaining table. Like Coleridge's Ancient Mariner, Mr. Harriman seems to be under some heavy compulsion to justify his failure to anyone who will listen. And the networks have shown themselves willing to give him all the air time he desires.

9   Now every American has a right to disagree with the President of the United States and to express publicly that disagreement. But the President of the United States has a right to communicate directly with the people who elected him, and the people of this country have the right to make up their own minds and form their own opinions about a Presidential address without having a President's words and thoughts characterized through the prejudices of hostile critics before they can even be digested.

10   When Winston Churchill rallied public opinion to stay the course against Hitler's Germany, he didn't have to contend with a gaggle of commentators raising doubts about whether he was reading public opinion right, or whether Britain had the stamina to see the war through. When President Kennedy rallied the nation in the Cuban missile crisis, his address to the people was not chewed over by a roundtable of critics who disparaged the course of action he'd asked America to follow.

11   The purpose of my remarks tonight is to focus your attention on this little group of men who not only enjoy a right of instant rebuttal to every Presidential address, but, more importantly, wield a free hand in selecting, presenting and interpreting the great issues in our nation.

12   First, let's define that power. At least 40 million Americans every night, it's estimated, watch the network news. Seven million of them view A.B.C., the remainder being divided between N.B.C. and C.B.S. According to Harris polls and other studies, for millions of Americans the networks are the sole source of national and world news. In Will Rogers' observation, what you knew was what you read in the newspaper. Today for growing millions of Americans, it's what they see and hear on their television sets.

13   Now how is this network news determined? A small group of men, numbering perhaps no more than a dozen anchormen, commentators and executive producers, settle upon the 20 minutes or so of film and commentary that's to reach the public. This selection is made from the 90 to 180 minutes that may be available. Their powers of choice are broad. They decide what 40 to 50 million Americans will learn of the day's events in the nation and in the world.

14   We cannot measure this power and influence by the traditional democratic standards, for these men can create national issues overnight. They can make or break by their coverage and commentary a moratorium on the war. They can elevate men from obscurity to national prominence within a week. They can reward some politicians with national exposure and ignore others.

15   For millions of Americans the network reporter who covers a continuing issue—like the ABM or civil rights—becomes, in effect, the presiding judge in a national trial by jury.

16   It must be recognized that the networks have made important contributions to the national knowledge—for news, documentaries and specials. They have often used their power constructively and creatively to awaken the public conscience to critical problems. The networks made hunger and black lung disease national issues overnight. The TV networks have done what no other medium could have done in terms of dramatizing the horrors of war. The networks have tackled our most difficult social problems with a directness and an immediacy that's the gift of their medium. They focus the nation's attention on its environmental abuses—on pollution in the Great Lakes and the threatened ecology of the Everglades.

17   But it was also the networks that elevated Stokely Carmichael and George Lincoln Rockwell from obscurity to national prominence.

18   Nor is their power confined to the substantive. A raised eyebrow, an inflection of the voice, a caustic remark dropped in the middle of a broadcast can raise doubts in a million minds about the veracity of a public official or the wisdom of a Government policy.

19   One Federal Communications Commissioner considers the powers of the networks equal to that of local, state and federal governments all combined. Certainly it represents a concentration of power over American public opinion unknown in history.

20   Now what do Americans know of the men who wield this power? Of the men who produce and direct the network news, the nation knows practically nothing. Of the commentators, most Americans know little other than that they reflect an urbane and assured presence seemingly well-informed on every important matter.

21   We do know that to a man these commentators and producers live and work in the geographical and intellectual confines of Washington, D. C., of New York City, the latter of which James Reston terms the most unrepresentative community in the entire United States. Both communities bask in their own provincialism, their own parochialism. We can deduce that these men read the same newspapers. They draw their political and social views from the same sources. Worse, they talk constantly to one another, thereby providing artificial reinforcement to their shared viewpoints.

22   Do they allow their biases to influence the selection and presentation of the news? David Brinkley states objectivity is impossible to normal behavior. Rather, he says, we should strive for fairness.

23   Another anchorman on a network news show contends, and I quote: "You can't expunge all your private convictions just because you sit in a seat like this and a camera starts to stare at you. I think your program has to reflect what your basic feelings are. I'll plead guilty to that."

24   Less than a week before the 1968 election, this same commentator charged that President Nixon's campaign commitments were no more durable than campaign balloons. He claimed that, were it not for the fear of hostile reaction, Richard Nixon would be giving in to, and I quote him exactly, "his natural instinct to smash the enemy with a club or go after him with a meat axe." Had this slander been made by one political candidate about another, it would have been dismissed by most commentators as a partisan attack. But this attack emanated from the privileged sanctuary of a network studio and therefore had the apparent dignity of an objective statement.

25   The American people would rightly not tolerate this concentration of power in Government. Is it not fair and relevant to question its concentration in the hands of a tiny, enclosed fraternity of privileged men elected by no one and enjoying a monopoly sanctioned and licensed by Government?

26   The views of the majority of this fraternity do not—and I repeat, not—represent the views of America. That is why such a great gulf existed between how the nation received the President's address and how the networks reviewed it. Not only did the country receive the President's address more warmly than the networks, but so also did the Congress of the United States. Yesterday, the President was notified that 300 individual Congressmen and 50 Senators of both parties had endorsed his efforts for peace.

27   As with other American institutions, perhaps it is time that the networks were made more responsive to the views of the nation and more responsible to the people they serve.

28   Now I want to make myself perfectly clear. I'm not asking for Government censorship or any other kind of censorship. I'm asking whether a form of censorship already exists when the news that 40 million Americans receive each night is determined by a handful of men responsible only to their corporate employers and is filtered through a handful of commentators who admit to their own set of biases.

29   The questions I'm raising here tonight should have been raised by others long ago. They should have been raised by those Americans who have traditionally considered the preservation of freedom of speech and freedom of the press their special provinces of responsibility. They should have been raised by those Americans who share the view of the late Justice Learned Hand that right conclusions are more likely to be gathered out of a multitude of tongues than through any kind of authoritative selection.

30   Advocates for the networks have claimed a First Amendment right to the same unlimited freedoms held by the great newspapers of America. But the situations are not identical. Where the *New York Times* reaches 800,000 people, N.B.C. reaches 20 times that number on its evening news. The average weekday circulation of the *Times* in October was 1,012,367; the average Sunday circulation was 1,523,558.

31   Nor can the tremendous impact of seeing television film and hearing commentary be compared with reading the printed page. A decade ago before the network news acquired such dominance over public opinion, Walter Lippmann spoke to the issue. He said there's an essential and radical difference between television and printing. The three or four competing television stations control virtually all that can be received over the air by ordinary television sets. But besides the mass circulation monthlies, out-of-town newspapers, and books. If a man doesn't like his newspaper, he can read another from out of town or wait for a weekly news magazine. It's not ideal, but it's infinitely better than the situation in television.

32   There if a man doesn't like what the networks are showing, all he can do is turn them off and listen to the phonograph. Networks, he stated, which are few in number, have a virtual monopoly of a whole media of communications. The newspapers of mass circulation have no monopoly on the medium of print.

33   Now a virtual monopoly of a whole medium of communication is not something that democratic people should blindly ignore. And we are not going to cut off our television sets and listen to the phonograph just because the airways belong to the networks. They don't. They belong to the people. As Justice Byron White wrote in his landmark opinion six months ago, it's the right of the viewers and listeners, not the right of the broadcasters, which is paramount.

34   Now it's argued that this power presents no danger in the hands of those who have used it responsibly. But, as to whether or not the networks have abused the power they enjoy, let us call as our first witness former Vice President Humphrey and the city of Chicago. According to Theodore White, television's intercutting of the film from the streets of Chicago with the current proceedings on the floor of the convention created the most striking and false political picture of 1968—the nomination of a man for the American Presidency by the brutality and violence of merciless police.

35   If we are to believe a recent report of the House of Representatives Commerce Committee, then television's presentation of the violence in the streets worked an injustice on the reputation of the Chicago police. According to the committee findings, one network in particular presented, and I quote, "a one-sided picture which in large measure exonerates the demontrators and protesters. Film of provocations of police that was available never saw the light of day while the film of a police response which the protesters provoked was shown to millions."

36   Another network showed virtually the same scene of violence from three separate angles without making clear it was the same scene. And, while the full report is reticent in drawing conclusions, it is not a document to inspire confidence in the fairness of the network news.

37   Our knowledge of the impact of network news on the national mind is far from complete, but some early returns are available. Again, we have enough information to raise serious questions about its effect on a democratic society. Several years ago Fred Friendly, one of the pioneers of network news, wrote that its missing ingredients were conviction, controversy and a point of view—the networks have compensated with a vengeance.

38   And in the networks' endless pursuit of controversy, we should ask: What is the end value—to enlighten or to profit? What is the end result—to inform or to confuse? How does the ongoing exploration for more action, more excitement, more drama serve our national search for internal peace and stability?

39   Gresham's Law seems to be operating in the network news. Bad news drives out good news. The irrational is more controversial than the rational. Concurrence can no longer compete with dissent. One minute of Eldridge Cleaver is worth 10 minutes of Roy Wilkins. The labor crisis settled at the negotiating table is nothing compared to the confrontation that results in a strike—or better yet, violence along the picket lines.

40   Normality has become the nemesis of the network news. Now the upshot of all this controversy is that a narrow and distorted picture of America often emerges from the televised news. A single dramatic piece of the mosaic becomes in the minds of millions the entire picture. And the American who relies upon television for his news might conclude that the majority of Americans feel no regard for their country. That violence and lawlessness are the rule rather than the exception on the American campus.

41   We know that none of these conclusions is true. Perhaps the place to start looking for a credibility gap is not in the offices of the Government in Washington but in the studios of the networks in New York.

42   Television may have destroyed the old stereotypes, but has it not created new ones in their places? What has this passionate pursuit of controversy done to the politics of progress through local compromise essential to the functioning of a democratic society?

43   The members of Congress or the Senate who follow their principles and philosophy quietly in a spirit of compromise are unknown to

many Americans, while the loudest and most extreme dissenters on
every issue are known to every man in the street. How many marches
and demonstrations would we have if the marchers did not know that
the ever-faithful TV cameras would be there to record their antics for
the next news show?

44   We've heard demands that Senators and Congressmen and judges
make known all their financial connections so that the public will know
who and what influences their decisions and their votes. Strong arguments can be made for that view. But when a single commentator or
producer, night after night, determines for millions of people how
much of each side of a great issue they are going to see and hear, should
he not first disclose his personal views on the issue as well?

45   In this search for excitement and controversy, has more than equal
time gone to the minority of Americans who specialize in attacking the
United States—its institutions and its citizens?

46   Tonight I've raised questions. I've made no attempt to suggest the
answers. The answers must come from the media men. They are challenged to turn their critical powers on themselves, to direct their energy,
their talent and their conviction toward improving the quality and objectivity of news presentation. They are challenged to structure their
own civic ethics to relate their great feeling with the great responsibilities they hold.

47   And the people of America are challenged, too, challenged to press
for responsible news presentations. The people can let the networks
know that they want their news straight and objective. The people can
register their complaints on bias through mail to the networks and
phone calls to local stations. This is one case where the people must
defend themselves; where the citizen not the Government, must be the
reformer; where the consumer can be the most effective crusader.

48   By way of conclusion, let me say that every elected leader in the
United States depends on these men of the media. Whether what I've
said to you tonight will be heard and seen at all by the nation is not my
decision, it's not your decision, it's their decision.

49   In tomorrow's edition of the *Des Moines Register* you'll be able
to read a news story detailing what I've said tonight. Editorial comment
will be reserved for the editorial page where it belongs. Should not the
same wall of separation exist between news and comment on the nation's
networks?

50   Now, my friends, we'd never trust such power, as I've described, over public opinion in the hands of an elected Government. It's time we questioned it in the hands of a small and unelected elite. The great networks have dominated America's airwaves for decades. The people are entitled to a full accounting of their stewardship.

Spiro Agnew delivered this address to the Montgomery, Alabama, Chamber of Commerce on November 20, 1969.

Address Extending Criticism
of News Coverage to the Press

1   Governor and Mrs. Brewer, Postmaster General and Mrs. Blount, Congressman Dickinson and the other distinguished members of the Alabama Legislature in the audience, officers, members of the board of directors and members of Alabama Chamber of Commerce and my Alabama friends all—I want to first express my very sincere appreciation to the people of Alabama for the very warm welcome which they have given to me and to my wife on our arrival here today.

2   And I particularly want to thank Governor Brewer for that very gracious and warm introduction. Governor Brewer and I never got to know each other as well as perhaps I would have liked because after he became Governor of this state, I didn't stay Governor much longer. But I want you to know one thing—that I did have a chance to serve with him and to be with him at a Southern Governors Conference, and I was tremendously impressed with the sincerity and the depth and the dedication of Governor Brewer, and I think the state of Alabama is very fortunate to have him.

3   As for the Postmaster General and his lovely wife, what can I say? He's taken us in Washington by storm, with his very perceptive feeling for people and his very warm concern about the problems of the country and, above all, his courage. Who else would dare to take on the monumental problems of reforming the postal division of the United States single-handed, other than Red Blount.

4   And to Red and Mary Kaye, also, a very, very warm thank you for opening your home to us and making us feel so welcome. I'm sorry we can't try that tennis court, but there just isn't time and the weather doesn't seem too conducive to that right now, anyhow.

5 I am really pleased that, included in the warmth of the welcome of the people of Alabama today was something that struck me as particularly significant and that was the fact that the young people at the airport were so enthusiastic. And it showed me beyond any doubt that young people, just as old people, refuse to be conformed and patterned into a specific mold and they have a right and a privilege and an obligation to think for themselves, and I'm glad to see how the young people of Alabama are thinking.

6 One week ago tonight I flew out to Des Moines, Iowa, and exercised my right to dissent. This is a great country—in this country every man is allowed freedom of speech, even the Vice President. Of course, there's been some criticism of what I said out there in Des Moines. Let me give you a sampling.

7 One Congressman charged me with, and I quote, "a creeping socialistic scheme against the free enterprise broadcast industry." Now this is the first time in my memory that anyone ever accused Ted Agnew of having socialist ideas.

8 On Monday, largely because of that address, Mr. Humphrey charged the Nixon Administration with a "calculated attack" on the right of dissent and on the media today. Yet it's widely known that Mr. Humphrey himself believes deeply that the unfair coverage of the Democratic convention in Chicago, by the same media, contributed to his defeat in November. Now his wounds are apparently healed, and he's casting his lot with those who were questioning his own political courage a year ago. But let's leave Mr. Humphrey to his own conscience. America already has too many politicians who would rather switch than fight.

9 There were others that charged that my purpose in that Des Moines speech was to stifle dissent in this country. Nonsense. The expression of my views has produced enough rugged dissent in the last week to wear out a whole covey of commentators and columnists.

10 One critic charged that the speech was disgraceful, ignorant and base; that leads us as a nation, he said, into an ugly era of the most fearsome suppression and intimidation. One national commentator, whose name is known to everyone in this room, said: "I hesitate to get in the gutter with this guy." Another commentator charges that "it was one of the most sinister speeches that I've ever heard made by a public official."

11   The president of one network said that it was an unprecedented attempt to intimidate a news medium which depends for its existence upon government licenses. The president of another charged me with an appeal to prejudice, and said that it was evident that I would prefer the kind of television that would be subservient to whatever political group happened to be in authority at the time.

12   And they say I have a thin skin.

13   Here indeed are classic examples of overreaction. These attacks do not address themselves to the questions I raised. In fairness, others, the majority of the critics and commentators, did take up the main thrust of my address. And if the debate that they have engaged in continues, our goal will surely be reached, our goal which of course is a thorough self-examination by the networks of their own policies and perhaps prejudices. That was my objective then, and that's my objective now.

14   Now let me repeat to you the thrust of my remarks the other night and perhaps make some new points and raise a few new issues. I'm opposed to censorship of television, of the press in any form. I don't care whether censorship is imposed by government or whether it results from management in the choice and presentation of the news by a little fraternity having similar social and political views. I'm against, I repeat, I'm against media censorship in all forms.

15   But a broader spectrum of national opinion should be represented among the commentators in the network news. Men who can articulate other points of view should be brought forward and a high wall of separation should be raised between what is news and what is commentary. And the American people should be made aware of the trend toward the monopolization of the great public information vehicles and the concentration of more and more power in fewer and fewer hands.

16   Should a conglomerate be formed that tied together a shoe company with a shirt company, some voice will rise up righteously to say that this is a great danger to the economy and that the conglomerate ought to be broken up. But a single company, in the nation's capital, holds control of the largest newspaper in Washington, D. C., and one of the four major television stations, and an all-news radio station, and one of the three major national news magazines—all grinding out the same editorial line—and this is not a subject that you've seen debated on the editorial pages of the *Washington Post* or the *New York Times*.

17   For the purpose of clarity, before my thoughts are obliterated in the smoking typewriters of my friends in Washington and New York, let me emphasize that I'm not recommending the dismemberment of the Washington Post Company, I'm merely pointing out that the public should be aware that these four powerful voices hearken to the same master. I'm raising these questions so that the American people will become aware of—and think of the implications of—the growing monopoly that involves the voices of public opinion, on which we all depend for our knowledge and for the basis of our views.

18   When the *Washington Times–Herald* died in the nation's capital, that was a political tragedy; and when the *New York Journal–American*, the *New York World–Telegram* and *Sun*, the *New York Mirror* and the *New York Herald Tribune* all collapsed within this decade, that was a great, great political tragedy for the people of New York. The *New York Times* was a better newspaper when they were all alive than it is now that they are gone.

19   And what has happened in the City of New York has happened in other great cities of America. Many, many strong, independent voices have been stilled in this country in recent years. And lacking the vigor of competition, some of those who have survived have—let's face it—grown fat and irresponsible.

20   I offer an example: When 300 Congressmen and 59 Senators signed a letter endorsing the President's policy in Vietnam, it was news—and it was big news. Even the *Washington Post* and the *Baltimore Sun*— scarcely house organs for the Nixon Administration—placed it prominently in their front pages. Yet the next morning the *New York Times*, which considers itself America's paper of record, did not carry a word. Why? Why?

21   If a theology student in Iowa should get up at a PTA luncheon in Sioux City and attack the President's Vietnam policy, my guess is that you'd probably find it reported somewhere in the next morning's issue of the *New York Times*. But when 300 Congressmen endorse the President's Vietnam policy, the next morning it's apparently not considered news fit to print.

22   Just this Tuesday when the Pope, the spiritual leader of half a billion Roman Catholics, applauded the President's effort to end the war in Vietnam, and endorsed the way he was proceeding, that news was on page 11 of the *New York Times*. The same day a report about some burglars who broke into a souvenir shop at St. Peter's and stole $9,000 worth of stamps and currency—that story made page 3. How's that for news judgment?

23　A few weeks ago here in the South I expressed my views about street and campus demonstrations. Here's how the *New York Times* responded:

> He (that's me) lambasted the nation's youth in sweeping and ignorant generalizations, when it's clear to all perceptive observers that American youth today is far more imbued with idealism, a sense of service ànd a deep humanitarianism than any generation in recent history, including particularly Mr. Agnew's generation.

24　That's what the *New York Times* said. Now that seems a peculiar slur on a generation that brought America out of the great depression without resorting to the extremes of communism or fascism. That seems a strange thing to say about an entire generation that helped to provide greater material blessings and more personal freedom—out of that depression—for more people than any other nation in history. We have not finished the task by any means—but we are still on the job.

25　Just as millions of young Americans in this generation have shown valor and courage and heroism fighting the longest, and least popular, war in our history, so it was the young men of my generation who went ashore at Normandy under Eisenhower, and with MacArthur into the Philippines. Yes, my generation, like the current generation, made its own share of great mistakes and great blunders. Among other things, we put too much confidence in Stalin and not enough in Winston Churchill.

26　But, whatever freedom exists today in Western Europe and Japan exists because hundreds of thousands of young men of my generation are lying in graves in North Africa and France and Korea and a score of islands in the Western Pacific. This might not be considered enough of a sense of service or a deep humanitarianism for the perceptive critics who write editorials for the *New York Times*, but it's good enough for me. And I'm content to let history be the judge.

27　Now, let me talk briefly about the younger generation. I have not and I do not condemn this generation of young Americans. Like Edmund Burke, I wouldn't know how to draw up an indictment against a whole people. After all, they're our sons and daughters. They contain in their numbers many gifted, idealistic and courageous young men and women. But they also list in their numbers an arrogant few who march under the flags and portraits of dictators, who intimidate and harass university professors, who use gutter obscenities to shout down speakers with whom they disagree, who openly profess their belief in the efficacy of violence in a democratic society.

28　Oh, yes, the preceding generation had its own breed of losers and our generation dealt with them through our courts, our laws and our system. The challenge is now for the new generation to put its house in order.

29   Today, Dr. Sydney Hook writes of "storm troopers" on the campus; that "fanaticism seems to be in the saddle." Arnold Beichman writes of "young Jacobins" in our schools who "have cut down university administrators, forced curriculum changes, halted classes, closed campuses and sent a nationwide chill of fear all through the university establishment." Walter Laqueur writes in *Commentary* that "the cultural and political idiocies perpetuated with impunity in this permissive age have gone clearly beyond the borders of what is acceptable for any society, however liberally it may be constructed."

30   George Kennan has devoted a brief, cogent and alarming book to the inherent dangers of what's taking place in our society and in our universities. Irving Kristol writes that our "radical students find it possible to be genuinely heartsick at the injustice and brutalities of American society, at the same time they are blandly approving of injustice and brutality committed in the name of 'the revolution.' " Or, as they like to call it, "the movement."

31   Now those are not names drawn at random from the letterhead of the Agnew–for–Vice President committee. Those are men more eloquent and erudite than I, and they raise questions that I've tried to raise.

32   For we must remember that among this generation of Americans there are hundreds who have burned their draft cards and scores who have deserted to Canada and Sweden to sit out the war. To some Americans, a small minority, these are the true young men of conscience in the coming generation. Voices are and will continue to be raised in the Congress and beyond asking that amnesty—a favorite word—amnesty should be provided for these young and misguided American boys. And they will be coming home one day from Sweden and from Canada and from a small minority of our citizens they will get a hero's welcome.

33   They are not our heroes. Many of our heroes will not be coming home; some are coming back in hospital ships, without limbs or eyes, with scars they shall carry for the rest of their lives. Having witnessed firsthand the quiet courage of wives and parents receiving posthumously for their heroes Congressional Medals of Honor, how am I to react when people say, "Stop speaking out, Mr. Agnew, stop raising your voice"?

34   Should I remain silent while what these heroes have done is vilified by some as "a dirty, immoral war" and criticized by others as no more than a war brought on by the chauvinistic anti-communism of Presidents Kennedy, Johnson and Nixon? These young men made heavy sacrifices so that a developing people on the rim of Asia might have a chance for freedom that they obviously will not have if the ruthless men who rule in Hanoi should ever rule over Saigon. What's dirty or immoral about that?

35   One magazine this week said that I'll go down as the "great polarizer" in American politics. Yet, when that large group of young Americans marched up Pennsylvania Avenue and Constitution Avenue last week, they sought to polarize the American people against the President's policy in Vietnam. And that was their right. And so it is my right, and my duty, to stand up and speak out for the values in which I believe.

36   How can you ask the man in the street in this country to stand up for what he believes if his own elected leaders weasel and cringe? It's not an easy thing to wake up each morning to learn that some prominent man or some prominent institution has implied that you're a bigot or a racist or a fool. I'm not asking immunity from criticism. This is the lot of a man in politics; we wouldn't have it any other way in a democratic society.

37   But my political and journalistic adversaries sometimes seem to be asking something more—that I circumscribe my rhetorical freedom while they place no restriction on theirs. As President Kennedy observed in a far more serious situation: This is like offering an apple for an orchard.

38   We do not accept those terms for continuing the national dialogue. The day when the network commentators and even the gentlemen of the *New York Times* enjoyed a form of diplomatic immunity from comment and criticism of what they said is over. Yes, gentlemen, the day is passed.

39   Just as a politician's words—wise and foolish—are dutifully recorded by press and television to be thrown up at him at the appropriate time, so their words should be likewise recorded and likewise recalled. When they go beyond fair comment and criticism they will be called upon to defend their statements and their positions just as we must defend ours. And when their criticism becomes excessive or unjust, we shall invite them down from their ivory towers to enjoy the rough and tumble of public debate.

40   I don't seek to intimidate the press, or the networks or anyone else from speaking out. But the time for blind acceptance of their opinions is past. And the time for naïve belief in their neutrality is gone. As to the future, each of us could do worse than to take as our own the motto of William Lloyd Garrison who said, and I'm quoting: "I am in earnest. I will not equivocate. I will not excuse. I will not retreat a single inch. And I will be heard."

Critique

An Exercise
in Manichean Rhetoric

From a national nonentity when nominated, from the apparently in-
sensitive bungler of the 1968 Presidential campaign, Spiro T. Agnew
emerged as one of the most significant rhetorical forces and became
perhaps the most formidable rhetorical weapon in the Administrative
armory.[1] Agnew's fame as a speaker dated from an address he made in
New Orleans on October 18, 1969, in which he characterized antiwar
demonstrators as "an effete corps of impudent snobs," and increased
with the "snobs and rotten apples" speech delivered at Harrisburg,
Pennsylvania on October 30, 1969.[2] However, his national notoriety was,
to a large extent, the product of live television coverage by all three
networks of his address at Des Moines, Iowa, criticizing television news
coverage. One week later at Montgomery, Alabama he amplified his
criticism to include newspapers. On January 30, 1970 he said he was
calling off his war on television broadcasters and then commented on
how pleased he was to be in Baltimore when the *Sun* papers were on
strike, even though the strike might cause a sanitation problem, because
"you know how they get rid of the garbage—they print it."[3] Subsequent
speeches,[4] letters to newspaper editors,[5] and a statement issued in response to press criticism[6] clearly indicated that Agnew was still deeply

---

[1] As of January 1970, Agnew had received 149,000 letters and telegrams in less
than four months, and all but 10,000 of them approved of him and of what he had
been saying (John Osborne, "Agnew's Effect," *New Republic*, Vol. 162 (February 28,
1970), p. 14). A Gallup Poll of late May 1970 reported that 49 percent of those questioned had a favorable impression of Agnew (*Los Angeles Times*, 21 June 1970, p.
E1). He is the most sought-after public speaker in the land, averaging 50 requests
per day, and the Republican Party's leading fund raiser (Jules Witcover, "Agnew:
The Step-by-Step Creation of a Conservative," *Los Angeles Times*, 10 May 1970, p.
G1).

[2] John Osborne, "Spiro Agnew's Mission," *New Republic*, Vol. 161 (November 15,
1969), pp. 17–18.

[3] "Agnew Calls Off TV War, Attacks Press," *Los Angeles Times*, 31 January 1970,
p. I3.

[4] Press reports of his speeches at Atlanta (Kenneth Reich, "Won't Be Quiet
Until Leftists Are—Agnew," *Los Angeles Times*, 22 February 1970, p. A16), at Houston
(Nicholas C. Chriss, "Not Muzzled by Nixon, Agnew Says as He Raps Press Again,"
Los Angeles Times, 15 May 1970, p. 1), at Los Angeles (Carl Greenberg, "News Media
Fail to Treat President Fairly, Agnew Says," *Los Angeles Times*, 9 June 1970, p.
I22), at Washington, D. C. (Don Irwin, "Some Media Slanting Reports on War—
Agnew," *Los Angeles Times*, 16 June 1970, p. I5), at Cleveland ("Agnew Assails
Critics Who 'Couldn't End or Win' War," *Los Angeles Times*, 21 June 1970, p. 1), and
at Denver ("Don't Hobble Nixon, Agnew Tells Critics," *Los Angeles Times*, 25 June
1970, p. I20) document his ongoing rhetorical war with the media and critics of the
Administration.

[5] Excerpts from his letters to the *Washington Post* and the *New York Times* may
be found in "Agnew Hits 2 Papers for Speech Criticism," *Los Angeles Times*, 24
June 1970, p. I5.

[6] "Agnew Strikes Back at Latest Criticism," *Los Angeles Times*, 5 July 1970,
p. A9.

engaged in a struggle with the mass media over the quality and fairness of news coverage and the criticism of Administrative statements and policies.

This analysis focuses on the speeches at Des Moines and Montgomery and draws three conclusions: (1) Administrative actions directly contradict Agnew's apparent intention of questioning the concentration and monopolization of the power of the mass media over American public opinion; (2) the real intent of these speeches is to discredit and/or limit critical analysis and evaluation of Administrative statements and policies; and (3) the power of Agnew's rhetoric lies in his ability to conceal a partisan attack on persons who dissent from Administrative policy behind a superficial analysis of a real and serious problem and to hide the exploitation of the fears and resentments of his audiences behind techniques that appear to be objective, scholarly, and rational. Agnew's ultimate objective is to discredit critical analysis and the disparate opinions it may produce so that his audiences will come to believe that, at least as regards overt and public dissent, "no true intellectual, no truly knowledgeable person, would so despise democratic institutions." [7]

The concentration and power of the mass media is indeed a compelling and serious problem. One quarter of all television stations are controlled by newspapers, and every commercial VHF television license in the top 10 United States markets is controlled by a network, a group owner, or a metropolitan newspaper chain. Over one half of all television revenue regularly goes to the 15 network-owned stations in the top 25 television markets.[8] Moreover more Americans receive their public affairs information from television than from any other source, and the 40 million nightly newswatchers *trust* television more than any other medium because they believe that its newsmen are impartial and nonpartisan and that the Federal Communications Commission effectively monitors television to keep its news treatment full, fair, and impartial. Agnew is accurate in saying that few men make the crucial decisions about television news coverage—probably somewhere between 75 and 100—and that these men of the networks plus another hundred or so wire service editors and officers [9] represent "a concentration of power over American public opinion unknown in history." However, the steadily increasing power of the media has been the subject of public criticism,[10] and Federal Communications Commissioner Nicholas Johnson in particular has been engaged in an extensive campaign to warn of the dangers and to inform

[7] "Snobs and Rotten Apples," *New Republic*, Vol. 161 (November 15, 1969), p. 18.
[8] John McLaughlin, "Public Regulation and the News Media," *America*, Vol. 121 (December 13, 1969), p. 586.
[9] Bernard Hennessy, "Welcome, Spiro Agnew," *New Republic*, Vol. 161 (December 13, 1969), pp. 13–14.
[10] See, for example, Robert Montgomery, *Open Letter From a Television Viewer* (New York: James H. Heineman, 1968).

citizens of the forms of recourse open to them.[11] Then why should a Republican Vice President select this issue and assume what appears to be an antiprivate power stance? At least in part the answer is that television networks and major newspapers are now clearly left of most political leaders in America.[12] The news media are in conflict with the Administration on many issues and constitute a powerful counterpersuasive force. In light of this rhetorical situation do Administrative statements and policies consistently reflect Agnew's purported concern for "the trend toward monopolization of the great public information vehicles and the concentration of more and more power over public opinion in fewer and fewer hands"? Strong evidence of inconsistency is provided by the Agnew's selection of certain media representatives as his targets and by the positions taken by the Administration on the Newspaper Preservation Act (S. 1520), the Pastore Bill (S. 2004), and the Federal Communications Commission *Policy Statement on Comparative Hearings Involving Regular Renewal Applications.*

At Montgomery, Agnew singled out the *Washington Post* for attack, a newspaper that exists in one of the three remaining large cities with more than one major newspaper under separate ownership.[13] He attacked the *Washington Post* ownership of WTOP–TV and radio but neglected to mention that there are four major television stations, three UHF stations, and 35 radio outlets in Washington, D. C.[14] He also failed to mention the obvious examples of news media concentration surrounding him as he spoke. The *Montgomery Advertiser* and the *Alabama Journal* are both owned by Multimedia, Inc. In Alabama, the Newhouse newspaper chain owns both dailies in Huntsville and Mobile, WAPI–TV, AM and FM radio stations in Birmingham, and CATV in Annison. Newhouse and another giant chain, Scripps–Howard, share ownership of the daily papers in Birmingham. In nearby areas Newhouse owns the dailies in New Orleans and Pascagoula, Mississippi, and Scripps–Howard owns the papers and WMC–TV in Memphis.[15] Agnew also neglected to mention a major media conglomerate generally well disposed to the President's Vietnam policy.[16] Along with the Hearst Corporation these media con-

---

[11] See, for example, *How to Talk Back to Your Television Set* (Boston: Little, Brown and Company, 1970); "Now Listen to This," *New Republic*, Vol. 161 (November 29, 1969), p. 9; "Two Views on the Regulation of Television: We Need the Pastore Bill—No We Don't," *New Republic*, Vol. 161 (December 6, 1969), pp. 16–19; "What Do We Do About Television?" *Saturday Review*, Vol. 53 (July 11, 1970), pp. 14 *ff;* "What You Can Do To Improve TV," *Harper's*, Vol. 238 (February 1969), pp. 14 *ff.*

[12] Tom Wicker, "Place Where All America Was Radicalized," *New York Times Magazine*, 24 August 1969, p. 95.

[13] Morton Mintz, "Spiro Agnew's Candles," *New Republic*, Vol. 162 (January 17, 1970), p. 14.

[14] "Response to Vice President's Attack," *New York Times*, 21 November 1969, p. 22.

[15] Mintz, "Spiro Agnew's Candles," pp. 13–14.

[16] "He neglected to mention, however, the New York News Co., with its interlocking ownership of WPIX–TV (New York), WGN–TV (Chicago), KDAL–TV (Duluth), KWGH–TV (Denver), WICC (Bridgeport, Conn.), and the Chicago *Tribune*

glomerates were active proponents of the Newspaper Preservation Act, a bill that repeals a Supreme Court decision and permits newspapers to violate certain antitrust laws, particularly profit pooling and price fixing. Ironically the *Washington Post* and the *New York Times*, the two newspapers Agnew singled out for criticism, are among the small number of newspapers that had the editorial courage to oppose this bill.[17] Agnew's failure to discuss this bill is itself somewhat unusual, considering his stated purpose. Even more unusual, however, is the history of Administrative behavior toward the bill. Initially the Justice Department testified against the bill before Congressional antitrust committees, and Richard McLaren, the Assistant Attorney General for Antitrust, stated that the bill would allow newspapers to share in the fruits of "an absolute monopoly." Subsequently, however, after Richard Berlin, president of the Hearst Corporation, made an apparently propitious visit to the White House, the Commerce Department unexpectedly endorsed the bill at a House antitrust committee hearing. Emanuel Cellar, chairman of the committee, said it was the first case in his 47 years in the House in which anyone except the Justice Department could speak for the White House on an antitrust bill. Later, aides to Nixon and Agnew, responding to questions about the bill, said that "the Administration supports it."[18] The President signed the bill into law on July 28, 1970.[19] Administrative action, in this case, seems directly contrary to Agnew's purported concern over newspaper monopolization.

A similarly contradictory situation existed in relation to the now-defunct Pastore bill, which would have protected and advanced concentration by making it virtually impossible for anyone to have a hearing to protest or compete with existing communications licensees at renewal time.[20] Robert Wells, the first broadcast station owner on the Federal Communications Commission since 1947, was on record as favoring the Pastore bill at the time of his appointment,[21] a fact indirectly indicating Administration support for the bill. This bill was allowed to die after it met with stiff and unexpected opposition from citizen groups.[22] However, the purpose of the bill has been realized in the *Policy Statement on Comparative Hearings Involving Regular Renewal Applications* of the Federal Communications Commission, which now includes the Nixon-appointed chairman, Dean Burch, and member, Robert Wells. The 1934 Communications Act provided for hearings in which incumbent and challenging applicants presented their conflicting claims;

—media that have been generally well disposed to the President's Viet Nam policy" (McLaughlin, "Public Regulation and the News Media," p. 587).

[17] Mintz, "Spiro Agnew's Candles," p. 14.

[18] *Ibid.*

[19] *Los Angeles Times*, 29 July 1970, p. 2.

[20] "Pastore's Pet," *New Republic*, Vol. 161 (October 25, 1969), pp. 10–11.

[21] "Dubious Appointments," *Nation*, Vol. 209 (October 6, 1969), p. 333.

[22] Robert Lewis Shayon, "Those Substantial Licenses," *Saturday Review*, Vol. 53 (February 7, 1970), p. 39.

licenses were to be awarded to applicants who demonstrated their willingness to do the better job of programming, a procedure intended to promote competition and produce the best possible service. As a result of the *Policy Statement*, the question of better service can arise only at a second hearing held if and only if the incumbent has been unable to show that his programming has been "substantially attuned to meeting the needs and interest" of the area he serves.[23] Agnew remained silent on the Pastore bill and the FCC policy statement. Once again the Administration seems to be on the side of concentration rather than decentralization of the mass media. Clearly there appears to be a serious discrepancy between the stated intent of Agnew's speeches and Administrative policy.

What then is Agnew's real purpose? A good case can be made for the conclusion that Agnew's attacks on the media are patently partisan, designed to discredit hostile news sources and limit criticism of Administrative policy. At Des Moines, Agnew's major example in his attack on television news coverage was the medium's treatment of the President's Vietnam War speech of November 3, 1969. Agnew's attitude toward criticism is evident in his statement that the President "has a right to communicate directly with the people who elected him," and those people, in turn:

> . . . have the right to make up their own minds and form their own opinions about a Presidential address without having the President's words and thoughts characterized through the prejudices of hostile critics before they can even be digested.

In short, Agnew implies that Presidential statements should be immune from prompt criticism before the immediate audience so that nothing will interfere with their persuasive impact. To be precluded are the speculations, interpretations, and objections of commentators that slow the persuasive process and encourage considered judgments essential to policy making in a democratic society. Although he has rejected the idea of prompt criticism before the immediate audience, Agnew goes on to attack the quality of network commentary on four grounds: The analyses were "instant"; the criticisms were "querulous"; the commentators had made up their minds in advance; and the majority of commentators were hostile. Clearly the analyses were "instant" in the sense that they were made immediately after the speech. Frank Stanton, president of CBS, responded that commentators had had more than two hours advance notice on the speech itself and the advantage of weeks of informed speculation on the content of the speech.[24] However, Agnew

[23] *Ibid.*, p. 38. The United States Court of Appeals has declared this policy to be "contrary to law." See "Court Rules FCC License Policy Illegal," *Los Angeles Times*, 13 June 1971, p. A3.

[24] Fred Ferretti, "President of C.B.S. Says Agnew Tries to Intimidate TV," *New York Times*, 26 November 1969, p. 1.

also argued the somewhat contradictory notion that their minds were made up in advance. This statement is true to the extent that they had advance notice of what was to be said or had speculated accurately about Presidential advocacy of the policy of Vietnamization. To demonstrate this point Agnew says:

> Those who recall the fumbling and groping that followed President Johnson's dramatic disclosure of his intention not to seek another term have seen these men in a genuine state of non-preparedness. This was not it.

If Stanton is correct, the commentators were and should have been prepared to analyze and evaluate the President's address. This was not the case with Johnson's speech, for the section in which Johnson said he would not run again was not released to the press prior to its delivery.[25] The two situations are significantly dissimilar.

Agnew supports his charges that the criticism was "querulous" and the critics hostile in his references to contradictions of "the President's statement about the exchange of correspondence with Ho Chi Minh" and to assertions "that the President was following a Pentagon line." He further maintains that facial expressions, gestures, and sarcasm by newsmen "made clear their sharp disapproval." He singles out Averell Harriman, former chief negotiator at Paris, as the paradigm of hostile network analysis. He says, sarcastically, that one network "trotted out" Harriman, who "waited in the wings" and then "recited perfectly." The "querulous" criticisms of Harriman were:

> He attacked the Thieu government as unrepresentative; . . . he twice issued a call to the Senate Foreign Relations Committee to debate Vietnam once again; he stated his belief that the Vietcong or North Vietnamese did not really want a military take-over of South Vietnam; and he told a little anecdote about a "very, very responsible" fellow he had met in the North Vietnamese delegation.

True, these statements are in opposition to those of the President, but whether they are "nit-picking" is open to serious question. Harriman's chief sin is that of:

> . . . challenging and contradicting the policies outlined by the President of the United States. Where the President had issued a call for unity, Mr. Harriman was encouraging the country not to listen to him.

[25] "Lyndon Johnson's renunciation of a second term as President dumbfounded all but a score of relatives and top aides. . . . It was not included in the advance text." [*Time*, Vol. 91 (April 12, 1969), p. 22].

If we accept Agnew's characterization,[26] Harriman is at fault simply because he is a critic—evaluating statements and policies in light of his experience, knowledge, and system of beliefs and then reaching a different conclusion from that of the President. The evil of his criticism is its call for dissent from the Presidential position and its lessening of the persuasive impact of the Presidential address. It is criticism as criticism, not the quality of the criticism, that is objectionable to Agnew.[27]

Agnew makes his final attack on network analysis: " . . . to a man these commentators and producers live and work in the geographical and intellectual confines of Washington, D. C., and New York City," communities that "bask in their own provincialism, their own parochialism." Consequently "the views of the majority of this fraternity do not—and I repeat, not—represent the views of America." Although many well-known newsmen come from small towns scattered throughout the United States,[28] whether the majority of newsmen accurately reflect the views of a majority of Americans is irrelevant. The important question is *what*, if anything, *should* the critic or commentator reflect? If Tom Wicker is right in his statement that "Agnew was really suggesting that television should serve Government's conception of the national interest and some consensus notion of 'the views of America,'" [29] there is a serious threat to free speech. Criticism and commentary are superfluous and indefensible if they mirror, simply and accurately, what is already known and believed. Critical statements that reflect and reinforce Administrative statements and policies will result in repression of the right to dissent, to question, and to evaluate—processes essential to any viable system of criticism. Finally, it should be noted that the Federal Communications Commission declared that the commentary following the President's speech was fair and impartial.[30]

The most significant issue is how effective Agnew's attacks on the media have been in limiting this form of criticism and commentary.

[26] Rather a different picture is given from reading some of Harriman's statements. See E. W. Kenworthy, "Agnew Charges News Distortion in TV Networks," *New York Times*, 14 November 1969, p. 1.

[27] Despite what Agnew characterized as hostile and inappropriate criticism, a Gallup Poll reported that 77 percent of those interviewed who had heard the President's speech supported the policies that he advocated (*Los Angeles Times*, 5 November 1969, p. I25).

[28] James Reston, "Are You an Agnewistic?" *New York Times*, 23 November 1969, p. E12.

[29] "Dr. Agnew's Patent Medicine," *New York Times*, 16 November 1969, p. E13. See also Fred W. Friendly, "Some Sober Second Thoughts on Vice President Agnew," *Saturday Review*, Vol. 52 (December 13, 1969), pp. 61 ff.

[30] The FCC made this declaration after its chairman, Dean Burch, called upon network news presidents for transcripts, an act more threatening than it appears, as the White House already had complete tape recordings of every word spoken on each network about the President's address collected by the Army Signal Corps detail assigned to the White House Communications Branch. CBS news reported that members of the Presidential staff made at least 20 calls to television stations on the night of November 3 to check on editorial comment ["Now Listen to This," *New Republic*, Vol. 161 (November 29, 1969), p. 9].

Agnew boasted publicly that "somehow when I look around the tube from time to time, I feel that I've had a modicum of success here and there." Agnew has been said to feel, as do many others at the White House:

> . . . that TV in particular treats him and the Administration generally with more care, that it carries more conservative and therefore friendly comment or noncomment on Administration pronouncements than it did before he opened up on it with his brutal reminders that it is a licensed business.[31]

Even commentators such as Eric Sevareid, who do not believe newsmen have consciously moderated their handling of Administrative and other news, concede that they are now forced to function in an atmosphere of public and official surveillance. Some affiliate stations have cancelled all post–Presidential address analyses, and a Washington, D. C., educational station cancelled a documentary critical of the Vietnam War.[32] Eric Sevareid has observed that perhaps discrediting the media could be one way for a government to protect itself from having its own credibility gap.[33] At several points Agnew seems to suggest that the problems of the Administration are caused by its critics: "Perhaps the place to start looking for a credibility gap is not in the offices of the government in Washington but in the studios of the networks in New York." Similarly he seems to place the blame for the problem of dissent on the media: "How many marches and demonstrations would we have if the marchers did not know that the ever-faithful TV cameras would be there to record their antics for the next news show?" The implication is that much dissent is exhibitionism rather than the outgrowth of legitimate grievances governments should confront and ameliorate.

Finally Presidential use of television subsequent to these speeches is notable. On February 1, 1970, Nixon made the unprecedented move of televising his veto of the educational appropriations bill, an act many commentators believe was the deciding factor in preventing a House override.[34] This veto message, despite its political implications, went undisputed because all three networks refused Democrats' requests for equal free time.[35] Nixon has used television more extensively than his predecessors. The political significance of unlimited access to the mass media and the power such access gives the Presidency have been the subject of hearings before the Senate communications subcommittee.[36]

[31] John Osborne, "Agnew's Effect," *New Republic*, Vol. 162 (February 28, 1970), p. 14.
[32] *Ibid.*, pp. 14–15.
[33] *Ibid.*, p. 15.
[34] Rowland Evans and Robert Novak, "How TV Aided the Veto," *Los Angeles Times*, 2 February 1970, p. II9.
[35] "Veto Answer Time Denied by Networks," *Los Angeles Times*, 31 January 1970, p. I3.
[36] "Presidential Access to TV," *Los Angeles Times*, 5 August 1970, p. I5.

Agnew's speeches have been eminently successful. They have effectively concealed a partisan attack upon the dissenting criticism of the "liberal" news media behind the real and serious problem of the increasing concentration and monopolization of news sources. The inconsistency between Agnew's statements and Administrative attitudes toward relevant legislation and FCC policy suggests that Agnew is primarily concerned with dissent by the news media and their criticism of Administrative statements and positions rather than with the power of the media. The danger is that:

> Mr. Agnew . . . seemed to be inviting not a thoughtful discussion of the very intricate problems of self-regulation but a partisan counterattack on broadcasters and the substitution of one small group of men whom the Vice President doesn't happen to like with another small group of men more hospitable to his own private vision of America.[37]

Regulation of the power of the media requires public discussion, but evidence indicates that Agnew has succeeded primarily in limiting the media in the amount and quality of criticism and analysis.

In response to considerable criticism of his speech making,[38] Agnew attempted to explain his theory of rhetoric and to justify his style and stratagems. Speaking before the International Association of Newspaper Publishers, he defined rhetoric as "the use of public discourse to persuade." He called for its "constructive use" to create "rational dissent" focused on an issue and open to debate, explaining that:

> . . . in the very act of encouraging peaceful argument, we automatically discourage violent protest. In agreeing to disagree, as reasonable people, we admit a unity of purpose.[39]

He has consistently called for presentation of "both sides" and defended his style by calling that of newsmen and extremist groups on the left "equally inflammatory."[40] Just prior to the speeches under consideration, Agnew justified his style, saying, "Outspokenness is the only way a

[37] Robert B. Semple, Jr., "Assent: Agnew Calls for Protest Against TV," *New York Times*, 16 November 1969, p. E1.
[38] See, for example, Jules Witcover, "Hickel, Mentioning Agnew, Hits Administration Policy on Youth," *Los Angeles Times*, 7 May 1970, p. 1; Kenneth Reich, "Agnew Plays It Cool in Georgia Dedication," *Los Angeles Times*, 10 May 1970, p. A14; "Finch Says Agnew Fed Unrest; Later Denies Quotation," *Los Angeles Times*, 10 May 1970, p. 1; Don Irwin, "New Dispute Flares Over Agnew Speeches," *Los Angeles Times*, 15 May 1970, p. I5; "Muskie Raps Agnew on Approach to Youth," *Los Angeles Times*, 25 May 1970, p. I7; "Agnew Talks Blamed in Student Alienation," *Los Angeles Times*, 24 June 1970, p. I16; "Agnew Words Wound Nation," *Los Angeles Times*, 24 June 1970, p. I16; "Agnew Elicits Radical Acts, Fulbright Says," *Los Angeles Times*, 6 July 1970, p. I22; John A. Averill, "Harriman Links Agnew Attacks to Nazi Tactics," *Los Angeles Times*, 9 July 1970, p. I4.
[39] Irwin, "Some Media Slanting . . ."
[40] Reich, "Won't Be Quiet . . ."; Chriss, "Not Muzzled by Nixon, . . ."

Vice President can hope to get attention." [41] More recently, complaining that his bland speeches were poorly reported, he said:

> So, in a desire to be heard, I have to throw them what people in American politics call a little red meat once in a while, and hope that in spite of the damaging context in which those remarks are often repeated, that other things that I think are very important will also appear.[42]

These bits of "red meat," "all packed into a trim two minutes that can be snipped out for TV, almost without having to review the tape," [43] are an effective device for attracting media coverage. Despite this admittedly deliberate stratagem, Agnew has objected to criticism based on such excerpts, contending he had been "misrepresented and misunderstood." [44] Considering his strategy and the difficulty involved in obtaining complete texts, at least for the general public, this plea seems inappropriate. As other rhetorical critics have argued, political figures can and should be held responsible for the highly predictable excerpting of controversial statements by the mass media.[45]

Agnew makes a sharp distinction between the substance and the style of his speeches, attacking media criticism of his rhetoric on the grounds that it "dealt with how he was saying something instead of what he was saying. . . . Nowhere do they come to grips with the inherent veracity of what I've been saying." [46] Such a distinction is always dubious but particularly so in a case in which stylistic techniques are deliberately employed to attract popular attention. Consequently the final stage in this analysis examines Agnew's rhetorical stratagems to show that they are designed to *simulate* rational deliberation and preclude "the intelligent judgment of its citizens" on which he says this nation depends.

Agnew is, for the most part, the mouthpiece for an array of sophisticated ghost writers,[47] who consciously choose techniques used in his

---

[41] "Agnew Finds a Role," *Newsweek*, Vol. 74 (November 17, 1969), p. 40.

[42] John Osborne, "Agnew and the Red Meat," *New Republic*, Vol. 163 (July 25, 1970), p. 12.

[43] Brock Brower, "Don't Get Agnew Wrong," *Life*, Vol. 68 (May 8, 1970), p. 66B.

[44] Osborne, "Agnew and the Red Meat," p. 11.

[45] Robert L. Scott and Wayne Brockriede, *The Rhetoric of Black Power* (New York: Harper & Row, 1969), pp. 78–81.

[46] "Agnew Gives Defense of His Style," *Los Angeles Times*, 1 July 1970, p. I6.

[47] "The Vice President's speeches, when they do not spring from his own pen (he wrote the New Orleans speech himself), are largely the work of a petite, auburn-haired former public-relations woman named Cynthia Rosenwald . . ." ("Agnew Finds a Role," p. 41). "Nixon's speech writers prize and acknowledge their assignments to draft Agnew speeches. Patrick Buchanan deplores reports that he has written some of the more abrasive ones, not because the reports are false, but because Agnew resents any indication that he is a mouthpiece for others and the stories might impair a working relationship that Buchanan and his colleagues have come to value" (Osborne, "Agnew's Effect," p. 13). In addition to his New Orleans speech, the speeches Agnew has authored, at least for the most part, include those delivered at Harrisburg, Pennsylvania; Atlanta, Georgia; and Minneapolis, Minnesota, although "Agnew admits to outside drafts on such important positional diatribes as that boomed at the TV networks last November 13" (Brower, "Don't Get Agnew Wrong," p. 66B).

speeches. Gerald Johnson, former editorial writer for the *Baltimore Sun*, comments:

> Persons who became familiar with the Vice President's syntax while he was a county executive, and then as the surprise Governor of Maryland, and who read his November 13 assault on the television news analysts, are convinced that Mr. Agnew has a new and better speech-writer. Never did such crisp and lucid English issue from the Towson courthouse or the Annapolis statehouse, during his tenure of those offices.[48]

However, there is little doubt that Agnew believes what he is saying. In reference to the Des Moines speech, Gerald Johnson wrote, "While the style of the speech was astonishingly improved, the content was entirely familiar. . . . His speeches may have been written by some other hand, but they express his sincere belief." [49]

The critical methodology of the following section is adapted from the noted Canadian literary critic, Northrop Frye, who makes a basic moral distinction between "genuine speech, . . . the expression of a genuine personality," [50] and "bastard speech," the voice of what he calls the ego. He explains that:

> . . . the ego has no interest in communication, but only in expression. . . . The ego is not the genuine individual, consequently it has nothing distinctive to express. It can express only the generic: food, sex, possessions, gossip, aggressiveness and resentments. Its natural affinity is for the ready-made phrase, the cliché, because it tends to address itself to the reflexes of its hearer, not to his intelligence or emotions.[51]

Frye describes the audience to which such speech is addressed and suggests an application of these concepts to political rhetoric:

> An aggregate of egos is a mob. A mob can only respond to reflex and cliché; it can only express itself, directly or through a spokesman, in reflex and cliché. A mob always implies some object of resentment, and political leaders who speak for the mob aspect of their society develop a special kind of tantrum style, a style constructed almost entirely out of unexamined clichés.[52]

Such characterization of Agnew's rhetoric may seem presumptuous to all but the most rabidly anti-Agnew primarily because he has refined this form of speech to conceal the nature of the rhetoric and maximize its effectiveness. His techniques include: (1) the use of Latinate and rela-

---

[48] Gerald W. Johnson, "The Old Agnew We Knew," *New Republic*, Vol. 161 (November 29, 1969), p. 13.
[49] *Ibid.*
[50] Northrop Frye, *The Well-Tempered Critic* (Bloomington: Indiana University Press, 1963), p. 41.
[51] *Ibid.*, pp. 41–42.
[52] *Ibid.*, p. 43.

tively esoteric language; (2) the use of literary or scholarly allusions; (3) the appearance of an attitude of fairness and objectivity; (4) the extensive use of specific examples and factual data in support of conclusions; and (5) the use of expert opinion, particularly from his opposition. These techniques suggest an argumentative rhetoric calling for rational deliberation, but they function instead to dignify and legitimize the invective of the speaker and the fears and resentments of his audience.

The terminology of Agnew's speeches is likely to challenge the well-educated individual, much less "the common man" he seems to be addressing. In his Des Moines speech, for example, he uses the words *querulous, gratuitous, disparaged, veracity, expunge,* and *nemesis.* At Montgomery he uses *efficacy, chauvinistic, vilified, erudite,* and *circumscribe.* Although these terms may not be so esoteric as to be unintelligible to the majority of Americans, many individuals would have difficulty defining them accurately. These terms serve two functions: They lend an aura of intellectualism to the speaker, and they serve to dignify the aggressive statements in which he uses them. Media criticism is not petty but *querulous;* Harriman's advice is not unrequested but *gratuitous;* newsmen do not belittle but *disparage,* and so on. In both speeches Agnew uses Latinate or esoteric terminology almost exclusively in extreme statements of praise or blame, whereas he uses simpler language in description or explanation. He makes a dignified appeal to the reflex and couches his invective in terminology that makes it appear less cliché, less directly angry and attacking. Yet despite their Latinate character these terms are clearly loaded and extreme.

Agnew uses allusions similarly. In the Des Moines speech he compares Averell Harriman to Coleridge's Ancient Mariner, as a man "under some heavy compulsion to justify his failure to anyone who will listen"; and without explaining the economic referent, he tells the audience that "Gresham's Law seems to be operating in the network news. Bad news drives out good news." At Montgomery, after citing an unfavorable *New York Times'* comment on his generation, Agnew says, "Like Edmund Burke, I wouldn't know how to draw up an indictment against a whole people." In each case he couches a personal or emotional attack in a form that gives it intellectual respectability.

Many statements in both speeches suggest his fairness and objectivity. In the Des Moines speech he gives credit to the media: "It must be recognized that the networks have made important contributions to the national knowledge." He asks, "Is it not fair and relevant to question . . . ?" as he does, and repeatedly states that he is "not asking for government censorship or any other kind of censorship. I'm asking whether a form of censorship already exists." His statement "Our knowledge of the impact of network news on the national mind is far from complete" and his insistence that he has only "raised questions" but made "no attempt to suggest the answers. The answers must come from the media men. . . . challenged to turn their critical powers on themselves" also imply objectivity. At Montgomery, after citing eight extreme examples of "critical overreaction" to his earlier speech, he says, "In fairness, others, the majority of critics and commentators, did take up the thrust of my address." He explains that his goal was only "a thorough self-examination by the networks of their own policies and perhaps prejudices." These and other statements create an aura of apparent impartiality. But the contradictions and omissions and the highly loaded language and examples with which he exploits the fears and resentments of his audience belie such objectivity. The network newsmen are a "small band of self-appointed analysts," a "gaggle" or "covey of commentators," "a tiny enclosed fraternity of privileged men," "a small and unelected elite" "responsible only to their corporate employers," who have "grown fat and irresponsible" and whom "the nation knows practically nothing." On an issue the newsman is "the presiding judge in a national trial by jury." The newsman's attacks have been protected because "they emanated from the privileged sanctuary of a network studio and therefore had the apparent dignity of an objective statement." These are the men who "elevated Stokely Carmichael and George Lincoln Rockwell from obscurity to national prominence," who say "one minute of Eldridge Cleaver is worth 10 minutes of Roy Wilkins" because they are engaged in an "endless" or "passionate pursuit of controversy." Such terms and illustrations are not designed to produce a fair or considered judgment. They are selected to induce an immediate, uncritical response.

Agnew's use of specific support materials creates the impression that he is knowledgeable about his subject. In his Des Moines speech he provides detailed instances of the criticism of Nixon's speech, data on the numbers of television viewers and polls indicating its impact. In his Montgomery speech he cites the *Washington Post* and delineates what it owns. He attacks the *New York Times* in terms of coverage of specific events. Agnew appears to have done thorough research and is prepared to present data to support his conclusions. Once again appearances are deceptive; the evidence he does *not* cite is significant. The evidence he does present is open to serious objection. He compares the situation of Nixon in relation to the Vietnam War with that of Winston Churchill during World War II and that of John Kennedy during the Cuban missile crisis to demonstrate that Nixon should be immune from dissenting criticism. He contrasts the critical preparedness of commentators on Nixon's speech with their shocked response to Johnson's announcement that he would not seek reelection in order to show that they had made up their minds in advance. Hypothetically, Agnew says, an attack on the President's Vietnam policy by a Sioux City, Iowa, theology student at a PTA meeting would have received *New York Times* coverage, whereas endorsement of that policy by 300 Congressmen did not.[53] These comparisons seem extremely dubious bases for the conclusions he draws. In addition he cites highly controversial statements of news commentators without any indication of the specific source; hence the typicality and significance of these statements are extremely difficult to judge in evaluating the quality of media commentary. Even a superficial examination indicates that the evidence provides a poor basis for the conclusions asserted.

Expert opinion, particularly from sources within the media, is employed in a similar fashion. In the Des Moines address Agnew cites James Reston on the unrepresentative character of New York City, David Brinkley on the impossibility of objectivity in normal behavior, and Walter Lippmann on the essential and radical differences between print and television. He claims that Supreme Court Justices argue for greater variety in points of view in news commentary and hold paramount the rights of viewers and listeners, not that of broadcasters. In his Montgomery address he cites statements by Sidney Hook, Arnold Beichman, Walter Laqueur, George Kennan, and Irving Kristol without providing any of their credentials. He merely adds: "Those are men more eloquent and erudite than I, and they raise questions that I've tried to raise." And, in a final and magnificent gesture, he has the temerity to conclude a speech in the deep South with a quotation from abolitionist William Lloyd Garrison: "I am in earnest. I will not equivocate. I will not excuse. I will not retreat a single inch. And I will be heard." In apparently the best traditions of argumentation Agnew has used expert opinion, even from opposing sources, to establish his case. However, the citation from Hook permits Agnew to call student demonstrators "storm troopers" among whom "fanaticism seems to be in the saddle"; the citation from Beichman permits him to call them "young Jacobins" who have "sent a nationwide chill of fear all through the university establishment." George Laqueur permits him to state that dissenters "have gone clearly beyond the borders of what is acceptable for any society," and Irving Kristol becomes the means for saying that "radical students . . . are blandly approving of injustice and brutality committed in the name of 'the revolution.'" These citations from experts do not provide insight into the problem of dissent but instead become the means to introduce

[53] "Mr. Agnew is again mistaken when he says that *The Times* did not 'carry a word' on the story about the Congressmen and Senators signing a letter endorsing the President's policy in Vietnam. *The New York Times* printed the story. Unfortunately, it failed to make the edition that reached Washington but was carried in a later edition of *The Times*. Moreover, *The Times* has given considerable attention to that story as it developed. . . . In the paper of November 13, there was the story to which the Vice President referred. In the paper of November 14, President Nixon's visit to the House and Senate to convey his appreciation to those who supported his Vietnam policy was the lead story. That story again reported the fact that more than 300 Congressmen and 59 Senators had signed the resolution" ("Response to Vice President's Attack: Mr. Sulzberger's Reply").

highly loaded language, even invective, into the address under the guise
of authoritative evidence. Agnew's arguments are clichés directed toward
the reflexes, but the means are carefully designed to legitimize the fears
and beliefs of the audience and dignify the most vicious attacks on the
dissenters.

Agnew's numerous references to himself even more directly support
the charge that this rhetoric is the voice of the ego. At the end of the
Des Moines speech, despite the fact that it was being carried live on all
three television networks, Agnew says: "Whether what I've said to you tonight will be heard and seen at all by the nation is not my decision; it's
not your decision; it's their decision." In his Montgomery address he says
that a week ago "I. . . exercised my right to dissent" and then cites eight
negative reactions, each of which becomes the basis for self-defense or
an attack on the critic. The comments Agnew selects make him appear as
a fearless white knight fighting against overwhelming odds. He asks:
"Should I remain silent while what these heroes have done is vilified by
some as 'a dirty, immoral war'?" and:

> How can you ask the man in the street in this country to stand up for
> what he believes if his own elected leaders weasel and cringe? It's not
> an easy thing to wake up each morning to learn that some prominent
> man or some prominent institution has implied that you're a bigot or a
> racist or a fool.

The tone of these remarks fits Frye's notion of the voice of the ego as a
monologue primarily concerned with self-expression and self-justification.
The tone is petty, shrill, and defensive, and such rhetoric is at the far-
thest extreme from "genuine speech," which, wherever spoken, "creates
a community." [54] "Positive" or not, the "polarization" is evident. [55]

The contradictions between these speeches and Administrative policy
and the omission of relevant data and supporting materials substan-
tiates the charge that this is "bastard speech." John McLaughlin, in
summarizing Agnew's basic rhetorical choice, points out that the Vice
President "failed to call for reform through legislative or judicial process. Instead he politicized the issues by focusing on those media personalities—individual and collective—who in his view have been failing to
meet standards of fairness." Mr. McLaughlin continues by suggesting the
sorts of reform Agnew might have advocated. [56] Instead of such advocacy,
Agnew's attacks have been personal, political, and emotional, a rhetorical stance that seems to fulfill Northrop Frye's criteria.

Interestingly even sympathetic commentators have noted what Frye
terms the "tantrum style" of such rhetoric. Brock Brower, for example,
describes the typical Agnew speech as a "good old-fashioned parental

---

[54] Frye, 41. See also Richard B. Gregg, "The Ego-Function of the Rhetoric of
Protest," *Philosophy and Rhetoric*, Vol. 4 (Spring 1971), pp. 71–91.
[55] "Snobs and Rotten Apples," p. 18.
[56] McLaughlin, "Public Regulation and the News Media," pp. 587–588.

Talking-To," with the crux of the speech contained in "the tongue-lashing" and characterized by "nil politics, total moralization, big words, high-thoughts and a rabbit-punch ending." [57] No one can doubt that Agnew is angry, even furious, over questions of dissent from and criticism of Administrative policies and statements or that he sees his war with the press as a personal vendetta.[58]

The power of Agnew's rhetoric lies in his ability to conceal his exploitation of the resentments, fears, and hostilities of his audience behind the facade of a serious and real problem—in this case the power of the mass media and the quality of media news coverage. His power also derives from his ability to dignify and legitimize the use of clichés, invective, and highly personal attacks with Latinate language, literary allusions, specific data, citations from experts, and an appearance of objectivity. The danger of such rhetoric in a democracy, which does in fact rely heavily "on the intelligent judgment of its citizens," should be obvious. That danger is multiplied when such rhetoric is directed toward stifling dissent and criticism. The threat posed is even clearer when these discourses are contrasted with "genuine speech." Unlike Agnew's rhetoric, genuine speech "is the voice of the genuine individual reminding us of our genuine selves, and of our role as members of a society" and "is heard whenever a speaker is honestly struggling to express what his society, as a society, is trying to be and do." [59] Such rhetoric is unique, rather than cliché, giving the peculiar and private insight of an individual into the problems of our society. It calls on each person to transcend the known, the believed, and the familiar to find new ways of viewing and solving problems. Genuine rhetoric is inevitably the rhetoric of dissent and criticism, and Agnew's speeches are not merely "bastard speech" but are attempts to stifle "genuine speech." That intention is unmistakable in Agnew's own words:

> There are people in our society who should be separated and discarded. . . . Not in a callous way, but they should be separated as far as any idea that their opinion shall have any effect on the course we follow.[60]

[57] Brower, "Don't Get Agnew Wrong," p. 66B.
[58] Agnew is still deeply resentful of press treatment of him during the 1968 campaign and during his term as governor of Maryland (*Ibid.*, pp. 66, 72).
[59] Frye, pp. 44–45.
[60] Osborne, "Agnew and the Red Meat," p. 12.

For Further Discussion

1   Describe the different techniques used in the preceding critique and explain how each technique results in a particular evaluation. If this criticism were limited to any one of the approaches found herein, how would the end result differ?

2   What are the critic's perceptible biases, if any? Do they invalidate, wholly

or in part, the critical evaluations offered? How does the critic's evidence affect the validity of the conclusions reached?

3 Compare these addresses to others made by Agnew. Would similar critical techniques applied to those addresses result in similar evaluations?

4 Are there other concepts in Chapter 1 of Northrop Frye's *The Well-Tempered Critic* which you find applicable to these addresses or to others included in this book?

5 One year after these addresses Agnew took an active part in the 1970 Congressional campaigns. In light of those addresses and their effects, do you think that the Vice President is still one of the most formidable weapons in the Administration's rhetorical armory? Explain.

For Further Reading

Northrop Frye, *The Well-Tempered Critic* (Bloomington: Indiana University Press, 1963).

Maury Green, *Television News: Anatomy and Process* (Belmont, Calif.: Wadsworth Publishing Company, 1969).

Nicholas Johnson, "The Life Party," *New Republic*, Vol. 164 (April 10, 1971), pp. 21–23.

Jim G. Lucas, *Agnew: Profile in Conflict* (New York: Charles Scribner's Sons, 1970).

John Osborne, "Is Agnew Washed Up?" *New Republic*, Vol. 163 (November 14, 1970), pp. 11–12.

Seven

Paul Ehrlich

Paul Ehrlich, professor of biology at Stanford University, is one of the most vocal and dedicated ecological crusaders in America. He is, by his own testimony, a "doomsayer." His basic argument is that we have little time left, that if we do not stop our insane destruction of the world in which we live, the possibility of stopping the destruction will no longer exist. The following discourse is not Ehrlich's most violent attack on our antiecological policies, but it is of unusual interest because it bends a literary genre to rhetorical ends.

This essay is, of course, a rhetorical act. The term eschatology *means the study of the end time, of the final age, of the period before oblivion. If we do not respond to Professor Ehrlich's essay as a rhetorical event, we shall be forced to deal with it as an eschatological work. Ehrlich, like Wald, believes that we are "the apocalyptic generation."*

Eco-Catastrophe!

1 The end of the ocean came late in the summer of 1979, and it came even more rapidly than the biologists had expected. There had been signs for more than a decade, commencing with the discovery in 1968 that

DDT slows down photosynthesis in marine plant life. It was announced in a short paper in the technical journal, *Science,* but to ecologists it smacked of doomsday. They knew that all life in the sea depends on photosynthesis, the chemical process by which green plants bind the sun's energy and make it available to living things. And they knew that DDT and similar chlorinated hydrocarbons had polluted the entire surface of the earth, including the sea.

2   But that was only the first of many signs. There had been the final gasp of the whaling industry in 1973, and the end of the Peruvian anchovy fishery in 1975. Indeed, a score of other fisheries had disappeared quietly from over-exploitation and various eco-catastrophes by 1977. The term "eco-catastrophe" was coined by a California ecologist in 1969 to describe the most spectacular of man's attacks on the systems which sustain his life. He drew his inspiration from the Santa Barbara offshore oil disaster of that year, and from the news which spread among naturalists that virtually all of the Golden State's seashore bird life was doomed because of chlorinated hydrocarbon interference with its reproduction. Eco-catastrophes in the sea became increasingly common in the early 1970s. Mysterious "blooms" of previously rare microorganisms began to appear in offshore waters. Red tides—killer outbreaks of a minute single-celled plant—returned to the Florida Gulf coast and were sometimes accompanied by tides of other exotic hues.

3   It was clear by 1975 that the entire ecology of the ocean was changing. A few types of phytoplankton were becoming resistant to chlorinated hydrocarbons and were gaining the upper hand. Changes in the phytoplankton community led inevitably to changes in the community of zooplankton, the tiny animals which eat the phytoplankton. These changes were passed on up the chains of life in the ocean to the herring, plaice, cod, and tuna. As the diversity of life in the ocean diminished, its stability also decreased.

4   Other changes had taken place by 1975. Most ocean fishes that returned to fresh water to breed, like the salmon, had become extinct, their breeding streams so dammed up and polluted that their powerful homing instinct only resulted in suicide. Many fishes and shellfishes that bred in restricted areas along the coasts followed them as onshore pollution escalated.

5   By 1977 the annual yield of fish from the sea was down to 30 million metric tons, less than one-half the per capita catch of a decade earlier. This helped malnutrition to escalate sharply in a world where an estimated 50 million people per year were already dying of starvation. The United Nations attempted to get all chlorinated hydrocarbon in-

secticides banned on a worldwide basis, but the move was defeated by the United States. This opposition was generated primarily by the American petrochemical industry, operating hand in glove with its subsidiary, the United States Department of Agriculture. Together they persuaded the government to oppose the U.N. move—which was not difficult since most Americans believed that Russia and China were more in need of fish products than was the United States. The United Nations also attempted to get fishing nations to adopt strict and enforced catch limits to preserve dwindling stocks. This move was blocked by Russia, who, with the most modern electronic equipment, was in the best position to glean what was left in the sea. It was, curiously, on the very day in 1977 when the Soviet Union announced its refusal that another ominous article appeared in *Science*. It announced that incident solar radiation had been so reduced by worldwide air pollution that serious effects on the world's vegetation could be expected.

6   Apparently it was a combination of ecosystem destabilization, sunlight reduction, and a rapid escalation in chlorinated hydrocarbon pollution from massive Thanodrin applications which triggered the ultimate catastrophe. Seventeen huge Soviet-financed Thanodrin plants were operating in underdeveloped countries by 1978. They had been part of a massive Russian "aid offensive" designed to fill the gap caused by the collapse of America's ballyhooed "Green Revolution."

7   It became apparent in the early '70s that the "Green Revolution" was more talk than substance. Distribution of high yield "miracle" grain seeds had caused temporary local spurts in agricultural production. Simultaneously, excellent weather had produced record harvests. The combination permitted bureaucrats, especially in the United States Department of Agriculture and the Agency for International Development (AID), to reverse their previous pessimism and indulge in an outburst of optimistic propaganda about staving off famine. They raved about the approaching transformation of agriculture in the underdeveloped countries (UDCs). The reason for the propaganda reversal was never made clear. Most historians agree that a combination of utter ignorance of ecology, a desire to justify past errors, and pressure from agro-industry (which was eager to sell pesticides, fertilizers, and farm machinery to the UDCs and agencies helping the UDCs) was behind the campaign. Whatever the motivation, the results were clear. Many concerned people, lacking the expertise to see through the Green Revolution drivel, relaxed. The population-food crisis was "solved."

8   But reality was not long in showing itself. Local famine persisted in northern India even after good weather brought an end to the ghastly Bihar famine of the mid-'60s. East Pakistan was next, followed by a resurgence of general famine in northern India. Other foci of famine rapidly developed in Indonesia, the Philippines, Malawi, the Congo, Egypt, Colombia, Ecuador, Honduras, the Dominican Republic, and Mexico.

9   Everywhere hard realities destroyed the illusion of the Green Revolution. Yields dropped as the progressive farmers who had first accepted the new seeds found that their higher yields brought lower prices—effective demand (hunger plus cash) was not sufficient in poor countries to keep prices up. Less progressive farmers, observing this, refused to make the extra effort required to cultivate the "miracle" grains. Transport systems proved inadequate to bring the necessary fertilizer to the fields where the new and extremely fertilizer-sensitive grains were being grown. The same systems were also inadequate to move produce to markets. Fertilizer plants were not built fast enough, and most of the underdeveloped countries could not scrape together funds to purchase supplies, even on concessional terms. Finally, the inevitable happened, and pests began to reduce yields in even the most carefully cultivated fields. Among the first were the famous "miracle rats" which invaded Philippine "miracle rice" fields early in 1969. They were quickly followed by many insects and viruses, thriving on the relatively pest-susceptible new grains, encouraged by the vast and dense plantings, and rapidly acquiring resistance to the chemicals used against them. As chaos spread until even the most obtuse agriculturists and economists realized that the Green Revolution had turned brown, the Russians stepped in.

10   In retrospect it seems incredible that the Russians, with the American mistakes known to them, could launch an even more incompetent program of aid to the underdeveloped world. Indeed, in the early 1970's there were cynics in the United States who claimed that outdoing the stupidity of American foreign aid would be physically impossible. Those critics were, however, obviously unaware that the Russians had been busily destroying their own environment for many years. The virtual disappearance of sturgeon from Russian rivers caused a great shortage of caviar by 1970. A standard joke among Russian scientists at that time was that they had created an artificial caviar which was indistinguishable from the real thing—except by taste. At any rate the Soviet Union, observing with interest the progressive deterioration of relations between the UDCs and the United States, came up with a solution. It had recently developed what it claimed was the ideal insecticide, a highly lethal chlorinated hydrocarbon complexed with a special agent for penetrating the external skeletal armor of insects. Announcing that the new pesticide, called Thanodrin, would truly produce a Green Revolution, the Soviets entered into negotiations with various UDCs for the construction of massive Thanodrin factories. The USSR would bear all

the costs; all it wanted in return were certain trade and military concessions.

11   It is interesting now, with the perspective of years, to examine in some detail the reasons why the UDCs welcomed the Thanodrin plan with such open arms. Government officials in these countries ignored the protests of their own scientists that Thanodrin would not solve the problems which plagued them. The governments now knew that the basic cause of their problems was overpopulation, and that these problems had been exacerbated by the dullness, daydreaming, and cupidity endemic to all governments. They knew that only population control and limited development aimed primarily at agriculture could have spared them the horrors they now faced. They knew it, but they were not about to admit it. How much easier it was simply to accuse the Americans of failing to give them proper aid; how much simpler to accept the Russian panacea.

12   And then there was the general worsening of relations between the United States and the UDCs. Many things had contributed to this. The situation in America in the first half of the 1970's deserves our close scrutiny. Being more dependent on imports for raw materials than the Soviet Union, the United States had, in the early 1970's, adopted more and more heavy-handed policies in order to insure continuing supplies. Military adventures in Asia and Latin America had further lessened the international credibility of the United States as a great defender of freedom—an image which had begun to deteriorate rapidly during the pointless and fruitless Viet-Nam conflict. At home, acceptance of the carefully manufactured image lessened dramatically, as even the more romantic and chauvinistic citizens began to understand the role of the military and the industrial system in what John Kenneth Galbraith had aptly named "The New Industrial State."

13   At home in the USA the early '70s were traumatic times. Racial violence grew and the habitability of the cities diminished, as nothing substantial was done to ameliorate either racial inequities or urban blight. Welfare rolls grew as automation and general technological progress forced more and more people into the category of "unemployable." Simultaneously a taxpayers' revolt occurred. Although there was not enough money to build the schools, roads, water systems, sewage systems, jails, hospitals, urban transit lines, and all the other amenities needed to support a burgeoning population, Americans refused to tax themselves more heavily. Starting in Youngstown, Ohio in 1969 and followed closely by Richmond, California, community after community was forced to close its schools or curtail educational operations for lack of funds. Water supplies, already marginal in quality and quantity in many places by 1970, deteriorated quickly. Water rationing occurred in 1723 municipalities in the summer of 1974, and hepatitis and epidemic dysentery rates climbed about 500 per cent between 1970–1974.

14   Air pollution continued to be the most obvious manifestation of environmental deterioration. It was, by 1972, quite literally in the eyes of all Americans. The year 1973 saw not only the New York and Los Angeles smog disasters, but also the publication of the Surgeon General's massive report on air pollution and health. The public had been partially prepared for the worst by the publicity given to the U.N. pollution conference held in 1972. Deaths in the late '60s caused by smog were well known to scientists, but the public had ignored them because they mostly involved the early demise of the old and sick rather than people dropping dead on the freeways. But suddenly our citizens were faced with nearly 200,000 corpses and massive documentation that they could be the next to die from respiratory disease. They were not ready for that scale of disaster. After all, the U.N. conference had not predicted that accumulated air pollution would make the planet uninhabitable until almost 1990. The population was terrorized as TV screens became filled with scenes of horror from the disaster areas. Especially vivid was NBC's coverage of hundreds of unattended people choking out their lives outside of New York's hospitals. Terms like nitrogen oxide, acute bronchitis, and cardiac arrest began to have real meaning for most Americans.

15   The ultimate horror was the announcement that chlorinated hydrocarbons were now a major constituent of air pollution in all American cities. Autopsies of smog disaster victims revealed an average chlorinated hydrocarbon load in fatty tissue equivalent to 26 parts per million of DDT. In October, 1973, the Department of Health, Education and Welfare announced studies which showed unequivocally that increasing death rates from hypertension, cirrhosis of the liver, liver cancer, and a series of other diseases had resulted from the chlorinated hydrocarbon load. They estimated that Americans born since 1946 (when DDT usage began) now had a life expectancy of only 49 years, and predicted that if current patterns continued, this expectancy would reach 42 years by 1980, when it might level out. Plunging insurance stocks triggered a stock market panic. The president of a major pesticide producer, went on television to "publicly eat a teaspoonful of DDT" (it was really powdered milk) and announce HEW had been infiltrated by Communists. Other giants of the petrochemical industry, attempting to dispute the indisputable evidence, launched a massive pressure campaign on Congress to force HEW to "get out of agriculture's business." They were aided by the agro-chemical journals, which had decades of experience in misleading the public about the benefits and dangers of pesticides. But by now the public realized that it had been duped. The Nobel

Prize for medicine and physiology was given to Drs. J. L. Radomski and W. B. Deichmann, who in the late 1960s had pioneered in the documentation of the long-term lethal effects of chlorinated hydrocarbons. A Presidential Commission with unimpeachable credentials directly accused the agro-chemical complex of "condemning many millions of Americans to an early death." The year 1973 was the year in which Americans finally came to understand the direct threat to their existence posed by environmental deterioration.

16   And 1973 was also the year in which most people finally comprehended the indirect threat. Even the president of Union Oil Company and several other industrialists publicly stated their concern over the reduction of bird populations which had resulted from pollution by DDT and other chlorinated hydrocarbons. Insect populations boomed because they were resistant to most pesticides and had been freed, by the incompetent use of those pesticides, from most of their natural enemies. Rodents swarmed over crops, multiplying rapidly in the absence of predatory birds. The effect of pests on the wheat crop was especially disastrous in the summer of 1973, since that was also the year of the great drought. Most of us can remember the shock which greeted the announcement by atmospheric physicists that the shift of the jet stream which had caused the drought was probably permanent. It signalled the birth of the Midwestern desert. Man's air-polluting activities had by then caused gross changes in climatic patterns. The news, of course, played hell with commodity and stock markets. Food prices skyrocketed, as savings were poured into hoarded canned goods. Official assurances that food supplies would remain ample fell on deaf ears, and even the government showed signs of nervousness when California migrant field workers went out on strike again in protest against the continued use of pesticides by growers. The strike burgeoned into farm burning and riots. The workers, calling themselves "The Walking Dead," demanded immediate compensation for their shortened lives, and crash research programs to attempt to lengthen them.

17   It was in the same speech in which President Edward Kennedy, after much delay, finally declared a national emergency and called out the National Guard to harvest California's crops, that the first mention of population control was made. Kennedy pointed out that the United States would no longer be able to offer any food aid to other nations and was likely to suffer food shortages herself. He suggested that, in view of the manifest failure of the Green Revolution, the only hope of the UDCs lay in population control. His statement, you will recall, created an uproar in the underdeveloped countries. Newspaper editorials accused the United States of wishing to prevent small countries from becoming large nations and thus threatening American hegemony. Politicians asserted that President Kennedy was a "creature of the giant drug combine" that wished to shove its pills down every woman's throat.

18   Among Americans, religious opposition to population control was very slight. Industry in general also backed the idea. Increasing poverty in the UDCs was both destroying markets and threatening supplies of raw materials. The seriousness of the raw material situation had been brought home during the Congressional Hard Resources hearings in 1971. The exposure of the ignorance of the cornucopian economists had been quite a spectacle—a spectacle brought into virtually every American's home in living color. Few would forget the distinguished geologist from the University of California who suggested that economists be legally required to learn at least the most elementary facts of geology. Fewer still would forget that an equally distinguished Harvard economist added that they might be required to learn some economics, too. The overall message was clear: America's resource situation was bad and bound to get worse. The hearings had led to a bill requiring the Departments of State, Interior, and Commerce to set up a joint resource procurement council with the express purpose of "insuring that proper consideration of American resource needs be an integral part of American foreign policy."

19   Suddenly the United States discovered that it had a national consensus: population control was the only possible salvation of the underdeveloped world. But that same consensus led to heated debate. How could the UDCs be persuaded to limit their populations, and should not the United States lead the way by limiting its own? Members of the intellectual community wanted America to set an example. They pointed out that the United States was in the midst of a new baby boom: her birth rate, well over 20 per thousand per year, and her growth rate of over one per cent per annum were among the very highest of the developed countries. They detailed the deterioration of the American physical and psychic environments, the growing health threats, the impending food shortages, and the insufficiency of funds for desperately needed public works. They contended that the nation was clearly unable or unwilling to properly care for the people it already had. What possible reason could there be, they queried, for adding any more? Besides, who would listen to requests by the United States for population control when that nation did not control her own profligate reproduction?

20   Those who opposed population controls for the U. S. were equally vociferous. The military–industrial complex, with its all-too-human mixture of ignorance and avarice, still saw strength and prosperity in numbers. Baby food magnates, already worried by the growing nitrate pollution of their products, saw their market disappearing. Steel manufacturers saw a decrease in aggregate demand and slippage for that holy of holies, the Gross National Product. And military men saw, in the growing population–food–environment crisis, a serious threat to their carefully nurtured Cold War. In the end, of course, economic arguments held sway, and the "inalienable right of every American couple to determine the size of its family," a freedom invented for the occasion in the early '70s, was not compromised.

21   The population control bill, which was passed by Congress early in 1974, was quite a document, nevertheless. On the domestic front, it authorized an increase from 100 to 150 million dollars in funds for "family planning" activities. This was made possible by a general feeling in the country that the growing army on welfare needed family planning. But the gist of the bill was a series of measures designed to impress the need for population control on the UDCs. All American aid to countries with overpopulation problems was required by law to consist in part of population control assistance. In order to receive any assistance each nation was required not only to accept the population control aid, but also to match it according to a complex formula. "Overpopulation" itself was defined by a formula based on U.N. statistics, and the UDCs were required not only to accept aid, but also to show progress in reducing birth rates. Every five years the status of the aid program for each nation was to be re-evaluated.

22   The reaction to the announcement of this program dwarfed the response to President Kennedy's speech. A coalition of UDCs attempted to get the U.N. General Assembly to condemn the United States as a "genetic aggressor." Most damaging of all to the American cause was the famous "25 Indians and a dog" speech by Mr. Shankarnarayan, Indian Ambassador to the U.N. Shankarnarayan pointed out that for several decades the United States, with less than six per cent of the people of the world had consumed roughly 50 per cent of the raw materials used every year. He described vividly America's contribution to worldwide environmental deterioration, and he scathingly denounced the miserly record of United States foreign aid as "unworthy of a fourth-rate power, let alone the most powerful nation on earth."

23   It was the climax of his speech, however, which most historians claim once and for all destroyed the image of the United States. Shankarnarayan informed the assembly that the average American family dog was fed more animal protein per week than the average Indian got in a month. "How do you justify taking fish from protein-starved Peruvians and feeding them to your animals?" he asked. "I contend," he concluded, "that the birth of an American baby is a greater disaster for the world than that of 25 Indian babies." When the applause had died away,

Mr. Sorensen, the American representative, made a speech which said essentially that "other countries look after their own self-interest, too." When the vote came, the United States was condemned.

24   This condemnation set the tone of U. S.–UDC relations at the time the Russian Thanodrin proposal was made. The proposal seemed to offer the masses in the UDCs an opportunity to save themselves and humiliate the United States at the same time; and in human affairs, as we all know, biological realities could never interfere with such an opportunity. The scientists were silenced, the politicians said yes, the Thanodrin plants were built, and the results were what any beginning ecology student could have predicted. At first Thanodrin seemed to offer excellent control of many pests. True, there was a rash of human fatalities from improper use of the lethal chemical, but, as Russian technical advisors were prone to note, these were more than compensated for by increased yields. Thanodrin use skyrocketed throughout the underdeveloped world. The Mikoyan design group developed a dependable, cheap agricultural aircraft which the Soviets donated to the effort in large numbers. MIG sprayers became even more common in UDCs than MIG interceptors.

25   Then the troubles began. Insect strains with cuticles resistant to Thanodrin penetration began to appear. And as streams, rivers, fish culture ponds and onshore waters became rich in Thanodrin, more fisheries began to disappear. Bird populations were decimated. The sequence of events was standard for broadcast use of a synthetic pesticide: great success at first, followed by removal of natural enemies and development of resistance by the pest. Populations of crop-eating insects in areas treated with Thanodrin made steady comebacks and soon became more abundant than ever. Yields plunged, while farmers in their desperation increased the Thanodrin dose and shortened the time between treatments. Death from Thanodrin poisoning became common. The first violent incident occurred in the Canete Valley of Peru, where farmers had suffered a similar chlorinated hydrocarbon disaster in the mid-'50s. A Russian advisor serving as an agricultural pilot was assaulted and killed by a mob of enraged farmers in January, 1978. Trouble spread rapidly during 1978, especially after the word got out that two years earlier Russia herself had banned the use of Thanodrin at home because of its serious effects on ecological systems. Suddenly Russia, and not the United States, was the *bête noir* in the UDCs. "Thanodrin parties" became epidemic, with farmers, in their ignorance, dumping carloads of Thanodrin concentrate into the sea. Russian advisors fled, and four of the Thanodrin plants were leveled to the ground. Destruction of the plants in Rio and Calcutta led to hundreds of thousands of gallons of Thanodrin concentrate being dumped directly into the sea.

26   Mr. Shankarnarayan again rose to address the U.N., but this time it was Mr. Potemkin, representative of the Soviet Union, who was on the hot seat. Mr. Potemkin heard his nation described as the greatest mass killer of all time as Shankarnarayan predicted at least 30 million deaths from crop failures due to overdependence on Thanodrin. Russia was accused of "chemical aggression," and the General Assembly, after a weak reply by Potemkin, passed a vote of censure.

27   It was in January, 1979, that huge blooms of a previously unknown variety of diatom were reported off the coast of Peru. The blooms were accompanied by a massive die-off of sea life and of the pathetic remainder of the birds which had once feasted on the anchovies of the area. Almost immediately another huge bloom was reported in the Indian ocean, centering around the Seychelles, and then a third in the South Atlantic off the African coast. Both of these were accompanied by spectacular die-offs of marine animals. Even more ominous were growing reports of fish and bird kills at oceanic points where there were no spectacular blooms. Biologists were soon able to explain the phenomena: the diatom had evolved an enzyme which broke down Thanodrin; that enzyme also produced a breakdown product which interfered with the transmission of nerve impulses, and was therefore lethal to animals. Unfortunately, the biologists could suggest no way of repressing the poisonous diatom bloom in time. By September, 1979, all important animal life in the sea was extinct. Large areas of coastline had to be evacuated, as windrows of dead fish created a monumental stench.

28   But stench was the least of man's problems. Japan and China were faced with almost instant starvation from a total loss of the seafood on which they were so dependent. Both blamed Russia for their situation and demanded immediate mass shipments of food. Russia had none to send. On October 13, Chinese armies attacked Russia on a broad front. . . .

29   A pretty grim scenario. Unfortunately, we're a long way into it already. Everything mentioned as happening before 1970 has actually occurred; much of the rest is based on projections of trends already appearing. Evidence that pesticides have long-term lethal effects on human beings has started to accumulate, and recently Robert Finch, Secretary of the Department of Health, Education and Welfare expressed his extreme apprehension about the pesticide situation. Simultaneously the petrochemical industry continues its unconscionable poison-peddling. For instance, Shell Chemical has been carrying on a high-pressure campaign to sell the insecticide Azodrin to farmers as a killer of cotton pests. They continue their program even though they know that Azodrin is not only ineffective, but often *increases* the pest density. They've covered themselves nicely in an advertisement which states, "Even if an overpowering migration [*sic*] develops, the flexibility of Azodrin lets you regain control fast. Just increase the dosage according to label recommendations." It's a great game—get people to apply the poison and kill the natural enemies of the pests. Then blame the increased pests on "migration" and sell even more pesticide!

30   Right now fisheries are being wiped out by over-exploitation, made easy by modern electronic equipment. The companies producing the equipment know this. They even boast in advertising that only their equipment will keep fishermen in business until the final kill. Profits must obviously be maximized in the short run. Indeed, Western society is in the process of completing the rape and murder of the planet for economic gain. And, sadly, most of the rest of the world is eager for the opportunity to emulate our behavior. But the underdeveloped peoples will be denied that opportunity—the days of plunder are drawing inexorably to a close.

31   Most of the people who are going to die in the greatest cataclysm in the history of man have already been born. More than three and a half billion people already populate our moribund globe, and about half of them are hungry. Some 10 to 20 million will starve to death *this year*. In spite of this, the population of the earth will increase by 70 million souls in 1969. For mankind has artificially lowered the death rate of the human population, while in general birth rates have remained high. With the input side of the population system in high gear and the output side slowed down, our fragile planet has filled with people at an incredible rate. It took several million years for the population to reach a total of two billion people in 1930, while a *second two billion will have been added by 1975!* By that time some experts feel that food shortages will have escalated the present level of world hunger and starvation into famines of unbelievable proportions. Other experts, more optimistic, think the ultimate food–population collision will not occur until the decade of the 1980's. Of course more massive famine may be avoided if other events cause a prior rise in the human death rate.

32   Both worldwide plague and thermonuclear war are made more probable as population growth continues. These, along with famine, make up the trio of potential "death rate solutions" to the population problem—solutions in which the birth rate–death rate imbalance is redressed by a rise in the death rate rather than by a lowering of the birth rate. Make no mistake about it, *the imbalance will be redressed*. The shape of the population growth curve is one familiar to the biologist. It is the outbreak part of an outbreak-crash sequence. A population grows rapidly in the presence of abundant resources, finally runs out of food or some other necessity, and crashes to a low level or extinction. Man is not only running out of food, he is also destroying the life support systems of the Spaceship Earth. The situation was recently summarized very succinctly: "It is the top of the ninth inning. Man, always a threat at the plate, has been hitting Nature hard. It is important to remember, however, that NATURE BATS LAST."

Critique

An Exercise
in the Rhetoric of
Science Fiction, Fantasy, and Fact

The cover of the September 1969 issue of *Ramparts* magazine shows a tombstone inscribed as follows:

THE OCEANS
Born, Circa
3,500,000,000 B.C.
Died, 1979 A.D.
"The Lord Gave,
and Man Hath Taken
Away, Cursed Be the
Name of Man"

Paul Ehrlich, professor of biology at Stanford University, announces the death of the oceans in an article entitled "Eco-Catastrophe." Although Ehrlich has authored many speeches, articles, and books,[1] "Eco-Catastrophe" merits special attention because in this essay Ehrlich recognizes and tries to overcome the most significant rhetorical problems confronting ecological persuaders.

"Earth Days," conferences, teach-ins, documentaries, and numerous articles and books have made the nature, variety, and scope of earth's ecological problems minutely and horribly familiar. At the same time little has been or is being done to change the conditions and procedures leading to disaster. This unique essay demonstrates an unusually penetrating insight into a fundamental barrier to attitude change confronting those who seek to fight pollution and conserve the earth's ecological balance. The barrier is that science *fiction* has become scientific *reality* and predictions about the future of life on earth, which seem to be the ravings of a mad scientist, are actually systematically developed inferences based on processes already in motion. In this critique I shall contrast science fiction with science fantasy, examine the persuasive difficulties that arise from the resemblance between science fiction and

[1] Ehrlich's addresses are not available in written form. His best-known work is *The Population Bomb* (New York: Ballantine Books, 1968).

ecological rhetoric, and analyze Ehrlich's attempts to overcome these difficulties.

Strictly speaking, science fiction is defined as an "almost step by step development of possibilities from known scientific or social data,"[2] a process illustrated in such science fiction classics as Arthur Clarke's *The Sands of Mars*[3] and George Orwell's *1984*.[4] Science fantasy, on the other hand, knows no such restrictions. "Obeying the sole requirement of dramatic plausibility, it permits the imagination not only to go beyond what is known and proved but to contradict it when that is necessary,"[5] as illustrated in Ray Bradbury's *Martian Chronicles*.[6] These two different genres are often combined in what is loosely referred to as "science fiction." Because works of science fiction and science fantasy are widely read and often confused, the first problem of the speaker or writer on ecology is to demonstrate that he is systematically extrapolating from what is known and proved in predicting future catastrophes, rather than fantasizing and exaggerating for the sake of dramatic or persuasive effect. The problem arises because ecological rhetoric is similar to science fiction in strictly defined terms.

The literature of science fiction has four additional characteristics: (1) It is set in the future; (2) It deals with technological changes, which in turn produce biological, psychological, and/or cultural changes altering man's life in the future radically and qualitatively; (3) To contemporary man, whether as a character in the story or as a reader, these changes appear to be mysterious, irrational, or even humorous in relation to his cultural background and experience; (4) The author, the narrator, or some character in the story is "scientifically expert." Similarities between science fiction and ecological rhetoric are immediately apparent. Both genres deal with prediction about the future, the time period for which proof is most difficult. Both explore technological changes that will produce biological or social changes in man and other species. Both predict and describe radical changes in the quality of life so that the predictions in both may seem impossible and unbelievable to the contemporary audience. Finally, like authors of science fiction, speakers and writers examining ecological problems are, for the most part, scientists or scientifically expert.

These similarities intensify the rhetorical problems involved in the fight against pollution and overpopulation. It is extraordinarily difficult to persuade people to take thought for the future, to protect the earth for unborn generations. Self-interest in the immediate present is a

[2] Reginald Bretnor, "Science Fiction," *Encyclopaedia Britannica*, Vol. 20, 1966, p. 124.
[3] Arthur Clarke, *The Sands of Mars* (New York: Harper & Row, 1952).
[4] George Orwell, *1984* (New York: Harcourt, Brace & World, 1963).
[5] Bretnor, "Science Fiction," p. 124.
[6] Ray Bradbury, *Martian Chronicles* (Garden City, New York: Doubleday & Company, 1958).

powerful motive strengthened by needs experienced here and now. Often the gulf between the scientifically expert persuader and his largely inexpert audience adds to his difficulty in translating scientific data and explaining scientific processes in understandable terms for his audience to internalize. Finally the radical changes he predicts are outside the audience's experience; they are, literally, unimaginable and so may be dismissed or ignored. Who among us can really imagine a world in which the oceans are dead? What layman quickly recognizes that the death of all marine life spells the inevitable death of all life?

Ehrlich systematically designed "Eco-Catastrophe" to overcome the obstacles that beset the ecologist attempting to persuade a lay audience it must change its cultural and political ways if it wishes to survive. He uses four basic strategies. His primary stratagem, of course, is the use of a science fiction format so that he can make use of the audience's tendency to treat ecological predictions as if they were fiction or fantasy. Then Ehrlich shifts the style abruptly, telling us that this fiction is fact or systematic inference from cycles already in motion or trends already in existence. He carefully distinguishes what has occurred and what must occur if present policies continue unchanged. Under such circumstances the audience can hardly treat the predictions as fantastic or impossible. The author uses the narrative style of prose fiction to create and describe events in the future imaginatively so that they come alive for the reader in some detail.

Within this basic format, the author is careful to make use of information and events known to the lay audience. The offshore oil disaster at Santa Barbara in 1969 received national attention, and the effects of oil slicks on marine life and on beaches have become a national concern. Most people have become familiar with data about the widespread pollution of DDT and other pesticides, and control of their use now indicates recognition of their effects. California mothers may know of the lethal danger to infants of high nitrate concentration in their water supply.[7] The use of material known to all or part of the audience lends credibility to the apparent "fiction" of the first part of the article. The sense of verisimilitude combats the notion of unreality.

Similarly in his predictions about future events the author selects situations, political figures, and incidents that have parallels in the past or are consistent with our knowledge of domestic and international politics. We can easily believe that smog disasters might occur in 1973, given published levels of pollution in urban areas and in light of past disasters.[8] The "fictional" Surgeon-General's report on air pollution and

---

[7] For a discussion of this problem, see Barry Commoner, "Can We Survive?" *The Washington Monthly*, Vol. 1 (December 1969), pp. 14–17.

[8] William Wise, *Killer Smog: The World's Worst Air Pollution Disaster* (Chicago: Rand McNally & Company, 1968); Helmuth Schrenk, "Air Pollution in Donora, Pa., epidemiology of the unusual smog episode of October 1948," Washington, Federal Security Agency, Public Health Service, Bureau of State Services, Division of Industrial Hygiene, 1949.

health is an uncomfortable reminder of a previous, slowly heeded report on smoking and health. We can imagine that the efforts of the powerful petrochemical industry lobby in the United States might thwart a United Nations attempt to ban pesticides and might persuade Americans that such a ban is unnecessary because they are less dependent on fish than is Russia or Japan. We can easily believe that the solution to the population–food crisis lies in a "Green Revolution" created by "miracle" grains and special pesticides, partly because the Food and Agricultural Organization of the United Nations have made such claims [9] and partly because we tend to believe that technology can find answers to most or all of our problems. We can imagine a United States president, such as Edward Kennedy, making a speech, shortly after the next election, on population control in the underdeveloped nations and the attacks from the opposition that he is a "creature of the giant drug combine," which wants to "shove its pills down every woman's throat." We can conceive that a population bill might be passed in 1974 calling for "family planning" in the United States and making economic aid to underdeveloped nations contingent on their ability to show progress in reducing birth rates. We can visualize a "fictional" Indian Ambassador to the United Nations, who bears a marked similarity to Krishna Menon, rising to denounce the United States as a "genetic aggressor" and to state the uncomfortable facts that, for several decades, the United States, with less than 6 percent of the world's population, has consumed nearly half of the raw materials used each year and that the average American family dog eats more protein in a week than the average Indian in a month. How easy to imagine that Russia might capitalize on such a situation by announcing the development of a new pesticide and declaring her willingness to build plants to produce it in developing nations. How easy to imagine, in light of past experience, that, in the words of the author, "the sequence of events was standard for the use of a synthetic pesticide; great success at first followed by removal of natural enemies and development of resistance by the past." [10] In this sequence worldwide famine, death, and the extinction of species follow, with revolts not far behind. The United Nations condemns Russia as a "chemical aggressor." Meanwhile new blooms or "red tides" appear in the oceans similar to those now appearing as a result of pesticide and nitrate pollution, [11] and all marine life dies. And how easy to believe that the inevitable result would be world war. The political processes and

---

[9] Richard Critchfield, "Can Politics Keep Up With Technology? Feeding the Hungry," New Republic, Vol. 161 (October 25, 1969), pp. 16–19.

[10] The current "mosquito" crisis in California and the consequent potential for an encephalitis epidemic illustrates this cyclical process. See Sandra Blakeslee, "Two Mosquito Species on Coast Immune to Pesticides," New York Times, 8 August 1971, p. 47.

[11] Commoner, "Can We Survive," pp. 16–17. See also Jon Novdheimer, "Gulf Coast of Florida Alerted for New Outbreak of Red Tide," New York Times, 8 August 1971, p. 50.

events are imagined, but they recall similar past occurrences; the political figures are fictional, but they are familiar. The future depicted seems uncomfortably real.

Finally Ehrlich can rely on his authority as a scientist. He is not a novelist using scientific data for dramatic purposes. He is a population biologist who has chosen to spend many hours and travel many miles to tell this grim story. In addition Ehrlich recognizes that he must create an audience with some understanding of scientific data and processes, and he uses his expertise to teach the basic scientific principles essential to effective action.

The author's conclusion is an inference based on two facts: the limited resources of Spaceship Earth and current rates of resource pollution, species extinction and human malnutrition–starvation. Given these facts we infer that the imbalance between the death rate and the birth rate of the species man *will be redressed,* either by the death rate solutions of war, famine, and plague or by lowering the birth rate. In addition Ehrlich argues that the problem of ecology is not technological but attitudinal, not scientific but social. Technological advances in food production cannot solve the problem because, as the author suggests by the examples of "miracle" grains and Thanodrin, they are likely to create new, more serious problems.[12] Overpopulation and pollution are themselves the results of technology combined with attitudes toward consumption characteristic of developed nations. As a consequence unless attitudes change, technological processes cannot become benign. Also, from the author's point of view, even if technology were capable of solutions to these problems, *there is just no time.* Speaking directly, he tells us that more optimistic experts "think the ultimate population–food collision will not occur until the decade of the 1980s," but less optimistic experts predict it by 1975, a date that is frighteningly near. Conceivably science may find ways to prevent the extinction of more species, to reduce the lethal effects of pollution, and to improve agricultural production, although Ehrlich does not seem to believe such means are possible. Whatever the case, even these solutions become impossible unless immediate social decisions are made to give scientists time—time that can be bought only through massive programs for zero or minus population growth and equally massive programs to decrease ecological destruction sharply, particularly on the part of this society, the most damaging and polluting in the world.[13] Ehrlich asks for drastic and far-reaching programs. He suggests elimination of the internal com-

[12] See, for example, William Murdoch and Joseph Connell, "All About Ecology," *The Center Magazine,* Vol. 3 (January 1970), pp. 56–63, and Lord Ritchie-Calder, "Polluting the Environment," *The Center Magazine,* Vol. 2 (May 1969), pp. 7–12.
[13] In an address to the student body of the University of California, San Diego, March 5, 1970, Ehrlich states that the ecological impact of the average white American is fifty times that of an Indian and three hundred times that of an Indonesian.

bustion engine; bans on the use of pesticides, nitrate fertilizers, and detergents; recycling of all products; and an end to the production of indestructible wastes. Major economic and social changes would be necessary to make such programs effective, and they would involve personal as well as political decisions. Ehrlich implies that our society requires a revolution of "declining expectations" to transform this ever more ecologically dangerous culture into one that, from Ehrlich's point of view, holds the potential for human survival.[14] The author does not spell out the details of such programs because his purpose is the more general one of confronting the reader with the urgency and scope of the crisis. This omission may lead to "false persuasion" because the audience may come to believe that catastrophe is imminent without committing itself to the drastic actions required if the catastrophe is to be averted.

To argue that eco-catastrophe is imminent is to become a prophet of doom, and such prophets are frequently ignored. How real, then, is the danger? How much time do we have? Ehrlich provides an answer in his words, but even more clearly in his actions. He is by profession a biologist, yet he devotes much time and travels many miles each year to warn Americans of the dangers of overpopulation and pollution.[15] The danger is real. In this essay he says, "Most of the people who are going to die in the greatest cataclysm in the history of man have already been born." The time is short. In this essay he predicts catastrophe within a decade, but in a recent interview Ehrlich stated: "When you reach a point where you realize further efforts will be futile, you may as well look after yourself and your friends and enjoy what little time you have left. That point for me is 1972." [16]

---

[14] In addresses to the student bodies at the University of California, Los Angeles, February 4, 1970 and the University of California, San Diego, March 5, 1970, Ehrlich is optimistic that an effective program could be developed but pessimistic that it would be. The only society which, apparently, has made a long-term national commitment to environmental protection is the People's Republic of China. For a description of that program, see Leo A. Orleans and Richard F. Suttmeier, "The Mao Ethic and Environmental Quality," *Science*, Vol. 170 (December 11, 1970), pp. 1173–1176.

[15] David M. Rorvik, "Ecology's Angry Lobbyist," *Look* (April 21, 1970), p. 42.

[16] *Ibid.*, p. 44.

For Further Discussion

1   Carefully describe the techniques used in the preceding critique and set up an alternative approach that would result in different evaluations.

2   What are the perceptible biases, if any, of the critic? Do they invalidate, wholly or in part, the critical evaluations offered?

3   Compare this essay with Ehrlich's book *The Population Bomb*. Discuss the differences in style between the two and assess their relative effectiveness as rhetorical acts.

4 This critique emphasizes the particular problems inherent in the genre of ecological rhetoric. Are there other rhetorical genres which have similar rhetorical problems?

5 Read Maynard Mack's "The Muse of Satire," consider this essay as an example of the genre of satire, and evaluate its strengths and weaknesses as a satirical discourse. Compare the satirical elements of Ehrlich's essay with those found in Emmet Hughes' essay in Chapter 12.

For Further Reading

Paul R. Ehrlich, *The Population Bomb* (New York: Ballantine Books, 1968).

Paul R. Ehrlich and Anne H. Ehrlich, *Population, Resources, Environment* (San Francisco: W. H. Freeman & Company, 1970).

Richard A. Falk, *This Endangered Planet: Prospects and Proposals for Human Survival* (New York: Random House, 1971).

Harold W. Helfrich, Jr., ed., *The Environmental Crisis* (New Haven, Conn.: Yale University Press, 1970).

G. Evelyn Hutchinson *et al.*, "The Biosphere," *Scientific American*, Vol. 223 (September 1970), entire issue.

John Lear *et al.*, "Environment and the Quality of Life," *Saturday Review*, Vol. 54 (January 2, 1971), pp. 63–69.

Maynard Mack, "The Muse of Satire," in *The Practice of Criticism*, eds. Sheldon P. Zitner, James D. Kissane, and M. M. Liberman (Glenview, Ill.: Scott, Foresman and Company, 1966), pp. 15–24.

Gunnar Myrdal, *The Challenge of World Poverty* (New York: Pantheon Books, 1970).

Eight

Eldridge Cleaver

Eldridge Cleaver, perhaps the most articulate spokesman for the Black Panther Party for Self-Defense, has spent much of his adult life in California prisons. To avoid further incarceration he fled to Algeria in 1968. He is the author of Soul On Ice, Post-Prison Writings and Speeches, *and numerous articles, most of which have appeared in* Ramparts *magazine.*

Cleaver is respected and admired by many blacks and some whites, particularly militants. Significantly, many middle-class blacks who disavow the use of obscenity and the advocacy of violent self-defense also express high regard for the courage and audacity of the Panthers. "It's not my style," says a successful black professional leader in San Francisco: "This violence and this filthy talk isn't my bag. And it's got the police built up into a regular militia these days. But man, it makes me PROUD *they stand up." "Any black man knows the Panthers are speaking for him," a successful black politician says. "They are saying what we don't have the guts to say. . . ." ** *

*To use Cleaver's metaphor, the Black Panthers "talk shit," saying what has been unsayable, stripping away euphemistic, sanitized rhetorical statements to reveal with shocking bluntness that equal power is essential if blacks are to achieve liberty and equality. When asked why they persisted in using so-called dirty words, Bobby Seale answered, "Because the filthiest word I know is 'kill' and this is what other men have done to the Negro for years." ** *

This essay was handwritten in Vacaville Prison where Cleaver was incarcerated after the April 1968 shootout between Panthers and police in

---

* Cited in Mary Ellen Leary, "The Uproar Over Cleaver," *New Republic*, Vol. 160 (November 30, 1969), p. 24.
** *Ibid.*

which Bobby Hutton was killed. It was smuggled out of his cell for publication in Ramparts. *Of all the rhetorical discourses in this book, it makes the most extensive use of dramatic form and poetic allusion.*

The Courage to Kill:
Meeting the Panthers

1   I fell in love with the Black Panther Party for Self-Defense immediately upon my first encounter with it; it was literally love at first sight. It happened one night at a meeting in a dingy little storefront on Scott Street in the Fillmore district, the heart of San Francisco's black ghetto. It was February 1967. The meeting was the latest in a series of weekly meetings held by a loose coalition functioning under the name of the Bay Area Grassroots Organizations Planning Committee. The purpose of the coalition was to coordinate three days of activities with the worthy ambition of involving the total black community in mass action commemorating the fourth anniversary of the assassination of Malcolm X. The highlight and culmination of the memorial was to be the appearance of Sister Betty Shabazz, Malcolm X's widow, who was to deliver the keynote speech at a mass meeting at the Bayview Community Center in Hunter's Point.

2   Among the topics on the agenda for this fortuitous meeting was the question of providing security for Sister Betty during the twenty-four hours she was to be our guest in the Bay Area. There was a paranoia around—which I did not share—that assassins by the dozens were lurking everywhere for the chance to shoot Sister Betty down. This fear, real or imagined, kept everybody uptight.

3   I had arrived at the meeting late, changing at the last minute a previous decision not to attend at all. I was pissed off at everyone in the room. Taking a seat with my back to the door I sat there with, I'm sure, a scornful frown of disdain upon my face. Roy Ballard (if the normal brain had three cylinders his would have one) sat opposite me, across the circle formed by the placement of the chairs. He, above all, understood the expression on my face, for he had done the most to put it there; this accounted, I thought, for the idiot grin on his own.

4   On Roy's left sat Ken Freeman, chairman of the now defunct Black Panther Party of Northern California, who always looked to me

From *Eldridge Cleaver: Post-Prison Writings and Speeches*, edited by Robert Scheer. Copyright © 1967, 1968, 1969 by Eldridge Cleaver. Reprinted by permission of Random House, Inc.

like Dagwood, with his huge round bifocals and the bald spot in the front of his natural. On Roy's right sat a frightened-looking little mulatto who seemed to live by the adage, "It's better to remain silent and be thought a fool than to open one's mouth and remove all doubt." He probably adopted that rule from observing his big fat yellow wife, who was seated on his right and who had said when I walked in, just loud enough for me to hear, "Shit! I thought we agreed after last week's meeting that *he* wouldn't be allowed to attend any more meetings!"

5   Next to her sat Jack Trueblood, a handsome, earnest youth in a black Russian cap who represented San Francisco State College's Black Students Union and who always accepted whatever tasks piled upon him, insuring that he would leave each weekly meeting with a heavy load. On his right sat a girl named Lucky. I could never tell why they called her that—not, I'm sure, because she happened to be Roy Ballard's old lady; maybe because she had such a beautiful smile.

6   Between Lucky and myself sat Marvin Jackmon, who was known as a poet, because after Watts went up in flames he had composed a catchy ditty entitled, "Burn, Baby, Burn!" and a play entitled *Flowers for the Trashman*. (It is hard for me to write objectively about Marvin. My association with him, dating from the third week of December 1966, ended in mutual bitterness with the closing of the Black House. After getting out of prison that month, he was the first person I hooked up with. Along with Ed Bullins, a young playwright who now has a few things going for himself off-Broadway, and Willie Dale, who had been in San Quentin with me and was trying to make it as a singer, we had founded the Black House in January 1967. Within the next two months the Black House, located in San Francisco, became the center of non-Establishment black culture throughout the Bay Area.)

7   On my right sat Bill Sherman, an ex-member of the Communist Party and at that time a member of the Central Committee of the Black Panther Party of Northern California. Next to Bill was Victoria Durant, who dressed with what the black bourgeoisie would call "style" or, better yet, "class." She seemed so out of place at those meetings. We were supposed to be representing the common people—grassroots—and here was Victoria ready to write out a $50 check at the drop of a hat. She represented, as everyone knew, the local clique of black Democrats who wanted inside info on everything even hinting of "organizing" in their stomping grounds—even if the price of such info was a steady flow of $50 checks.

8   Then there was Marianne Waddy, who kept everybody guessing because no one was ever sure of where or what she really was. One day she'd be dressed in flowing African gowns with her hair wrapped up in a pretty *skashok*, the perfect picture of the young Afro-American lady who had established a certain identity and relationship to traditional African culture. The next day she would be dressed like a man and acting like a man who would cut the first throat that got in his way.

9   Next to Marianne sat a sneaky-looking fellow called Nasser Shabazz. Sitting between Nasser and Ken Freeman, completing the circle, was Vincent Lynch, as smooth and black as the ebony statues he had brought back from his trip to Nigeria and the only member of the Black Panther Party of Northern California I ever liked or thought was sincere. Somewhere in the room, too, was Ann Lynch, Vincent's wife, with their bright-eyed little son, Patrice Lumumba Lynch. Ann was the head of Black Care, the women's auxiliary to this Black Panther Party. These sisters spent all of their time talking about the impending violent stage of the black revolution, which was inevitable, and how they, the women, must be prepared to care for the men who would be wounded in battle.

10   I had come out of prison with plans to revive the Organization of Afro-American Unity, the vehicle finally settled upon by Malcolm X to spearhead the black revolution. The OAAU had never really got off the ground, for it was stopped by the assassin's bullets that felled Malcolm on the stage of the Audubon Ballroom in New York City. I was amazed that no one else had moved to continue Malcolm's work in the name of the organization he had chosen, which seemed perfect to me and also logically necessary in terms of historical continuity. The three-day memorial, which was but part of the overall plan to revive the OAAU, was to be used as a forum for launching the revival. In January, I had put the plan on paper and circulated it throughout the Bay Area, then issued a general call for a meeting to establish a temporary steering committee that would see after things until the start of the memorial. At this time we would have a convention, found the Bay Area branch of the Organization of Afro-American Unity, and elect officers whom Sister Betty Shabazz would install, giving the whole effort her blessings in a keynote address on the final day of the memorial.

11   By February the plan had been torn to shreds. If the plan was a pearl, then I had certainly cast it before swine, and the biggest swine of all, Roy Ballard, had hijacked the plan and turned it into a circus. It soon became clear that if the OAAU was to be reborn, it would not be with the help of this crew, because all they could see was the pageantry of the memorial. Beyond that, their eyes blotted out all vision. Far from wanting to see an organization develop that would put an end to the archipelago of one-man showcase groups that plagued the black community with division, they had each made it their sacred cause to insure the survival of their own splinter group.

12   From the beginning, when the plan was first put before them, they took up each separate aspect and chewed it until they were sure it was either maimed for life or dead. Often after an idea had gone around the circle, if it still showed signs of life they would pounce upon it and rend it some more. When they finished, all that was left of the original plan was a pilgrimage to the site where a sixteen-year-old black youth, Matthew Johnson, had been murdered by a white cop; putting some pictures of Malcolm X on the walls of the Bayview Community Center; a hysterical speech by Ken Freeman; and twenty-four hours of Sister Betty Shabazz's time.

13   In all fairness, however, I must confess that the whole plan was impossible to achieve, mostly because it did not take into account certain negative aspects of the black man's psychological heritage from four hundred years of oppression here in Babylon. Then, too, I was an outsider. Having gone to prison from Los Angeles, I had been paroled to San Francisco. I was an interloper unfolding a program to organize *their* community. Fatal. It didn't matter to them that we were dealing with the concept of the Black Nation, of colonized Afro-America, and that all the boundaries separating our people were the stupid impositions of the white oppressors and had to be obliterated. Well, no matter; I had failed. Proof of my failure was Roy Ballard, sitting there before me like a gaunt buzzard, presiding over the carcass of a dream.

14   Suddenly the room fell silent. The crackling undercurrent that for weeks had made it impossible to get one's point across when one had the floor was gone; there was only the sound of the lock clicking as the front door opened, and then the soft shuffle of feet moving quietly toward the circle. Shadows danced on the walls. From the tension showing on the faces of the people before me, I thought the cops were invading the meeting, but there was a deep female gleam leaping out of one of the women's eyes that no cop who ever lived could elicit. I recognized that gleam out of the recesses of my soul, even though I had never seen it before in my life: the total admiration of a black woman for a black man. I spun round in my seat and saw the most beautiful sight I had ever seen: four black men wearing black berets, powder blue shirts, black leather jackets, black trousers, shiny black shoes—and each with a gun! In front was Huey P. Newton with a riot pump shotgun in his right hand, barrel pointed down to the floor. Beside him was Bobby Seale, the handle of a .45 caliber automatic showing from its holster on his right hip, just below the hem of his jacket. A few steps behind Seale was Bobby Hutton, the barrel of his shotgun at his feet. Next to him was Sherwin Forte, an M1 carbine with a banana clip cradled in his arms.

15   Roy Ballard jumped to his feet. Licking his lips, he said, "For those of you who've never met the brothers, these are the Oakland Panthers."

16   "You're wrong," said Huey P. Newton. "We're not the Oakland Panthers. We happen to live in Oakland. Our name is the Black Panther Party for Self-Defense."

17   With that the Panthers seated themselves in chairs along the wall, outside the circle. Every eye in the room was riveted upon them. What amazed me was that Roy Ballard did not utter one word in contradiction, nor was there any other yakkity-yak around the room. There was absolute silence. Even little Patrice Lumumba Lynch seemed to sit up and take notice.

18   Where was my mind at? Blown! Racing through time, racing through the fog of a perspective that had just been shattered into a thousand fragments. Who are these cats? I wondered at them, checking them out carefully. They were so cool and it seemed to me not unconscious of the electrifying effect they were having on everybody in the room. Then I recalled a chance remark that Marvin Jackmon had once made. We were discussing the need for security at the Black House because the crowds were getting larger and larger and we had had to bodily throw out a cat who was high and acting like he owned the place. I said that Marvin, Ed, Dale and I had better each get ourself a gun. As I elaborated on the necessity as I saw it, Marvin said: "You need to forget about the Black House and go across the bay and get with Bobby Seale." And then he laughed.

19   "Who is Bobby Seale?" I asked him.

20   At first he gave no answer, he seemed to be carefully considering what to say. Finally he said, "He's arming some brothers across the bay." Though I pressed him, he refused to go into it any further, and at the time it didn't seem important to me, so I forgot about it. Now, sitting there looking at those Panthers, I recalled the incident with Marvin. I looked at him. He seemed to have retreated inside himself, sitting there looking like a skinny black Buddha with something distasteful and menacing on his mind.

21   "Do you brothers want to make a speech at the memorial?" Roy Ballard asked the Panthers.

22   "Yes," Bobby Seale said.

23   "O.K.," said Ballard. "We have the program broken down into subjects: Politics, Economics, Self-Defense and Black Culture. Now which section do you brothers want to speak under?" This was the sort of question which in my experience had always signaled the beginning of a two-hour debate with this group.

24   "It doesn't matter what section we speak under," Huey said. "Our message is one and the same. We're going to talk about black people arming themselves in a political fashion to exert organized force in the political arena to see to it that their desires and needs are met. Otherwise there will be a political consequence. And the only culture worth talking about is a revolutionary culture. So it doesn't matter what heading you put on it, we're going to talk about political power growing out of the barrel of a gun."

25   "O.K.," Roy Ballard said. He paused, then added, "Let's put it under Politics." Then he went on to start the specific discussion of security for Sister Betty, who would pick her up at the airport, etc. Bobby Seale was jotting down notes in a little black book. The other Panthers sat quietly, watchfully.

26   Three days before the start of the memorial, I received a phone call from Los Angeles. The man on the other end identified himself as Hakim Jamal, Malcolm X's cousin by marriage. He would be arriving with Sister Betty, he said, and both of them wanted to talk with me. They had liked, it turned out, an article on Malcolm that I had written and that was published in *Ramparts*. We agreed that when they got in from the airport I would meet them at the *Ramparts* office in San Francisco.

27   On the day that Sister Betty and Hakim Jamal were to arrive in San Francisco, I was sitting in my office tinkering with some notes for an article. One of the secretaries burst through the door. Her face was white with fear and she was shouting, "We're being invaded! We're being invaded!"

28   I couldn't tell just who her invaders were. Were the Chinese coming? Had the CIA finally decided to do *Ramparts* in? Then she said, "There are about twenty men outside with guns!"

29   I knew that Hakim Jamal and Sister Betty had arrived with their escort of armed Black Panthers.

30   "Don't worry," I said, "they're friends."

31   *"Friends?"* she gasped. I left her there with her eyes bugging out of her head and rushed to the front of the building.

32   I waded through *Ramparts* staff jammed into the narrow hallway, fending off the frightened inquiries by repeating, "It's all right, it's all right." The lobby resembled certain photographs coming out of Cuba the day Castro took Havana. There were guns everywhere, pointed toward the ceiling like metallic blades of grass growing up out of the sea of black faces beneath the black berets of the Panthers. I found Hakim Jamal and Sister Betty surrounded by a knot of Panthers, who looked calm and self-possessed in sharp contrast to the chaotic reactions their appearance had set off. Outside where Broadway ran in four lanes to feed the freeway on-ramp and to receive the heavy traffic from the off-ramp, a massive traffic jam was developing and sirens could be heard screaming in the distance as cops sped our way.

33   I took Jamal and Sister Betty to an office down the hall. We talked for about fifteen minutes about Malcolm. Sister Betty, her eyes concealed behind dark glasses, said nothing after we were introduced. She looked cool enough on the surface, but it was clear that she felt hard-pressed. Huey P. Newton was standing at the window, shotgun in hand, looking down into the upturned faces of a horde of police. I left the room to get Sister Betty a glass of water, squeezing past Bobby Seale and what seemed like a battalion of Panthers in the hall guarding the door. Seale's face was a chiseled mask of determination.

34   A few yards down the hall, Warren Hinckle III, editor of *Ramparts*, was talking to a police lieutenant.

35   "What's the trouble?" the lieutenant asked, pointing at the Black Panthers with their guns.

36   "No trouble," Hinckle said. "Everything is under control."

37   The policeman seemed infuriated by this answer. He stared at Bobby Seale for a moment and then stalked outside. While I was in the lobby a TV cameraman, camera on his shoulder, forced his way through the front door and started taking pictures. Two white boys who worked at *Ramparts* stopped the TV man and informed him that he was trespassing on private property. When he refused to leave they picked him up and threw him out the door, camera and all.

38   When it was agreed that it was time to leave, Huey Newton took control. Mincing no words, he sent five of his men out first to clear a path through the throng of spectators clustered outside the door, most of whom were cops. He dispatched a phalanx of ten Panthers fast on their heels, with Hakim Jamal and Sister Betty concealed in their midst. Newton himself, along with Bobby Seale and three other Panthers, brought up the rear.

39   I went outside and stood on the steps of *Ramparts* to observe the departure. When Huey left the building, the TV cameraman who had been tossed out was grinding away with his camera. Huey took an envelope from his pocket and held it up in front of the camera, blocking the lens.

40   "Get out of the way!" the TV man shouted. When Huey continued to hold the envelope in front of the lens, the TV man started cursing, and reached out and knocked Huey's hand away with his fist. Huey coolly turned to one of the score of cops watching and said:

41   "Officer, I want you to arrest this man for assault."

42   An incredulous look came into the cop's face, then he blurted out: "If I arrest anybody it'll be you!"

43   Huey turned on the cameraman, again placing the envelope in front of the lens. Again the cameraman reached out and knocked Huey's hand away. Huey reached out, snatched the cameraman by the collar and slammed him up against the wall, sending him spinning and staggering down the sidewalk, trying to catch his breath and balance the camera on his shoulder at the same time.

44   Bobby Seale tugged at Huey's shirt sleeve. "C'mon, Huey, let's get out of here."

45   Huey and Bobby started up the sidewalk toward their car. The cops stood there on the point, poised as though ready to start shooting at a given signal.

46   "Don't turn your backs on these back-shooting dogs!" Huey called out to Bobby and the other three Panthers. By this time the other Panthers with Sister Betty and Jamal had gotten into cars and melted into the traffic jam. Only these five were still at the scene.

47   At that moment a big, beefy cop stepped forward. He undid the little strap holding his pistol in his holster and started shouting at Huey, "Don't point that gun at me! Stop pointing that gun at me!" He kept making gestures as though he was going for his gun.

48   This was the most tense of moments. Huey stopped in his tracks and stared at the cop.

49   "Let's split, Huey! Let's split!" Bobby Seale was saying.

50   Ignoring him, Huey walked to within a few feet of the cop and said, "What's the matter, you got an itchy finger?"

51   The cop made no reply.

52   "You want to draw your gun?" Huey asked him.

53   The other cops were calling out for this cop to cool it, to take it easy, but he didn't seem to be able to hear them. He was staring into Huey's eyes, measuring him.

54   "O.K.," Huey said. "You big fat racist pig, draw your gun!"

55   The cop made no move.

56   "Draw it, you cowardly dog!" Huey pumped a round into the chamber of the shotgun. "I'm waiting," he said, and stood there waiting for the cop to draw.

57   All the other cops moved back out of the line of fire. I moved back, too, onto the top step of *Ramparts*. I was thinking, staring at Huey surrounded by all those cops and daring one of them to draw, "Goddam, that nigger is c-r-a-z-y!"

58   Then the cop facing Huey gave it up. He heaved a heavy sigh and lowered his head. Huey literally laughed in his face and then went off up the street at a jaunty pace, disappearing in a blaze of dazzling sunlight.

59   "Work out, soul brother!" I was shouting to myself. "You're the baddest motherfucker I've ever seen!" I went back into *Ramparts* and we all stood around chattering excitedly, discussing what we had witnessed with disbelief.

60   "*Who was that?*" asked Vampira, Warren Hinckle's little sister.

61   "That was Huey P. Newton," I said, "Minister of Defense of the Black Panther Party for Self-Defense."

62   "Boy, is he gutsy!" she said dreamily.

63   "Yeah," I agreed. "He's out of sight!"

64   The quality in Huey P. Newton's character that I had seen that morning in front of *Ramparts* and that I was to see demonstrated over and over again after I joined the Black Panther Party for Self-Defense was *courage*. I had called it "crazy," as people often do to explain away things they do not understand. I don't mean the courage "to stand up and be counted," or even the courage it takes to face certain death. I speak of that revolutionary courage it takes to pick up a gun with which to oppose the oppressor of one's people. That's a different kind of courage.

65   Oppressed people, Fanon points out, kill each other all the time. A glance through any black newspaper will prove that black people in America kill each other with regularity. This is the internalized violence of oppressed people. Angered by the misery of their lives but cowed by the overt superior might of the oppressor, the oppressed people shrink from striking out at the true objects of their hostility and strike instead at their more defenseless brothers and sisters near at hand. Somehow this seems safer, less fraught with dire consequences, as though one is less dead when shot down by one's brother than when shot down by the oppressor. It is merely criminal to take up arms against one's brother, but to step outside the vicious circle of the internalized violence of the oppressed and take up arms against the oppressor is to step outside of life itself, to step outside of the structure of this world, to enter, almost alone, the no-man's-land of revolution.

66   Huey P. Newton took that step. For the motto of the Black Panther Party for Self-Defense he chose a quotation from Mao Tse-tung's *Little Red Book:* "We are advocates of the abolition of war; we do not want war; but war can only be abolished through war; and in order to get rid of the gun it is necessary to pick up the gun."

67   When I decided to join the Black Panther Party for Self-Defense the only hang-up I had was with its name. I was still clinging to my conviction that we owed it to Malcolm to pick up where he left off. To me, this meant building the organization that he had started. Picking up where Malcolm left off, however, had different meanings for different people. For cats like Marvin Jackmon, for instance, it meant returning to the ranks of Elijah Muhammad's Nation of Islam, denouncing Malcolm as a heretic and pledging loyalty to Elijah, all in Malcolm's name. For Huey, it meant implementing the program that Malcolm advocated. When that became clear to me, I knew what Huey P. Newton was all about.

68   For the revolutionary black youth of today, time starts moving with the coming of Malcolm X. Before Malcolm, time stands still, going down in frozen steps into the depths of the stagnation of slavery. Malcolm talked shit, and talking shit is the iron in a young nigger's blood.

Malcolm mastered language and used it as a sword to slash his way through the veil of lies that for four hundred years gave the white man the power of the word. Through the breach in the veil, Malcolm saw all the way to national liberation, and he showed us the rainbow and the golden pot at its end. Inside the golden pot, Malcolm told us, was the tool of liberation. Huey P. Newton, one of the millions of black people who listened to Malcolm, lifted the golden lid off the pot and blindly, trusting Malcolm, stuck his hand inside and grasped the tool. When he withdrew his hand and looked to see what he held, he saw the gun, cold in its metal and implacable in its message: Death–Life, Liberty or Death, mastered by a black hand at last! Huey P. Newton is the ideological descendant, heir and successor of Malcolm X. Malcolm prophesied the coming of the gun to the black liberation struggle. Huey P. Newton picked up the gun and pulled the trigger, freeing the genie of black revolutionary violence in Babylon.

69 The genie of black revolutionary violence is here, and it says that the oppressor has no rights which the oppressed are bound to respect. The genie also has a question for white Americans: which side do you choose? Do you side with the oppressor or with the oppressed? The time for decision is upon you. The cities of America have tested the first flames of revolution. But a hotter fire rages in the hearts of black people today: total liberty for black people or total destruction for America.

70 The prospects, I confess, do not look promising. Besides being a dumb nation, America is mad with white racism. Whom the gods would destroy, they first make mad. Perhaps America has been mad far too long to make any talk of sanity relevant now. But there is a choice and it will be made, by decision or indecision, by action or inaction, by commission or omission. Black people have made their choice; a revolutionary generation that has the temerity to say to America that Huey P. Newton must be set free, also invested with the courage to kill, pins its hopes on the revolutionary's faith and says, with Che: "Wherever death may surprise us, it will be welcome, provided that this, our battlecry, reach some receptive ear, that another hand reach out to pick up weapons, and that other fighting men come forward to intone our funeral dirge with the staccato of machine guns and new cries of battle and victory."

Critique

An Exercise
in the Rhetoric of Poetic Injustice

Rhetoric of dissent, confrontation, alienation, and revolution poses the most difficult problems for the critic of contemporary persuasive discourse. Such rhetoric challenges and threatens the most basic values underlying social institutions and policies, and society is quick to retaliate and punish. Surely no body of dissenting rhetoric demonstrates this reaction more clearly than that of spokesmen associated with radical Black Protest. Arrests, trials, and imprisonment are frequent occurrences, as the circumstances under which Eldridge Cleaver's essay was written remind us. One notable example is that of H. Rap Brown, who was charged with inciting to riot and arson as a result of a speech delivered in the summer of 1967 to some 400 blacks of Cambridge, Maryland. He said, "It's time for Cambridge to explode, baby. . . . If this town don't come around, this town should be burnt down." Shortly after his speech, Brown led about 40 followers toward downtown Cambridge. They were met by police, who shouted at them to halt and then, while they were still at some distance, fired a shotgun that inflicted a minor wound on Brown's forehead. Rioting broke out, and by morning there were 700 National Guardsmen in Cambridge. A fugitive warrant was issued for Brown's arrest, and Spiro Agnew, then Governor of Maryland, said that he hoped whoever caught Brown would "lock him up and throw away the key." The Cambridge incident is significant because Congress subsequently cited it in passing a new federal law prohibiting the crossing of state lines with the purpose of inciting to riot—the law later used in prosecuting the Chicago Eight.[1]

During the trial of the then Chicago Seven, Bobby Seale, chairman of the Black Panther Party for Self-Defense, was called to testify in order to explain the "language of the ghetto." In a speech to demonstrators at the 1968 Democratic Convention, Seale had said: "Pick up a gun. And pull that spike out from the wall. Because if you pull it out and if you shoot well, all I'm gonna do is pat you on the back and say 'Keep on shooting.'" In his testimony Seale stated that he had been using a special rhetoric in which words do not necessarily have their normal, literal meanings and that this passage was meant as a call for black people to assert their rights and defend themselves against "any racist bigoted person" who attacked them "unjustly." In the speech itself Seale had said: "There are many kinds of guns. Many, many kinds of guns. But the strongest weapon we have, all individually, is all of us.

[1] Peter A. Jay, "Rap Brown Trial Opens Today in Uneasy Town," *Los Angeles Times*, 9 March 1970, p. I8.

Unite in opposition." Seale and others contend that "apparently inflammatory statements . . . are only the special oratory of the movement."[2] Such claims have historical precedents because "violent language has been almost universal in emotionally oriented agitation, but violence is not its inevitable consequence."[3] These trials raise fundamental questions: Does a causal relationship exist between speeches and subsequent civil disorder? Should speakers and writers be protected in their utterances, no matter how angry?

The answers to these questions depend largely on one's ability to understand the nature of radical black rhetoric. In their book *The Rhetoric of Black Power*, Robert Scott and Wayne Brockriede argue that the uncritical responses of white liberals to media excerpts from this rhetoric play an important role in widening the gulf between blacks and whites.[4]

I address the following discussion to the white population in an attempt to provide grounds for a less threatening and divisive interpretation of Black Protest rhetoric. Let me state, unequivocally, that because I am white, I am necessarily racist, despite the fact that I have fought and am fighting the good fight with myself. In short this critique is a dialogue among whites who live in a racist society and who, by action and inaction, perpetuate that racism. I hope that this analysis will permit those whites in good faith to fight against their racism through a deeper understanding of Black Protest rhetoric.

In the words of Page Smith, well-known historian and provost of Cowell College at Santa Cruz, the function of Black Protest rhetoric for blacks is "to reclaim themselves from their patrons, and in so doing, to themselves as authentic beings, to claim their full humanity."[5] Or, in the words of Stokely Carmichael, the purpose of such rhetoric is to develop "a sense of peoplehood . . . and an attitude of brotherly communal responsibility among all black people for one another."[6] Cleaver's description of the meeting in the first section of the essay and the reasons he gives for the failure of his plan to revive the OAAU vividly illustrate the problem of disunity among blacks.

First, to develop a sense of community or cultural integrity, Black Protest rhetoric must create a new term sufficiently powerful to act as a rallying cry for social change. The new term must unify diverse individuals into a people, subordinating individual differences and clearly

[2] Richard T. Cooper, "Seale 'Explains' Ghetto Talk at Chicago Trial," *Los Angeles Times*, 30 January 1970, p. 117.

[3] Charles Lomas, " 'Incitement to Violence' Not New," *Los Angeles Times*, 11 March 1970, p. II7.

[4] Robert L. Scott and Wayne Brockriede, *The Rhetoric of Black Power* (New York: Harper & Row, 1969), pp. 124–131.

[5] Page Smith, "Women, Blacks, Students: Unquenchable Fires," *Los Angeles Times*, 23 November 1969, p. G3.

[6] Stokely Carmichael and Charles V. Hamilton, *Black Power: The Politics of Liberation in America* (New York: Vintage Books, 1967), p. viii.

distinguishing them from all other people in the society. Also the new unifying term must symbolize pride and power to confront the name of the dominant group in the society. In other words the self-identifying term must be the symbolic agency through which an oppressed and subservient group changes its self-concept as a preface to and prerequisite for the struggle for economic and political equality. For Carmichael the primary struggle is "whether or not black people have the right to use the words they want to use without white people giving their sanction for it." [7] Cleaver recognizes the critical role of rhetorical redefinition: "Malcolm mastered the language and used it as a sword to slash his way through the veil of lies that for four hundred years gave the white man the power of the word." Consequently black rhetoricians have spent much time redefining the meanings of the terms *Negro* and *black* in relation to the term *white*. They start from the meaning of the term *white* that Malcolm X defined by saying, "When he says he's white, he means he's boss. That's right. That's what white means in this language." [8] To his black audience the black rhetorician argues that *Negro* is the name given them by whites: "White people . . . define us by calling us Negroes, which means apathetic, lazy, stupid and all those other things . . . "; [9] *black* is the name they choose for themselves. Negroes are the descendants of the house Negroes of the plantations who identified with their masters; blacks are the descendants of the masses of field Negroes who hated their masters and in turn were hated and feared. Whites are comfortable with the term *Negro;* *black* frightens them. Negro leaders are acceptable to the white establishment; black spokesmen are not. Negro is the badge of slavery; black is the badge of pride. Negroes seek integration; blacks seek self-determination. Negroes are ashamed of their color and ancestry; blacks are proud of their African heritage, color, and racial characteristics. The importance of the struggle over terms is apparent in Malcolmn X's statement to a white audience:

> If you call yourself "white," why should I not call myself "black"? Because you have taught me that I am a "Negro"! Now then, if you ask a man his nationality. . . . the term he uses to identify himself connects him with a nation, a language, a culture and a flag. Now if he says his nationality is "Negro" he has told you nothing—except possibly that he is not good enough to be "American." . . . If Frenchmen are of France and Germans are of Germany, where is "Negroland"? I'll tell you: it's in the mind of the white man.[10]

[7] Stokley Carmichael, "Black Power," in Charles Lomas, ed., *The Agitator in American Society* (Englewood Cliffs, N. J.: Prentice-Hall, 1968), p. 140.

[8] George Breitman, ed., *Malcolm X Speaks* (New York: Grove Press, 1965), p. 163.

[9] Stokely Carmichael, "Speech at Morgan State College," in Haig A. Bosmajian and Hamida Bosmajian, eds., *The Rhetoric of the Civil-Rights Movement* (New York: Random House, 1969), p. 114.

[10] Cited by C. Eric Lincoln, *The Black Muslims in America* (Boston: Beacon Press, 1961), pp. 68–69.

To whites, the sharp juxtaposition of the terms *white* and *black* may seem threateningly divisive. To the black rhetorician, it creates a symbolic confrontation, which permits economic and political struggles to begin. In the words of Malcolm X, "black will fight white for the right to make decisions that affect the struggle in order to arrive at their manhood and respect." [11] It is in this sense that Cleaver states: "Huey P. Newton is the ideological descendant, heir, and successor of Malcolm X."

Second, the black rhetorician must engage in restructuring the experienced realities of his black audience. The appropriation of terms associated with international colonialism illustrates the process of restructuring. However, as one white critic has recognized:

> . . . most Whites probably have difficulty thinking of the ghetto as a colony. The label just does not seem to fit. All this raises the question: How does the Black Power speaker go about making the label seem proper? Perhaps the question itself, no matter how well intentioned, illustrates the deep gulf between the viewpoints of the White liberal and the Black revolutionary. Judging from what the latter says, there is no question. Black people are exploited; colonialism is the means of exploitation; the ghettos are colonies. That line of thought apparently is connection enough to make the symbol a consummation of reality. [12]

Perhaps we can understand the significance of this linguistic restructuring if we recognize what it does for the black audience. Calling the ghetto a colony transforms American blacks from a national minority into an international majority, aligns them with the Third World nations struggling for independence from a dying Western white colonialism, and validates their experience as universal. It places blame on the white power structure, explaining grim social, political, and economic facts in ways that allow blacks to retain a sense of worth while confronting the ugly realities of their condition. Whether ghettos in the United States are *literally* comparable to colonies is less significant than the fact that many blacks, including the late Martin Luther King, Jr., [13] accept this language as accurate and that this redefinition brings reinforcement, hope, and dignity to these people. Cleaver's use of quotations from Franz Fanon, Mao Tse-tung, and Che Guevara reflects identification of the struggle of blacks in America with the struggles of oppressed peoples throughout the world. By relabeling and redefining, Black Protest rhetoric restructures black experience so that blacks can deal with the effects of white racism and unite to resist it.

---

[11] Breitman, *Malcolm X Speaks*, pp. 207–208.
[12] Robert L. Scott, "Justifying Violence—The Rhetoric of Black Power," *Central States Speech Journal*, Vol. 19 (Summer 1968), p. 100.
[13] "The President's Address to the Tenth Anniversary Convention of the Southern Christian Leadership Conference, Atlanta, Georgia, August 16, 1967," in Robert L. Scott and Wayne Brockriede, *The Rhetoric of Black Power* (New York: Harper & Row, 1969), p. 152.

Finally, and crucially, the critic of Black Protest rhetoric must explore what whites perceive as the "advocacy of violence" in discourses such as Cleaver's. That radical Black Protest rhetoric contains the threat of violent *self-defense* is clear; Cleaver's essay is a vivid illustration. That such threats frighten the white community is indisputable. Despite pervasive appeals to democratic and humanitarian values, these spokesmen seek radical changes in American social institutions.

However, there is a special and significant "speaker–audience" relationship involved here. These discourses are acts of symbolic violence, and they have a peculiar self-creating and self-defining value. In these statements the means are the end—the threat is the whole act, an end in itself. Franz Fanon, the black Algerian psychiatrist to whom Cleaver refers, wrote that "at the level of individuals, violence is a cleansing force. It frees the native from his inferiority complex and from his despair and inaction; it makes him fearless and restores his self-respect." [14] Fanon argues that the ends of freedom and equality cannot be achieved solely through peaceful acts because the oppressed individual requires a change of self effected only through an act that unequivocally demonstrates his equality and manhood. Acts of symbolic violence perform this function, for they demonstrate unmistakably to the actor and spectator that the rhetorician is equal to, as powerful as, the oppressor he assaults or threatens. The confrontation between Huey P. Newton and the policeman, which is described in the third section of Cleaver's essay, vividly illustrates this concept. In fact Cleaver's essay itself is an act of symbolic violence; its threat is stated explicitly: "Total liberty for black people or total destruction for America." In similar acts Stokely Carmichael threatens his white audience, "Move over, or we'll move over you," [15] and Malcolm X advises his black listener, "If someone puts his hand on you, send him to the cemetery." [16] If Fanon is correct in his argument, Newton, Cleaver, Carmichael, and Malcolm X are performing self-transforming acts of symbolic violence that threaten and frighten whites and assure the black actor of his equality and manhood. To carry a gun and to advocate violent self-defense may be an end in itself, a self-creating act by which the rhetorician prepares himself and his black audience to struggle with whites as equals. If this analysis is correct, these angry utterances must be permitted and protected, for they serve as an essential means by which blacks act to experience and achieve the sense of equality necessary to effect political, economic, and social change.

The spokesmen for black power recognize that their rhetoric alienates

[14] Franz Fanon, *The Wretched of the Earth,* trans. Constance Farrington (New York: Grove Press, 1963), p. 73. See also Richard B. Gregg, "The Ego-Function of the Rhetoric of Protest," *Philosophy and Rhetoric,* Vol. 4 (Spring 1971), pp. 71–91.
[15] Carmichael, "Black Power," p. 151.
[16] Breitman, *Malcolm X Speaks,* p. 12.

many whites; and many persons, black and white, argue that such rhetoric is self-defeating for a minority requiring tolerance, if not support, of the majority controlling the institutions and processes of social change. However, radical black spokesmen reject the criterion of white approval or acceptance in selecting arguments or appeals or in judging effectiveness. Traditional views of rhetoric have emphasized "adjusting ideas to people and people to ideas" [17] as primary functions of persuasive discourse. Robert Scott and Donald Smith describe the critical problem:

> Since the time of Aristotle, academic rhetorics have been, for the most part, an instrument of established society, presupposing the "goods" of order, civility, reason, decorum, and civil or theocratic law. . . . A rhetorical theory suitable to our age must take into account the charge that civility and decorum serve as masks for the preservation of injustice, that they condemn the dispossessed to non-being, and that as transmitted in a technological society they become the instrumentalities of power for those who have.[18]

Cleaver's essay is an unusual and complex response to "adjustive" and "confrontative" requirements because it combines dramatic narrative and discursive argument. It illustrates the special role that poetic elements play in rhetorical discourse.

The structure of the essay is dramatic. The opening section is a prologue that sets the scene, introduces the characters, and provides historical background for the subsequent scenes. "Suddenly the room fell silent . . ." initiates Act I; "Three days before the start of the memorial . . ." marks the beginning of Act II. The final section is an epilogue in which the narrator steps off the stage to address the audience directly and discursively.

The essay is not adjustive rhetoric in any traditional sense. For the most part the mode of presentation is neither adjustive nor confrontative; it is dramatic and poetic. As drama it speaks in a manner essentially different from the concepts implied by both terms. The dramatic mode is inherently organic and holistic, characteristics that make it difficult to dissect and explain discursively.

In the first three sections Cleaver is not primarily concerned with communicating to an audience. Rather he is artistically selecting and forming his experiences into an organic whole for himself. As readers we are permitted to observe only the events he has decided were critical in shaping his attitudes toward the Black Panther Party for Self-Defense; we encounter his inner world as he now perceives it. Through an artistic process Cleaver identifies his feelings, determines the meanings of his

---

[17] Donald C. Bryant, "Rhetoric: Its Functions and Its Scope," *Quarterly Journal of Speech*, Vol. 39 (December 1953), p. 413.
[18] Robert L. Scott and Donald K. Smith, "The Rhetoric of Confrontation," *Quarterly Journal of Speech*, Vol. 55 (February 1969), pp. 7–8.

experiences, and allows us to share them as they have been formed dramatically. The artistic mode is primarily intrapersonal and self-persuasive; Cleaver is discovering and determining the meaning of his experiences for himself.

Private experience, however, becomes accessible to an audience as aesthetic experience because, as ordered and identified, it has a form that allows others to participate vicariously. The dramatic form is most evident at two points. The first point is the dramatic metaphor that climaxes the heightening tension at the beginning of Act I: ". . . there was a deep female gleam leaping out of one of the women's eyes. . . . I recognized that gleam out of the recesses of my soul, even though I had never seen it before in my life; the total admiration of a black woman for a black man." In one stroke these lines present the symbolic experience, altering consciousness so that the narrator moves to a different level of perceived reality. By implication they create a context for the author: an unloved, lonely man in the presence of the admiration and respect he so desperately seeks. He is now profoundly aware of the men who have called it forth, and he desires to know them, to be like them; they are the most beautiful sight he has ever seen. His mind? "Blown! Racing through time, racing through the fog of a perspective that had just been shattered into a thousand fragments."

The second point is the confrontation between Huey P. Newton and the policeman, a symbolic replay of the shootouts that climax Western dramas. Like the Western hero, Newton is an underdog facing the superior force of corrupt representatives of law and order. Because of his courage he can face them down. Symbolically Cleaver reenacts the drama in which the hero, because of his moral superiority, can overcome the numerical superiority of the forces of evil. Again he shapes the scene dramatically to reveal the process of altering consciousness, the experience that radically changes his way of perceiving reality.

The reader can share these experiences as Cleaver presents them in dramatic form because they become archetypal instances of recurring human feelings and values. In the first case loneliness and lovelessness are archenemies; and reaching out for love, especially the love of a woman, is a basic part of this culture's teaching for men. To be loved a man must be worthy of love, capable of eliciting admiration and respect. In the second case courageousness is a quality with which anyone can identify, and the lonely figure who faces down the mob is part of the deepest levels of American folklore. In this form the author's private experiences become part of the ongoing human drama in which everyone can aesthetically participate.

Retroactively the first three sections become rhetorical because of the nature of the epilogue. The final section is direct address, explicitly discursive and explanatory. It specifies the content of this altered consciousness: "the revolutionary courage it takes to pick up a gun with which to oppose the oppressor of one's people." It argues that violent self-defense is the logical outcome of the ideology of national liberation and the essential means toward its achievement. It confronts the audience with a choice between total liberty for blacks or total destruction for America—the only possible alternatives given the commitment of a revolutionary generation symbolized by Newton and his followers. However, even in the final section Cleaver speaks in mythic and poetic terms: "Huey P. Newton . . . lifted the golden lid off the pot and blindly, trusting Malcolm, stuck his hand inside and grasped the tool. . . . Huey P. Newton picked up the gun and pulled the trigger, freeing the genie of black revolutionary violence in Babylon." To describe Newton's actions in this manner is to make him the mythic successor to Siegfried and his sword *Nothung*, to King Arthur and Excalibur—a destined hero with special moral powers. Similarly Babylon represents both the place where a chosen people are exiled and suffer and a place of moral corruption and sterility where a hero is required if transformation is to occur. Despite its poetic component, the epilogue emphasizes the rhetorical thread that runs through the entire essay. It alters the reader's perception so that earlier sections are interpreted as persuasive discourse. The epilogue is indubitably confrontative rhetoric; it challenges, threatens, and perhaps alienates. The rejection of the "goods" of "order, civility, reason, decorum, and civil or theocratic law" is evident. In this essay Cleaver tempers the harshness of the confrontation by the use of a dramatic form that permits us to share aesthetically his experiences. In a more generic sense, all rhetoric, no matter how angry, is an alternative to physical violence; and Black Protest rhetoric affirms and reaffirms that prior white violence justifies black violence. In this sense black spokesmen adhere to the traditional concept of rhetoric as justificatory; it is argumentation that gives good reasons for action or attitude.[19]

Many whites never become aware of this traditional grounding of Black Protest rhetoric because the processes of symbolic confrontation and symbolic self-transformation and self-definition are intrinsically threatening to them. These processes, or strategies, include the development of a new, strong, self-identifying term with which to confront whites, a symbolic restructuring of black experience that allows blacks to transcend the horrors of their condition in concerted action, and the use of symbolic violence to demonstrate that black speakers and audiences are equal to their white oppressors.

The rage of black Americans is evident in these discourses. Some whites have reacted to this rage by charging that radical Black Protest is black racism. In evaluating that charge let us not forget that blacks have hundreds of years of good and real reasons to hate and fear whites,

[19] Robert L. Scott, "Justifying Violence—The Rhetoric of Black Power," pp. 96–104.

whereas whites have hated and assaulted blacks, individually and in-
stitutionally, solely because they are black. That act alone is racism. Even
those persons who do not make such charges are puzzled by the principle
underlying militant demands. As Carmichael states it: "You can never
give anyone their independence. All men are born free. They are enslaved
by other men." [20] Cleaver poses "a question for white Americans: which
side do you choose? Do you side with the oppressor or with the oppressed?" Two highly respected black psychiatrists articulate the principle
similarly:

> What is the problem?
> *The white man has crushed all but the very life from blacks from the
> time they came to these shores to this very day.*
> What is the solution?
> *Get off their backs.*
> How?
> *By simply doing it—now.*[21]

In Carmichael's words, "The only thing a white liberal can do for me is to
help civilize other whites, because they need to be civilized." [22]

For nearly 400 years black Americans have lived in a violent, threat-
filled world created entirely by white Americans. The threats have been
and are symbolic: "boy," "darky," "nigger," "colored," "Negro," "you are
only ten percent of the population"; the threats have been and are entirely
real: job and housing restrictions, inaccessible or second-rate education,
as well as physical violence and death. White Americans have rejected
order, civility, and justice; we have lynched many hundreds of black
Americans, and we have never sentenced a convicted lyncher to death.[23]

If we refuse to honor the rhetoric of radical Black Protest, not only will
we have created a threat-filled world for black Americans, but we will now
have proposed the further threat of forbidding black Americans to use
words because these words threaten us. And why do we react this way?
Because, threaten others as we may, we white Americans assume that no
one has the right to threaten us.

Finally let us not forget that many black Americans have been arrested,
tried and imprisoned for their statements—words that have made blacks
proud and hopeful, that have helped them to transform themselves, reclaim themselves as human beings, and unite to demand equality and
dignity. And for this reason they must be punished? Because they have
dared to frighten *us?*

[20] Stokely Carmichael, "Black Power," in Ray Fabrizio, Edith Karas, and Ruth
Menmuir, eds., *The Rhetoric of No* (New York: Holt, Rinehart and Winston, 1970),
p. 67.

[21] William H. Grier and Price M. Cobbs, *Black Rage* (New York: Basic Books,
1968), pp. 202–203.

[22] Carmichael, "Black Power," *The Rhetoric of No*, p. 67.

[23] John Davis, ed., *The American Negro Reference Book* (Englewood Cliffs, N. J.:
Prentice-Hall, 1966), pp. 516–517.

For Further Discussion

1 Carefully describe the techniques used in the preceding critique and set up an alternative approach to radical Black Protest rhetoric that would result in a different evaluation.

2 What are the perceptible biases, if any, of the critic? Do they invalidate, wholly or in part, the critical evaluations offered?

3 Read *The Rhetoric of Black Power* and then discuss the special rhetorical problems of the black speaker who is likely to be labeled a "racist" by whites if he addresses himself wholly to black audiences and who is likely to be labeled an "Uncle Tom" by blacks if he addresses himself to white audiences. Compare the ways in which different black speakers have attempted to overcome these problems.

4 Discuss the special problems of the white critic who attempts to analyze and evaluate radical Black Protest rhetoric. Such rhetoric is clearly an important force in contemporary America and thus should not be ignored. Yet how does the critic transcend his condition as part of the audience that is being confronted and condemned?

5 Selec an address made by Malcolm X and one by Stokely Carmichael. Test the adequacy of this critique as "genre criticism" by applying the approach used in the preceding critique to those addresses.

6 The rhetoric of Martin Luther King, Jr. is generally thought to be essentially different in style and argument from radical Black Protest rhetoric. Test this assumption by comparing his Presidential Address to the Tenth Anniversary Convention of the Southern Christian Leadership Conference, Atlanta, Georgia, August 16, 1967 (*Rhetoric of Black Power*, pp. 146–165) with this address by Eldridge Cleaver.

For Further Reading

Haig A. Bosmajian and Hamida Bosmajian, eds., *The Rhetoric of the Civil-Rights Movement* (New York: Random House, 1969).

George Breitman, ed., *Malcolm X Speaks* (New York: Grove Press, 1965).

Parke G. Burgess, "The Rhetoric of Black Power: A Moral Demand?" *Quarterly Journal of Speech*, Vol. 54 (April 1968), pp. 122–133.

Eldridge Cleaver, *Soul on Ice* (New York: McGraw-Hill Book Company, 1968).

John Illo, "The Rhetoric of Malcolm X," *The Columbia University Forum*, Vol. 9 (Spring 1966), pp. 5–12.

Mary Ellen Leary, "The Uproar Over Cleaver," *New Republic*, Vol. 160 (November 30, 1968), pp. 21–24.

Louis E. Lomax, *When the Word Is Given* (New York: Signet Books, 1963).

Robert Scheer, ed., *Eldridge Cleaver: Post-Prison Writings and Speeches* (New York: Random House, 1969).

Robert L. Scott and Wayne Brockriede, *The Rhetoric of Black Power* (New York: Harper & Row, 1969).

Arthur L. Smith, *Rhetoric of Black Revolution* (Boston: Allyn and Bacon, 1969).

Nine

Jo Freeman

Jo Freeman is a leading women's liberation historian and a most effective organizer in the movement. She was instrumental in establishing a center in Chicago where women could study the feminist problem with the aid of pertinent materials and documents.

With the possible exception of racism, the issue of women's liberation confronts the critic with the most profound difficulties in the form of personal bias, prejudice, and fear: The female critic must be dispassionate in the face of issues that directly affect her; the male critic must be dispassionate enough to consider whether the arguments that confront him are legitimate.

Although Miss Freeman is a militant feminist, this particular discourse is an essentially traditional rhetorical transaction that relies primarily on argument and evidence to justify its conclusions.

The Building
of the Gilded Cage

1   Hidden somewhere in the byways of social science is an occasionally discussed, seldom studied, frequently employed, and rarely questioned field generally referred to as social control. We have so thoroughly ab-

From *The Second Wave: A Magazine of the New Feminism*, Vol. 1 (Spring 1971). Reprinted by permission of the author.

sorbed our national ideology about living in a "free society" that whatever else we may question, as radicals or academics, we are reluctant to admit that all societies, ours included, do an awful lot of controlling of *everyone's* lives. We are even more reluctant to face the often subtle ways that our own attitudes and our own lives are being controlled by that same society.

2   This is why it has been so difficult for materially well-off, educated whites—women as well as men—to accept the idea that women are oppressed. "Women can have a career (or do something else) if they really want to" is the oft-heard refrain. "Women are where they are because they like it" is another. There are many more. "Women are their own worst enemies," "Women prefer to be wives and mothers rather than compete in the hard, aggressive male world." "Women enjoy being feminine. They like to be treated like ladies." These are just variations on the same "freedom of choice" argument which maintains that women are free (don't forget, we are living in a *free* society) to do what they want and never question why they think they want what they say they want.

3   But what people think they want is precisely what society must control if it is to maintain the *status quo.* As the Bems put it, "We overlook the fact that the society that has spent twenty years carefully marking the woman's ballot for her has nothing to lose in that twenty-first year by pretending to let her cast it for the alternative of her choice. Society has controlled not her alternatives but her motivation to choose any but one of those alternatives." [1]

4   There are many mechanisms of social control and some are more subtle than others. The socialization process, the climate of opinion in which people live, the group ideology (political or religious), the kind of social structures available, the legal system, and the police are just some of the means society has at its disposal to channel people into the roles it finds necessary for its maintenance. They are all worthy of study, but here we are only going to look at two of them—one overt and one covert—to see what they can tell us about women.

5   The easiest place to start when trying to determine the position of any group of people is with the legal system. This may strike us as a little strange since our national ideology also says that "all men are equal under the law" until we remember that the ideology is absolutely correct in its restriction of this promise to "men." Now there are three groups who have never been accorded the status and the rights of manhood—blacks, children (minors), and women. Children at least are considered to be in their

---

[1] Sandra Bem and Daryl Bem, "We're All Non-Conscious Sexists," *Psychology Today*, Vol. 4 (November 1970), p. 26.

inferior, dependent status only temporarily because some of them (white males) eventually graduate to become men. Blacks (the 47% who are male) have "been denied their manhood" since they were kidnapped from Africa and are currently demanding it back. But women (51% of the population, black and white)—how can a woman have manhood?

6   This paradox illustrates the problem very well; because there is a long-standing legal tradition, reaching back to early Roman law, which says that women are perpetual children and the only adults are men. This tradition, known as the "Perpetual Tutelage of Women" [2] has had its ups and downs, been more or less enforced, but the definition of women as minors who never grow up, who therefore must always be under the guidance of a male (father, brother, husband, or son), has been carried down in modified form to the present day and vestiges of it can still be seen in our legal system.

7   Even Roman law was an improvement over Greek society. In that cradle of democracy only men could be citizens in the polis. In fact most women were slaves, and most slaves were women.[3] In ancient Rome both the status of women and slaves improved slightly as they were incorporated into the family under the rule of *Patria potestas,* or Power of the Father. This term designated not so much a familial relationship as a property relationship. All land was owned by families, not individuals, and was under the control of the oldest male. Women and slaves could not assume proprietorship and in fact frequently were considered to be forms of property. The woman in particular had to turn any income she might receive over to the head of the household and had no rights to her own children, to divorce, or to any life outside the family. The relationship of woman to man was designated by the concept of *manus* (hand) under which the woman stood. Women had no rights under law—not even legal recognition. In any civil or criminal case she had to be represented by the *Pater* who accepted legal judgment on himself and in turn judged her according to his whims. Unlike slaves, women could not be *emancipated* (removed from under the hand). She could only go from under one hand to another. This was the nature of the marital relationship (from which comes our modern practice "to ask a woman's father for her *hand* in marriage"). At marriage women were "born again" into the household of the bridegroom's family and became the "daughter of her husband." [4]

8   Although later practice of Roman Law was much less severe than the ancient rules, some of the most stringent aspects were incorporated into Canon Law and from there passed to the English Common Law. In-

---

[2] Sir Henry Sumner Maine, *Ancient Law* (London: John Murray, 1905), p. 135.
[3] Alvin W. Gouldner, *Enter Plato* (New York: Basic Books, 1965), p. 10.
[4] Numa Denis Fustel de Coulanges, *The Ancient City* (Garden City, N. Y.: Doubleday & Company, 1873), pp. 42–94.

terpretation and spread of the Roman Law varied throughout Europe, but it was through the English Common Law that it was brought to this country and made part of our own legal tradition.

9   Even here history played tricks on women. Throughout the sixteenth and seventeenth centuries tremendous liberalizations were taking place in the Common Law attitude toward women. This was particularly true in the American colonies where rapidly accelerating commercial expansion often made it profitable to ignore the old social rules. In particular, the development of property other than land facilitated this process as women had always been held to have some right in *movable* property while only male heirs could inherit the family lands.[5]

10   But when Blackstone wrote his soon-to-be-famous *Commentaries on the Laws of England,* he chose to ignore these new trends in favor of codifying the old Common Law rules. Published in 1765, his work was used in Britain as a textbook. But in the Colonies and new Republic it became a legal bible. Concise and readable, it was frequently the only book to be found in most law libraries in the United States up until the middle of the nineteenth century, and incipient lawyers rarely delved past its pages when seeking the roots of legal tradition.[6] Thus when Edward Mansfield wrote the first major analysis of *The Legal Rights, Liabilities and Duties of Women* in 1845, he still found it necessary to pay homage to the Blackstone doctrine that "the husband and wife are as one and that one is the husband." As he saw it three years before the Seneca Falls Convention would write the *Woman's Declaration of Independence,* "it appears that the husband's control over the person of his wife is so complete that he may claim her society altogether; that he may reclaim her if she goes away or is detained by others; that he may use constraint upon her liberty to prevent her going away, or to prevent improper conduct; that he may maintain suits for injuries to her person; that she cannot sue alone; and that she cannot execute a deed or valid conveyance without the concurrence of her husband. In most respects she loses the power of personal independence, and altogether that of separate action in legal matters."[7] The husband also had almost total control over all the wife's real and personal property or income.

11   Legal traditions die hard even when they are mythical ones. So the bulk of the activities of feminists in the nineteenth century were spent chipping away at the legal nonexistence that Blackstone had defined for

[5] Richard B. Morris, *Studies in the History of American Law* (Philadelphia: Mitchell & Co., 1959), pp. 126–128.
[6] Mary Beard, *Woman as Force in History* (New York: The Macmillan Company, 1946), pp. 108–109.
[7] Edward Mansfield, *The Legal Rights, Liabilities and Duties of Women* (Salem, Mass.: Jewett & Co., 1845), p. 273.

married women. Despite the passage of Married Women's Property Acts and much other legislative relief during the nineteenth century, the core idea of the Common Law that husbands and wives have reciprocal—not equal—rights and duties remains. The husband must support the wife and children, and she in return must render services to the husband. Thus the woman is legally required to do the domestic chores, to provide marital companionship and sexual consortium. Her first obligation is to him. If he moves out of town, she cannot get unemployment compensation if she quits her job to follow him, but he can divorce her on grounds of desertion if she doesn't. Likewise, unless there has been a legal separation, she cannot deny him access to their house even if she has good reason to believe that his entry on a particular occasion would result in physical abuse to her and her children. He must maintain her, but the amount of support beyond subsistence is at his discretion. She has no claim for direct compensation for any of the services rendered.[8]

12   Crozier commented on this distribution of obligations: "clearly, that economic relationship between A and B whereby A has an original ownership of B's labor, with the consequent necessity of providing B's maintenance, is the economic relationship between an owner and his property rather than that between two free persons. It was the economic relationship between a person and his domesticated animal. In the English Common Law the wife was, in economic relationship to the husband, his property. The financial plan of marriage law was founded upon the economic relationship of owner and property."[9]

13   This basic relationship still remains in force today. The "domesticated animal" has acquired a longer leash, but the legal chains have yet to be broken. Common Law practices, assumptions, and attitudes still dominate the law. The property, real and personal, brought by the woman to the marriage now remains her separate estate, but such is not always the case for that acquired during the marriage.

14   There are two types of property systems in the United States— common law and community. In the nine community property states (Arizona, California, Hawaii, Idaho, Louisiana, Nevada, New Mexico, Texas, and Washington) all property or income acquired by either husband or wife is community property and is equally divided upon divorce. However, "the general rule is that the husband is the head of the 'community' and the duty is his to manage the property for the benefit of his wife and family. Usually, as long as the husband is capable of managing the community, the wife has no power of control over it and, acting alone,

---

[8] Sophonisba Breckinridge, *The Family and the State* (Chicago: University of Chicago Press, 1934), pp. 109–110.
[9] Blanche Crozier, "Marital Support," *Boston University Law Review*, Vol. 15, (1935).

cannot contract debts chargeable against it." [10] In two of the states (Texas and Nevada) the husband can even dispose of the property without his wife's consent. Included in the property is the income of a working wife which, under the law, is managed by the husband with the wife having no legal right to a say in how it shall be spent.

15   In common law states each spouse has a right to manage his own income and property. However, unlike community property states, this principle does not recognize the contribution made by a wife who works only in the home. Although the wife generally contributes domestic labor to the maintenance of the home far in excess of that of her husband she has no right to an allowance, wages or an income of any sort. Nor can she claim joint ownership upon divorce.[11]

16   Marriage incurs a few other disabilities as well. A married woman cannot contract on the same basis as her husband or a single woman in most states. In only five states does she have the same right to her own domicile. In many states a married woman can now live separately from her husband, but his domicile is still her address for purposes of taxation, voting, jury service, etc.[12]

17   Along with the domicile regulations, those concerning names are most symbolic of the theory of the husband's and wife's legal unity. Legally, every married woman's surname is that of her husband and no court will uphold her right to go by a different name. Pragmatically, she can use another name only so long as her husband does not object. If he were legally to change his name, hers would automatically change too, though such would not necessarily be the case for the children. "In a very real sense, the loss of a woman's surname represents the destruction of an important part of her personality and its submersion in that of her husband." [13]

18   When we move out of the common law and into the statutory law, we find an area in which, until recently, the dual legal status of women has increased in the last seventy years. This assault was particularly intense around the turn of the century, but has solidified considerably since then. Some of the earliest sex discriminatory legislation was against prostitutes; but this didn't so much prohibit the practice of their profession as regulate their hours and place of work. The big crackdown against prostitutes

---

[10] Philip Francis, *The Legal Status of Women* (New York: Oceana Publications, 1963), p. 23.
    [11] Citizens Advisory Council on the Status of Women, *Report of the Task Force on Family Law and Policy*, 1968, p. 2.
    [12] *Ibid.*, p. 39.
    [13] Leo Kanowitz, *Women and the Law: The Unfinished Revolution* (Albuquerque: University of New Mexico Press, 1969), p. 41.

didn't come until World War I when there was fear that the soldiers would contact venereal disease.[14]

19   There was also a rise in the abortion laws. Originally abortion was illegal only when performed without the husband's consent and the only crime was a "wrong to the husband in depriving him of children." [15] Prior to passage of the nineteenth century laws which made it a criminal offense it was largely regarded as a Church offense punishable by religious penalties.[16]

20   The most frequent new laws were sex specific labor legislation. Under common law and in the early years of this country there was very little restrictive legislation on the employment of women. It was not needed. Custom and prejudice alone sufficed to keep the occupations in which women might be gainfully employed limited to domestic servant, factory worker, governess, and prostitute. As women acquired education and professional skills in the wake of the Industrial Revolution, they increasingly sought employment in fields which put them in competition with men. In some instances men gave way totally, and the field became dominated by women, losing prestige, opportunities for advancement and pay in the process. The occupation of secretary is the most notable. In most cases men fought back and were quick to make use of economic, ideological, and legal weapons to reduce or eliminate their competition. "They excluded women from trade unions, made contracts with employers to prevent their hiring women, passed laws restricting the employment of married women, caricatured working women, and carried on ceaseless propaganda to return women to the home or to keep them there." [17]

21   The restrictive labor laws were the main weapon. Among the earliest were those prohibiting women from practicing certain professions, such as law and medicine. But most were directed toward regulating work conditions in factories. Initially such laws were aimed at protecting both men and women workers from the sweatshop conditions that prevailed during the nineteenth century. The extent to which women, and children, were protected more than men varied from state to state, but in 1905 the heated struggle to get the state to assume responsibility for the welfare of workers received a major setback. The Supreme Court invalidated a New York law that no male or female worker could be required or permitted to

[14] George Gould and Ray F. Dickenson, The American Social Hygiene Association, *Digest of State and Federal Laws Dealing with Prostitution and Other Sex Offenses*, 1942.
[15] Bernard M. Dickens, *Abortion and the Law* (Bristol: MacGibbon & Kee, Ltd., 1966), p. 15.
[16] Alan F. Guttmacher, "Abortion—Yesterday, Today and Tomorrow," in Alan F. Guttmacher, ed., *The Case for Legalized Abortion Now* (Berkeley: Diablo Press, 1967), p. 4.
[17] Helen Mayer Hacker, "Women as a Minority Group," *Social Forces*, Vol. 31 (October 1951), p. 67.

work in bakeries more than sixty hours a week and in so doing made all such protective laws unconstitutional.[18]

22 Three years later the Court upheld an almost identical Oregon statute that applied to females only, on the grounds that their physical inferiority and their function as "mothers to the race" justified special class legislation.[19] With this decision as a precedent, the drive for protective legislation became distorted into a push for laws that applied to women only. It made some strange allies, who had totally opposing reasons for supporting such laws. On the one hand social reformers and many feminists were in favor of them on the principle that half a loaf was better than none and the hope that at some time in the future the laws would apply to men as well.[20] Many male union leaders were also in favor of them, but not because they would protect women. As President Strasser of the International Cigarmakers Union expressed it, "We cannot drive the females out of the trade but we can restrict this daily quota of labor through factory laws." [21]

23 Strasser soon proved to be right, as the primary use of "protective" laws has been to protect the jobs of men by denying overtime pay, promotions, and employment opportunities to women. The Supreme Court has long since rejected its ruling that prevented protective legislation from applying to men yet there has been no move by male workers to have the laws extended to them. Most of the real benefits made available by such laws have been obtained through federal law or collective bargaining, while the state restrictive laws have been quoted by unions and employers alike to keep women in an inferior competitive position. The dislike of these laws felt by the women they affect can be seen in the numerous cases challenging their legitimacy that have been filed since Title VII of the Civil Rights Act was passed (prohibiting sex discrimination in employment).

24 These laws do more than restrict the hours which women may work. An examination of the state labor laws reveals a complex, confusing, inconsistent chaos. Thirteen states have minimum wage laws which apply only to women and minors, and two which apply only to women. Adult women are prohibited from working in specified occupations or under certain working conditions considered hazardous in twenty-six states; in ten of these women cannot work in bars.[22]

---

[18] *Lockner* v. *New York*, 198 U. S. 45 (1905).

[19] *Mueller* v. *Oregon*, 208 U. C. 412 (1908).

[20] British feminists always opposed such laws for their country on the grounds that any sex specific laws were fraught with more evil than good.

[21] Alice Henry, *The Trade Union Woman* (New York: Appleton and Co., 1915), p. 24.

[22] U. S. Department of Labor, *Summary of State Labor Laws for Women*, February 1967, passim.

25   Laws restricting the number of hours a woman may work—generally to eight per day and forty-eight per week—are found in forty-one states and the District of Columbia. Twenty states prohibit night work and limitations are made in twelve on the amount of weight that can be lifted by a woman. These maximums range from fifteen to thirty-five pounds (the weight of a small child).[23]

26   The "weight and hours" laws have proved to be the most onerous and are the ones usually challenged in the courts. In *Mengelkoch et al.* v. *the Industrial Welfare Commission of California and North American Aviation, Inc.* the defending corporation has admitted that the women were denied overtime and promotions to positions requiring overtime, justifying their actions by the California maximum hours law. In *Roig* v. *Southern Bell Telephone and Telegraph Co.*, the plaintiffs are protesting that their current job is exempt from the Louisiana maximum hours but that the higher paying job to which they were denied promotion is not. One major case which challenged the Georgia weight-lifting law is *Weeks* v. *Southern Bell Telephone and Telegraph.* It received a favorable ruling from the Fifth Circuit Court, but the plaintiff has yet to be given the promotion for which she sued.

27   But perhaps most illustrative of all is an Indiana case,[24] in which the company tried to establish maximum weight-lifting restrictions even though its plant and the plaintiffs were located in a state which did not have such laws. By company policy, women were restricted to jobs whose highest pay rate was identical with the lowest pay rate for men. Many of the women, including the defendants, were laid off, while men with less seniority were kept on, on the grounds that the women could not lift over 35 pounds. This policy resulted in such anomalies as women having to lift seventeen and one-half tons of products a day in separate ten-pound loads, while the male supervisors sat at the head of the assembly line handling the controls and lifting one forty-pound box of caps each hour. "In a number of other instances, women were doing hard manual labor until the operations were automated; then they were relieved of their duties, and men were employed to perform the easier and more pleasant jobs." [25] In its defense, the company claimed it reached this policy in accordance with the union's wishes, but the Seventh Circuit Court unanimously ruled against it anyway. This is only one of many instances in which corporations and male-run unions have taken advantage of "protective" legislation in order to protect themselves from giving women equal job opportunities and equal pay.

[23] *Ibid.*
[24] *Sellers, Moore and Case* v. *Colgate Palmolive Co. and the International Chemical Workers Union, Local No. 15,* 272 Supp. 332; *Minn. L. Rev.* Vol. 52, p. 1091.
[25] *Brief for the Plaintiffs/ Appellants in the Seventh Circuit Court of Appeals,* No. 16, 632, p. 5.

28   With the passage of Title VII the restrictive labor legislation is slowly being dissolved by the courts. But these laws are just vestiges of what has been an entirely separate legal system applicable particularly to women. At their base lies the fact that the position of women under the Constitution is not the same as that of men. The Supreme Court has ruled several times that the Fourteenth Amendment prohibits any arbitrary class legislation, except that based on sex. The last case was decided in 1961, but the most important was in 1874. In *Minor* v. *Happerset* (88 U. S. 21 Wall. 162 1873), the Court first defined the concept of "second-class citizenship" by saying that some citizens could be denied rights which others had. The "equal protection" clause of the Fourteenth Amendment did not give women equal rights with men.

29   Other groups in society have also had special bodies of law created for them as a means of social control. Thus an examination of the statutes can clearly delineate those groups which society feels it necessary to control.

30   The statutes do not necessarily indicate *all* of the groups which a particular society excludes from full participation, but they do show those which it most adamantly excludes. In virtually every society that has existed, the caste cleavages, as distinct from the class lines, have been imbedded in the law. Differentiating between class and caste is often difficult as the two differ in degree that only at the extremes is seen as a difference in kind. It is made more difficult by our refusal to acknowledge that castes exist in our society. Here too we have allowed our thinking to be subverted by our national ideology. Our belief in the potentiality, if not the current existence, of high social mobility determined only by the individual's talents, leads us to believe that mobility is hampered by one's socio-economic origins but not that it is made impossible if one comes from the wrong caste. Only recently have we reluctantly begun to face the reality of the "color-line" as a caste boundary. Our consciousness of the caste nature of the other boundaries, particularly that of sex, is not yet this high.

31   The law not only shows the caste boundaries, it also gives a fairly good history of the changes in boundaries. If the rigidity of caste lines fades into more permeable class lines, the legislation usually changes with it. The Middle Ages saw separate application of the law to the separate estates. In the early years of this country certain rights were reserved to those possessing a minimum amount of property. Today, nobility of birth or amount of income may affect the treatment one receives from the courts, but it is not expressed in the law itself. For the past 150 years, the major caste divisions have been along the lines of age, sex, and ethnic origin; these have been the categories for which special legislation has existed.

32   The law further indicates when restricted castes are seen to be most threatening and the ways in which they are felt to be threatening. If members of a group will restrict their own activities, or these activities are inconsequential, law is unnecessary. No law need be made to keep people out of places they never considered going. It is when certain prerogatives are threatened by an outgroup that it must be made illegal to violate them. Thus Jim Crow laws were not necessary during slavery and restrictive labor legislation was not extensively sought for until women entered the job market in rapidly accelerating numbers at the end of the nineteenth century.

33   Frequently, members of the lower castes are lumped together and the same body of special law applied to all. Most of the labor legislation discussed earlier applies to "women and minors." The state of New York once worded its franchise law to include everyone but "women, minors, convicts and idiots." When a legal status had to be found for Negro slaves in the seventeenth century, the "nearest and most natural analogy was the status of women." [26] But the clearest analogy of all was stated by the Southern slave-owning class when trying to defend the system prior to the Civil War. One of the most widely read rationalizations was that of George Fitzhugh who wrote in his 1854 *Sociology for the South* that "The kind of slavery is adapted to the men enslaved. Wives and apprentices are slaves, not in theory only, but often in fact. Children are slaves to their parents, guardians, and teachers. Imprisoned culprits are slaves. Lunatics and idiots are slaves also." [27]

34   The progress of "out castes," particularly those of the wrong race and sex, also has been parallel. The language of the Nineteenth Amendment was borrowed directly from that of the Fifteenth. The "sex" provision of Title VII (only the second piece of corrective legislation pertaining to women that has been passed) [28] was stuck into the Civil Rights Act of 1964 as a joke by octogenarian representative Howard W. Smith of Virginia.[29]

35   Many of the same people were involved in both movements as well. Sojourner Truth and Douglass were staunch feminists. Douglass urged the first Convention at Seneca Falls in 1848 to demand the franchise when many of the women were reluctant to do so. Similarly, the early feminists were ardent abolitionists. The consciousness of two of the most active is

[26] Gunnar Myrdal, *An American Dilemma* (New York: Harper & Row, Publishers, 1944), p. 1073.
[27] George Fitzhugh, *Sociology for the South* (Richmond, Va.: A. Morris, 1854), p. 86.
[28] The first was the Equal Pay Act of 1963 which took 94 years to get through Congress.
[29] Caroline Bird, *Born Female: The High Cost of Keeping Women Down* (New York: David McKay Co., 1968), chapter I.

dated from the World Anti-Slavery Convention in London in 1840 when Lucretia Mott and Elizabeth Cady Stanton were compelled to sit in the galleries rather than participate in the convention.[30] Many of today's new feminists also come out of an active background in the civil rights and other social movements.[31] Almost without exception, when one of the lower castes in our society begins to revolt, the others quickly perceive the similarities to their own condition and start the battle on their own grounds.

36 Thus it is not surprising that these groups quickly find that they have more in common than having a similar legal situation. All of them, when comparing themselves to the culture of the middle-aged white male,[32] find that they are distinctly in the minority position. This minority position involves a good deal more than laws and a good deal more than economic and social discrimination. Discrimination *per se* is only one aspect of oppression and not always the most significant one. There are many other social and psychological aspects. Likewise, being subject to separate laws and poorer access to the socio-economic system are only some of the characteristics of being in a minority group. This point has been well explored by Hacker.[33]

37 The Negro analogy has been challenged many times on the grounds that women do not suffer from the same overt segregation as blacks. This point is well noted. But it is important to realize that blatant discrimination is just one mechanism of social control. There are many more subtle ones employed long before such coercion becomes necessary. It is only when these other methods fail to keep a minority group in its place that harsher means must be found. Given that a particular society needs the subservience of several different groups of people it will use its techniques to a different degree with each of them depending on what is available and what they are most susceptible to. It is a measure of the blacks' resistance to the definition which white society has tried to impose on them that such violent extremes have had to be used to keep the caste lines intact.

38 Women, however, have not needed such stringent social chains. Their bodies can be left free because their minds are chained long before they became functioning adults. Most women have so thoroughly internalized the social definitions that their only significant role is to serve men as wives and raise the next generation of men and their servants that no laws are necessary to enforce this.

[30] Eleanor Flexner, *Century of Struggle* (New York: Atheneum, 1959), p. 71. They were joined by one white and one black man, William Lloyd Garrison and John Cronan.

[31] Jo Freeman, "The New Feminists," *Nation*, Vol. 208 (February 24, 1969), p. 242.

[32] Myrdal, p. 1073.

[33] Hacker, pp. 10–19.

39   The result is that women, even more than other minority groups, have their identities derived first as members of a group and only second, if at all, as unique persons. "Consider the following—When a boy is born, it is difficult to predict what he will be doing twenty-five years later. We cannot say whether he will be an artist or a doctor or a college professor because he will be permitted to develop and fulfill his own identity. But if the newborn child is a girl, we can predict with almost complete certainty how she will be spending her time twenty-five years later. Her individuality does not have to be considered; it is irrelevant." [34]

40   Yet until very recently, most women have refused to recognize their own oppression. They have openly accepted the social definition of who and what they are. They have refused to be conscious of the fact that they are seen and treated, before anything else, as women. Many still do. This very refusal is significant because no group is so oppressed as one which will not recognize its own oppression. Women's denial that they must deal with their oppression is a reflection of just how far they still have to go.

41   There are many reasons why covert mechanisms of social control have been so much more successful with women than with most other minority groups. More than most they have been denied any history. Their tradition of subjection is long, and even this history is purged from the books so women cannot compare the similarities of their current condition with that of the past. In a not-so-subtle way both men and women are told that only men make history and women are not important enough to study.

42   Further, the agents of social control are much nearer to hand than those of any other group. No other minority lives in the same household with its master, separated totally from its peers and urged to compete with them for the privilege of serving the majority group. No other minority so thoroughly accepts the standards of the dominant group as its own and interprets any deviance from those values as a sign of degeneracy. No other minority so readily argues for the maintenance of its own position as one that is merely "different" without questioning whether one must be the "same" to be equal.

43   Women reach this condition, this acceptance of their secondary role as right and just, through the most insidious mechanism of social control yet devised—the socialization process. That is the mechanism that we want to analyze now.

44   To understand how most women are socialized we must first understand how they see themselves and are seen by others. Several studies

---

[34] Bem and Bem, p. 7.

have been done on this. Quoting one of them, McClelland stated that "the female image is characterized as small, weak, soft and light. In the United States it is also dull, peaceful, relaxed, cold, rounded, passive and slow." [35] A more thorough study which asked men and women to choose out of a long list of adjectives those which most clearly applied to themselves showed that women strongly felt themselves to be such things as uncertain, anxious, nervous, hasty, careless, fearful, full, childish, helpless, sorry, timid, clumsy, stupid, silly, and domestic. On a more positive side women felt they were: understanding, tender, sympathetic, pure, generous, affectionate, loving, moral, kind, grateful, and patient.[36]

45   This is not a very favorable self-image, but it does correspond fairly well with the social myths about what women are like. The image has some nice qualities, but they are not the ones normally required for that kind of achievement to which society gives its highest social rewards. Now one can justifiably question both the idea of achievement and the qualities necessary for it, but this is not the place to do so. Rather, because the current standards are the ones which women have been told they do not meet, the purpose here will be to look at the socialization process as a mechanism to keep them from doing so. We will also need to analyze some of the social expectations about women and about what they define as a successful *woman* (not a successful person) because they are inextricably bound up with the socialization process. All people are socialized to meet the social expectations held for them, and it is only when this process fails to do so (as is currently happening on several fronts) that it is at all questioned.

46   First, let us further examine the effects on women of minority group status. Here, another interesting parallel emerges, but it is one fraught with more heresy than any previously observed. When we look at the *results* of female socialization we find a strong similarity between what our society labels, even extols, as the typical "feminine" character structure and that of oppressed peoples in this country and elsewhere.

47   In his classic study *The Nature of Prejudice* Allport devotes a chapter to "Traits Due to Victimization." Included are such personality characteristics as sensitivity, submission, fantasies of power, desire for protection, indirectness, ingratiation, petty revenge and sabotage, sympathy, extremes of both self and group hatred and self and group glorification, display of flashy status symbols, compassion for the underprivileged, identification with the dominant group's norms, and passivity.[37] Allport

[35] David McClelland, "Wanted: A New Self-Image for Women," in Robert J. Lifton, ed., *The Woman in America* (Boston: Beacon Press, 1965), p. 173.
[36] Edward M. Bennett and Larry R. Cohen, "Men and Women: Personality Patterns and Contrasts," *Genetic Psychology Monographs*, Vol. 59 (1959), pp. 101–155.
[37] Gordon W. Allport, *The Nature of Prejudice* (Reading, Mass.: Addison-Wesley Publishing Co., 1954), pp. 142–161.

was primarily concerned with Jews and Negroes, but compare his characterization with the very thorough review of the literature on sex differences among young children made by Terman and Tyler. For girls, they listed such traits as: sensitivity, conformity to social pressures, response to environment, ease of social control, ingratiation, sympathy, low levels of aspiration, compassion for the underprivileged, and anxiety. They found that girls compared to boys were more nervous, unstable, neurotic, socially dependent, submissive, had less self-confidence, lower opinions of themselves and of girls in general, and were more timid, emotional, ministrative, fearful, and passive.[38] These are also the kinds of traits found in the Indians when under British rule,[39] in the Algerians under the French,[40] and elsewhere.

48   Two of the most essential aspects of this "minority group character structure" are the extent to which one's perceptions are distorted and one's group is denigrated. These two things in and of themselves are very effective means of social control. If one can be led to believe in one's own inferiority, then one is much less likely to resist the status that goes with that inferiority.

49   When we look at women's opinion of women, we find the notion that they are inferior prevalent just about everywhere. Young girls get off to a very good start. They begin speaking, reading, and counting sooner. They articulate more clearly and put words into sentences earlier. They have fewer reading and stuttering problems. Girls are even better in math in the early school years. They also make a lot better grades than boys do until late high school. But when they are asked to compare their achievements with those of boys, they rate boys higher in virtually every respect. Despite factual evidence to the contrary, girls' opinion of girls grows progressively worse with age, while their opinion of boys and boys' abilities grows better. Boys, likewise, have an increasingly better opinion of themselves and worse opinion of girls as they grow older.[41]

50   These distortions become so gross that, according to Goldberg, by the time girls reach college they have become prejudiced against women. He gave college girls sets of booklets containing six identical professional articles in traditional male, female, and neutral fields. The articles were identical, but the names of the authors were not. For example, an article in one set would bear the name "John T. McKay" and in another set the same article would be authored by "Joan T. McKay." Questions at the

---

[38] Lewis M. Terman and Leona E. Tyler, "Psychological Sex Differences," in Leonard Carmichael, ed., *Manual of Child Psychology* (New York: John Wiley & Sons, 1954), pp. 1080–1100.

[39] Lewis Fisher, *Gandhi* (New York: New American Library, 1954).

[40] Franz Fanon, *The Wretched of the Earth* (New York: Grove Press, 1963).

[41] S. Smith, "Age and Sex Differences in Children's Opinion Concerning Sex Differences," *Journal of Genetic Psychology*, Vol. 54 (1939), pp. 17–25.

end of each article asked the students to rate the articles on value, persuasiveness, and profundity and the authors for writing style and competence. The male authors fared better in every field, even in such "feminine" areas as Art History and Dietetics. Goldberg concluded that "Women are prejudiced against female professionals and, regardless of the actual accomplishments of these professionals, will firmly refuse to recognize them as the equals of their male colleagues." [42]

51 But these unconscious assumptions about women can be very subtle and cannot help but to support the myth that women do not produce high-quality professional work. If the Goldberg findings hold in other situations, and the likelihood is great that they do, it explains why women's work must be of a much higher quality than that of men to be acknowledged as merely equal. People in our society simply refuse to believe that a woman can cross the caste lines and be competent in a "man's world."

52 However, most women rarely get to the point of writing professional articles or doing other things which put them in competition with men. They seem to lack what psychologists call the "Achievement Motive." [43] When we look at the little research that has been done, we can see why this is the case. Horner's recent study of undergraduates at the University of Michigan showed that 65 percent of the women but only 10 percent of the men associated academic success with having negative consequences. Further research showed that these college women had what Horner termed a "motive to avoid success" because they perceived it as leading to social rejection and role conflict with their concept of "femininity." [44] Lipinski has also shown that women students associate success in the usual sense as something which is achieved by men but not by women. [45] Pierce suggested that girls did in fact have achievement motivation but that they had different criteria for achievement than did boys. He went on to show that high achievement motivation in high school women correlates much more strongly with early marriage than it does with success in school. [46]

53 Some immediate precedents for the idea that women should not achieve too much academically can be seen in high school, for it is here that the performance of girls begins to drop drastically. It is also at this time that peer group pressures on sex role behavior increase and con-

[42] Philip Goldberg, "Are Women Prejudiced Against Women?" *Transaction*, Vol. 5 (April 1968), pp. 28 *ff*.

[43] McClelland, passim.

[44] Matina S. Horner, "Woman's Will to Fail," *Psychology Today*, Vol. 3 (November 1969), p. 36. See also, Matina S. Horner, *Sex Differences in Achievement Motivation and Performance in Competitive and Non-Competitive Situations*. Unpublished doctoral dissertation, University of Michigan, 1968.

[45] Beatrice Lipinski, *Sex-Role Conflict and Achievement Motivation in College Women*. Unpublished doctoral dissertation, University of Cincinnati, 1965.

[46] James V. Pierce, "Sex Differences in Achievement Motivation of Able High School Students," Co-operative Research Project No. 1097, University of Chicago, December 1961.

ceptions of what is "properly feminine" or "masculine" become more narrow.[47] One need only recall Asch's experiments to see how peer group
pressures, coupled with our rigid ideas about "femininity" and "mas-
culinity," could lead to the results found by Horner, Lipinski, and Pierce.
Asch found that some 33 percent of his subjects would go contrary to the
evidence of their own senses about something as tangible as the comparative length of two lines when their judgments were at variance with those
made by the other group members.[48] All but a handful of the other 67 percent experienced tremendous trauma in trying to stick to their correct
perceptions.

54   These experiments are suggestive of how powerful a group can be
in imposing its own definition of a situation and suppressing the resistance
of individual deviants. When we move to something as intangible as sex
role behavior and to social sanctions far greater than simply the displeas-
ure of a group of unknown experimental stooges, we can get an idea of
how stifling social expectations can be. It is not surprising, in light of our
cultural norm that a girl should not appear too smart or surpass boys in
anything, that those pressures to conform, so prevalent in adolescence,
prompt girls to believe that the development of their minds will have only
negative results.

55   But this process begins long before puberty. It begins with the kind
of toys young children are given to play with, with the roles they see their
parents in, with the stories in their early reading books, and the kind of
ambitions they express or actions they engage in that receive rewards
from their parents and other adults. Some of the early differentiation
along these lines is obvious to us from looking at young children and
reminiscing about our own lives. But some of it is not so obvious, even
when we engage in it ourselves. It consists of little actions which parents
and teachers do every day that are not even noticed but can profoundly
affect the style and quality of a child's developing mind.

56   Adequate research has not yet been done which irrefutably links up
child-rearing practices with the eventual adult mind, but there is evidence
to support some hypotheses. Let us take a look at one area where strong
sex differences show up relatively early—mathematical reasoning ability.
No one has been able to define exactly what this ability is, but it has been
linked up with number ability and spatial perception, or the ability to
visualize objects out of their context. As on other tests, girls score higher
on number ability until late high school, but such is not the case with
analytic and spatial perception tests. These tests indicate that boys per-

[47] Lionel J. Neiman, "The Influence of Peer Groups Upon Attitudes Toward the
Feminine Role," *Social Problems*, Vol. 2 (1954), pp. 104–111.
[48] S. E. Asch, "Studies of Independence and Conformity. A Minority of One
Against a Unanimous Majority," *Psychological Monographs*, Vol. 70, No. 9 (1956).

ceive more analytically, while girls are more contextual—although the ability to "break set" or be "field independent" also does not seem to appear until after the fourth or fifth year.[49]

57   According to Maccoby, this contextual mode of perception common to women is a distinct disadvantage for scientific production. "Girls on the average develop a somewhat different way of handling incoming information—their thinking is less analytic, more global, and more perseverative—and this kind of thinking may serve very well for many kinds of functioning, but it is not the kind of thinking most conducive to high-level intellectual productivity, especially in science."[50]

58   Several social psychologists have postulated that the key developmental characteristic of analytic thinking is what is called early "independence and mastery training," or "whether and how soon a child is encouraged to assume initiative, to take responsibility for himself, and to solve problems by himself, rather than rely on others for the direction of his activities."[51] In other words, analytically inclined children are those who have not been subject to what Bronfenbrenner calls "over-socialization,"[52] and there is a good deal of indirect evidence that such is the case. Levy has observed that "overprotected" boys tend to develop intellectually like girls.[53] Bing found that those girls who were good at spatial tasks were those whose mothers left them alone to solve the problems by themselves, while the mothers of verbally inclined daughters insisted on helping them.[54] Witkin similarly found that mothers of analytic children had encouraged their initiative, while mothers of non-analytic children had encouraged dependence and discouraged self-assertion.[55] One writer commented on these studies that "this is to be expected, for the independent child is less likely to accept superficial appearances of objects without

[49] Eleanor E. Maccoby, "Sex Differences in Intellectual Functioning," in Eleanor Maccoby, ed., *The Development of Sex Differences* (Stanford University Press, 1966), p. 26 *ff*. The three most common tests are the Rod and Frame test, which requires the adjustment of a rod to a vertical position regardless of the tilt of a frame around it; the Embedded Figures Test, which determines the ability to perceive a figure embedded in a more complex field; and an analytic test in which one groups a set of objects according to a common element.
[50] Eleanor E. Maccoby, "Woman's Intellect" in Seymour M. Farber and Roger H. L. Wilson, eds., *Man and Civilization: The Potential of Women, A Symposium,* (New York: McGraw-Hill, 1963), p. 30.
[51] Maccoby, *Ibid.,* p. 31. See also Julia A. Sherman, "Problems of Sex Differences in Space Perception and Aspects of Intellectual Functioning," *Psychological Review,* Vol. 74 (July 1967), pp. 290–299; and Philip E. Vernon, "Ability Factors and Environmental Influences," *American Psychologist,* Vol. 20 (September 1965), pp. 723–733.
[52] Urie Bronfenbrenner, "Some Familial Antecedents of Responsibility and Leadership in Adolescents," in Luigi Petrullo and Bernard M. Bass, eds., *Leadership and Interpersonal Behavior* (New York: Holt, Rinehart and Winston, 1961), p. 260.
[53] D. M. Levy, *Maternal Overprotection* (New York: Columbia University Press, 1943).
[54] Maccoby, *Ibid.,* p. 31.
[55] Herman A. Witkin *et al., Psychological Differentiation* (New York: John Wiley & Sons, 1962).

exploring them for himself, while the dependent child will be afraid to reach out on his own and will accept appearances without question. In other words, the independent child is likely to be more *active*, not only psychologically but physically, and the physically active child will naturally have more kinesthetic experience with spatial relationships in his environment." [56]

59   When we turn to specific child-rearing practices, we find that the pattern repeats itself according to the sex of the child. Although comparative studies of parental treatment of boys and girls are not extensive, those that have been made indicate that the traditional practices applied to girls are very different from those applied to boys. Girls receive more affection, more protectiveness, more control, and more restrictions. Boys are subjected to more achievement demands and higher expectations.[57] In short, while girls are not always encouraged to be dependent *per se*, they are usually not encouraged to be *independent* and physically active. "Such findings indicate that the differential treatment of the two sexes reflects in part a difference in goals. With sons, socialization seems to focus primarily on directing and constraining the boys' impact on the environment. With daughters, the aim is rather to protect the girl from the impact of environment. The boy is being prepared to mold his world, the girl to be molded by it." [58]

60   This relationship holds true cross-culturally even more than it does in our own society. In studying child socialization in 110 non-literate cultures, Barry, Bacon, and Child found that "Pressure toward nurturance, obedience, and responsibility is most often stronger for girls, whereas pressure toward achievement and self-reliance is most often stronger for boys." [59] They also found that strong differences in socialization practices were consistent with highly differentiated adult sex roles.

61   These cross-cultural studies show that dependency training for women is widespread and has results beyond simply curtailing analytic ability. In all these cultures women were in a relatively inferior status position compared to males. In fact, there was a correlation with the degree of rigidity of sex-role socialization and the subservence of women to men.

62   In our society also, analytic abilities are not the only ones valued. Being person-oriented and contextual in perception are very valuable

[56] James Clapp, "Sex Differences in Mathematical Reasoning Ability," unpublished paper, 1968.
[57] Robert R. Sears *et al.*, *Patterns of Child Rearing* (Evanston, Ill.: Row and Peterson, 1957).
[58] Bronfenbrenner, *Ibid.*, p. 260.
[59] Herbert Barry, M. K. Bacon, and Irving L. Child, "A Cross-Cultural Survey of Some Sex Differences in Socialization," *Journal of Abnormal and Social Psychology*, Vol. 55 (November 1957), p. 328.

attributes for many fields where, nevertheless, very few women are found. Such characteristics are valuable in the arts and the social sciences where women are found more than in the natural sciences—yet even here their achievement is still not deemed equivalent to that of men. One explanation of this, of course, is the repressive effect of role conflict and peer group pressures discussed earlier. But when one looks further it appears that there is an earlier cause here as well.

63   As several studies have shown, the very same early independence and mastery training which has such a beneficial effect on analytic think-ing also determines the extent of one's achievement orientation [60]—that drive which pushes one to excel beyond the need of survival. And it is precisely this kind of training that women fail to receive. They are en-couraged to be dependent and passive—to be "feminine." In that process the shape of their mind is altered and their ambitions are dulled or channeled into the only socially rewarded achievement for a woman—marriage.

64   Now we have come almost full circle and can begin to see the vicious nature of the trap in which our society places women. When we become conscious of the many subtle mechanisms of social control—peer group pressures, cultural norms, parental training, teachers, role expecta-tions, and negative self-concept—it is not hard to see why girls who are better at most everything in childhood do not excel at much of anything as adults.

65   Only one link remains and that requires taking a brief look at those few women who do manage to slip through a chance loophole. Maccoby provided the best commentary on this when she noted that the girl who does not succumb to overprotection and develop the appropriate per-sonality and behavior for her sex has a major price to pay: the anxiety that comes from crossing the caste lines. She feels that "it is this anxiety which helps to account for the lack of productivity among those women who do make intellectual careers—because [anxiety] is especially damag-ing to creative thinking." The combination of all these factors together tell "something of a horror story." It would appear that even when a woman is suitably endowed intellectually and develops the right temperament and habits of thought to make use of her endowment, she must be fleet of foot indeed to scale the hurdles society has erected for her and to remain a whole and happy person while continuing to follow her intellectual bent.[61]

[60] Marian R. Winterbottom, "The Relation of Need for Achievement to Learning Experiences in Independence and Mastery," in Harold Proshansky and Bernard Seidenberg, eds., *Basic Studies in Social Psychology* (New York: Holt, Rinehart and Winston, 1965), pp. 294–307.
[61] Maccoby, *Ibid.*, p. 37.

66   The plot behind this horror story should by now be clearly evident. There is more to oppression than discrimination and more to the condition of women than whether or not they want to be free of the home. All societies have many ways to keep people in their places, and we have only discussed a few of the ones used to keep women in theirs. Women have been striving to break free of these bonds for many hundreds of years and once again are gathering their strength for another try. It will take more than a few changes in the legal system to significantly change the condition of women, although those changes will be reflective of more profound changes taking place in society. Unlike blacks, the women's liberation movement does not have the thicket of Jim Crow laws to cut through. This is a mixed blessing. On the one hand, the women's liberation movement lacks the simple handholds of oppression which the early civil rights movement had; but at the same time it does not have to waste time wading through legal segregation before realizing that the real nature of oppression lies much deeper. It is the more basic means of social control that will have to be attacked as women and men look into their lives and dissect the many factors that made them what they are. The dam of social control now has many cracks in it. It has held women back for years, but it is about to break under the strain.

Questions for Criticism and Discussion

1   Describe the two major arguments in this discourse by outlining the processes of development for each argument. How are the two arguments connected and how do they serve in combination to justify the major conclusion, or thesis?

2   Describe the supporting materials in this discourse. In light of the "rhetorical problem" faced by advocates of women's liberation, how would you evaluate the author's selection of evidence and argument?

3   In light of the evidence presented in the discourse, is your evaluation of the credibility of the supporting materials and arguments and the *ethos* of the author affected by the writer's being Jo, rather than Joe, Freeman?

4   Compare this discourse with a more militant or radical statement of the feminist position. Describe the audience for which each discourse would be effective and the different ways in which the "rhetorical problem" is approached.

5   Which of the basic criteria for evaluation (truth, effects, ethics, aesthetics) would most appropriately be applied to this discourse? In that application, what shortcomings, if any, do you find?

For Further Reading

Joanne Cooke, Charlotte Bunch-Weeks, and Robin Morgan, eds., *The New Women: A Motive Anthology on Women's Liberation* (Indianapolis: Bobbs-Merrill Company, 1971).

Cynthia Fuchs Epstein and William J. Goode, eds., *The Other Half: Roads to Women's . Equality* (Englewood Cliffs, N. J.: Prentice-Hall, 1971).

Vivian Gornick and Barbara K. Moran, *Woman in Sexist Society: Studies in Power and Powerlessness* (New York: Basic Books, 1971).

Michele Hoffnung Garskof, *Roles Women Play: Readings Toward Women's Liberation* (Belmont, Calif.: Brooks/Cole Publishing Company, 1971).

Germaine Greer, *The Female Eunuch* (New York: McGraw-Hill Book Company, 1971).

Hoffman R. Hays, *The Dangerous Sex, The Myth of Feminine Evil* (New York: G. P. Putnam's Sons, 1964).

Elizabeth Janeway, *Man's World, Woman's Place: A Study in Social Mythology* (New York: William Morrow and Company, 1971).

Robert Jay Lifton, ed., *The Woman in America* (Boston: Beacon Press, 1964).

Kate Millett, *Sexual Politics* (Garden City, N. Y.: Doubleday & Company, 1970).

Robin Morgan, ed., *Sisterhood is Powerful* (New York: Vintage Books, 1970).

Betty Roszak and Theodore Roszak, eds., *Masculine/Feminine* (New York: Harper Colophon Books, 1969).

Ten

Edgar Z. Friedenberg

Edgar Z. Friedenberg is a sociologist who has authored The Vanishing Adolescent, Coming of Age in America, The Dignity of Youth and Other Atavisms *and co-authored* Society's Children. *Friedenberg's interests and expertise concern the treatment of young people in America.*

This essay is a radical reinterpretation of the conflict between youth and their elders. It is rhetorically similar to George Wald's address in that it seeks to redefine and restructure the audience's perspective by unifying a series of problems in terms of a single principle. The author uses a blunt, cutting style that clearly reveals his attitudes. The essay is unusually "self-conscious" because the author is explicitly aware of the attitudes of the audience that this discourse will select.

Readers of Friedenberg's essay must face this question: If the argument presented here is correct, what actions can be taken to remedy these problems?

The Generation Gap

1   The idea that what separates us from the young is something so passive that it may justly be called a "generation gap" is, I believe, itself a misleading article of middle-aged liberal ideology, serving to allay

The Annals of the American Academy of Political and Social Science, Vol. 382 (March 1969), pp. 32–42. Reprinted by permission of the author and the American Academy of Political and Social Science.

anxiety rather than to clarify the bases of intergenerational conflict. It is true, to be sure, that the phrase is strong enough to describe the barrier that separates many young people from their elders, for a majority still accept our society as providing a viable pattern of life and expectations for the future. Liberalism dies hard, and most young people, like some Negroes even today, are still willing to attribute their difficulties with their elders and society to mutual misunderstanding.

2 I believe, however, that this is a false position. Though most adults maintain a benevolent posture in expressing their public attitudes toward youth and—though, I think, steadily fewer—young people still accept this as what their elders intend in principle, both young and old seem trapped in a false view of what is actually a profound conflict of interest in our society. What appears to be a consequence of mere cultural lag in responding to a new social and political maturity in the young, with distressing but unintended repressive consequences, is rather the expression of what has become genuine class-conflict between a dominant and exploitive older generation and youth who are slowly becoming more aware of what is happening to them as demands on them are, in the language of the time, escalated.[1]

Discontinuity in an Open Society

3 In all societies, so far as I know, young people enter the social system in subordinate roles while older people run things. This is true even in technically primitive cultures, where the crude physical strength of youth is still of real productive advantage. Is there always a generational conflict? And, if so, does it always reflect as profound a division, and as severe a conflict of interest, as generational conflict in America today?

4 There is, I believe, indeed an inherent basis for such a conflict in the fact that the old dominate the young and the young wish to replace them, but it is not as severe in most societies as in ours. Here, it has become different in kind, as the brightest and most articulate of the young declare that they will not even accept, when their turn comes, the kinds of roles—in the kind of society—which their parents have held. As Bruno Bettelheim[2] pointed out in a classic paper some years ago, factors that

---

[1] I am indebted to John and Margaret Rowntree of York University and the University of Toronto, respectively, for demonstrating in their paper "The Political Economy of Youth in the United States" the class-dynamics of generational conflict. This document, prepared for presentation at the First Annual Meeting of the Committee on Socialist Studies in Calgary, Alberta, in June 1968, was published in the Montreal quarterly journal *Our Generation*, Vol. 6, No. 1, 1968. Their radical analysis simplifies many apparent paradoxes in the relationship between the generations.

[2] Bruno Bettelheim, "The Problem of Generations," *Daedalus*, Vol. 91, No. 1 (Winter 1962), pp. 68–96.

have traditionally mitigated generational conflict have become feeble or inoperative even in this country. The family, for example, which is the context within which the strongest—albeit ambivalent—affectual ties between the generations are formed, plays a decreasing role in the lives of its members and, certainly, in the socialization of the young. It has less effect on their life chances than it once had. If the Victorian father or the head of a traditional rural household was often a tyrant, and more or less accepted as such by his neighbors and his children, he was also a man who felt that he could transmit his wealth, his trade, and his position in the community, by inheritance. His relationship to his sons was not purely competitive but complementary as well: it was they who would have to carry on his work as his own powers failed, and on whom he was therefore ultimately dependent if his accomplishment in life was to lead to anything permanent. The proper attitude of father to son—both the authority and the underlying tenderness—took account of this mutual though unequal dependency. And while excessive and inconsiderate longevity in a father might make his son's position grotesque, as that of mad old George III did to the Prince Regent's position, the problems of succession were usually made less abrasive by the recognition of mutual need.

5   Moreover, so long as society changed slowly, elders really knew more that was useful than the young did; they were wiser; their authority was based on real superiority in the subtle techniques of living. This was never a very strong bond between the generations in America, where the sons of immigrants have always been as likely to find their greenhorn parents a source of embarrassment as of enlightenment; and generational conflict has probably always been more severe here than in more stable cultures—or would have been had there not also been a continent to escape into and develop.

6   But, today, the older generation has become not merely an embarrassment, but often an obstructive irrelevance to the young. We cannot even defend our former functions with respect to youth; for the ethos of modern liberalism condemns as inequitable, and a violation of equal opportunity, the arrangements on which continuity between the generations has been based. Bourgeois emphasis on private property and the rights of inheritance gave to the family the function of providing this continuity, which, under feudal conditions, would have been shared among several institutions—apprenticeship, for example. But the development of an open, bureaucratic society has weakened the influence of the family, and has transferred the task of distributing status among claimants primarily to the schools, which profess to judge them, so far as possible, without regard to their antecedents.

7   Today, college admissions officers agree that the sons of alumni should not be favored over more gifted applicants who seek admission solely on the basis of their academic record and recommendations. But this amounts to redefining merit to mean the kind of performance and personality that high school teachers and, increasingly, counselors like. Counselors now virtually control many a high school student's future chances, by their decision whether to assign him to a college-preparatory course and by monitoring his applications for admission. Whether this whole process makes the contest more open, or merely changes the criteria for preferment, is hard to say.[3]

8   The effect of the high school, and especially of the counselor, on continuity of status between the generations, and hence on the bond between the generations, is the subject of a fascinating study—still little known after five years—by Aaron V. Cicourel and John I. Kitsuse.[4] While the entire work bears on this issue, one particular interview excerpt is worth quoting here because of the clarity with which it shows a high school student from an upper-status suburban home being punished for his lack of humility in school by restriction of his future chances. This young man had already been classed by his counselor as an "under-achiever." Here are some of the counselor's comments to Cicourel and Kitsuse's interviewer:

> *Counselor:* His mother says he's a pleasant outgoing boy. His teachers will say he's either a pleasant boy or that he's a pest. I think he's arrogant. He thinks he's handsome. He's nice-looking, but not handsome. He thinks he owns Lakeshore. He talks to his teachers as if they were stupid. He's a good student. He's in biology and algebra honors.
>
> *Interviewer:* Is he going to college?
>
> *Counselor:* He plans college. I think he said he plans to go East like M.I.T., Harvard, etc. He won't make it. He's a candidate for a midwestern school.[5]

9   This excerpt, of course, illustrates certain very positive reasons for conflict between youth and older people: the constraint imposed by the school and its basic disrespect for its young captive. But I have introduced it here specifically to call attention to the fact that the school is here destroying the basis for continuity in the home by making it a condition—for higher- as well as for lower-status students—that the student *unlearn* what the home has taught him about himself if he wishes to retain access to his family's present socioeconomic status. In this way, older middle-and upper-class life-patterns are made positively dysfunctional for the young, just as lower-class life-patterns are, in the equalizing process of the school. Unless the tendency of the home is toward docile acceptance of

[3] Christopher Jencks and David Riesman, in *The Academic Revolution* (Garden City, N. Y.: Doubleday & Company, 1968), pp. 146–154, provide a thoughtful, if rather gingerly, discussion of this issue.
[4] Aaron V. Cicourel and John I. Kitsuse, *The Educational Decision-Makers* (Indianapolis: Bobbs-Merrill, 1963).
[5] *Ibid.*, p. 72.

the common-man pattern of life and expectation, the school will run counter to its influence.

10   The influence of the school itself is, in a matter of this complexity, difficult to isolate and appraise. But it is clear—and, I think, significant—that disaffection in the young is heavily concentrated among both the bright middle-class and upper–middle-class youth, on the one hand, and the lower-class, especially Negro, youth, on the other. The working class, young and old, is, in contrast, much more likely to be hostile to dissent, and especially to demonstrations, and to regard the school as the pathway to opportunity; its children are more willing to put on a clean shirt and tie and await the pleasure of the draftboard or the interviewer from industry. For them, the school and family have worked together, and adult role-models retain their quite possibly fatal appeal.

Youth as a Discriminated-Against Class

11   I have already asserted that conflict between the generations is less a consequence of the ways in which old and young perceive, or misperceive, each other than of structurally created, genuine conflicts of interest. In this, as in other relationships, ideology follows self-interest; we impute to other people and social groups characteristics that justify the use we plan to make of them and the control over them that use requires. The subordinate group, in turn, often develops these very characteristics in response to the conditions that were imposed on them. Slaves, slum-dwellers, "teen-agers," and enlisted men do, indeed, often display a defensive stupidity and irresponsibility, which quickly abates in situations which they feel to be free of officious interference, with which they can deal, by means of their own institutions, in their own way.

12   For American youth, these occasions are few, and have grown relatively fewer with the escalation of the war in Vietnam. The Dominican intervention, the scale and permanence of our military investment in Southeast Asia, and the hunch that our economic system requires the engagement of its youth at low pay, or none, in a vast military–academic complex, in order to avoid disastrously widespread unemployment—even under present circumstances far greater among youth than among older persons—suggest to thoughtful young people that their bondage may be fundamental to the American political system and incapable of solution within its terms.

13   That bondage is remarkably complete—and so gross, in comparison to the way in which other members of the society are treated, that I find it difficult to accept the good faith of most adults who declare their sympathy with "the problems of youth" while remaining content to operate within the limits of the coercive system that deals with them, in any official capacity. To search for explanations of the problems of youth in America in primarily psychological terms while suggesting ways of easing the tension between them and the rest of society is rather like approaching the problem of "the American turkey in the late autumn" with the same benign attitude. Turkeys would have no problem, except for the use we make of them, though I can imagine clearly enough the arguments that a cadre of specialists in poultry-relations might advance in defense of Thanksgiving, all of them true enough as far as they went: that wild turkeys could not support themselves under the demanding conditions of modern life; that there are now more turkeys than ever before and their general health and nutritional status, if not their life-expectancy, is much more favorable than in the past; that a turkey ought to have a chance to fulfill its obligations and realize the meaning of its life as a responsible member of society; that, despite the sentimental outcries of reformers, most turkeys seem contented with their lot—those that are not content being best treated by individual clinical means and, if necessary, an accelerated program; and that the discontented are not the fattest, anyway, only the brightest.

14   Young men in America, like most Negroes, are excluded from any opportunity to hold the kind of job or to earn the kind of money without which members of this society committed to affluence are treated with gross contempt. In a sense, the plight of youth is more oppressive, for the means by which they are constrained are held to be lawful, while discrimination against Negroes is now proscribed by law and what remains, though very serious indeed, is the massive toxic residue of past practice rather than current public policy.

15   Students are not paid for attending school; they are held to be investing in their future—though if, in fact, they invested as capital the difference between the normal wage of an employed adult high school graduate for four to seven years and what little they may have received as stipends during their academic careers for the same length of time, the return accrued to them might easily exceed the increment a degree will bring. But, of course, they have not got it to invest, and are not permitted to get it to live on. The draft siphons off working-class youth, while middle-class youth are constrained to remain in college to avoid it. If there were no draft, their impact on the economy would probably be ruinous. Trade-union restrictions and child-labor laws, in any case, prevent their gaining the kind of experience, prior to the age of eighteen—even as part of a high school program—that would qualify them for employment as adults by the time they reach their legal majority, though young workers could be protected by laws relating to working conditions, hours, and wage-rates, if this protection were indeed the intent of restrictive legislation, without eliminating the opportunity for employment.

16   Even the concept of a legal majority is itself a social artifact, defining the time at which the social structure is ready to concede a measure of equality to those of its members whom youthfulness has kept powerless, without reference to their real qualifications which, where relevant, could be directly tested. Nature knows no such sharp break in competence associated with maturation, except in the sexual sphere; and comparatively little of our economic and political behavior is overtly sexual. Perhaps if more were, we would be more forthright and less spiteful. Nor is there any general maturational factor, gradual but portentous in its cumulative effect, which is relevant to society's demands.

17   Neither wisdom nor emotional stability is particularly characteristic of American adults, as compared to the young; and where, in this country, would the electoral process become less rational if children were permitted to vote: southern California? Washington, D. C.? If there should be any age limitation on voting, it ought to apply, surely, to those so old that they may reasonably expect to escape the consequences of their political decisions, rather than to those who will be burdened and perhaps destroyed by them. Certainly, the disfranchisement of youth is impossible to square, morally, with the Selective Service Act—though politically, there is no inconsistency: the second implies the first. But the draft is pure exploitation, in a classical Marxian sense. The question of the need for an army is not the issue. A volunteer army could be raised, according to the conservative economist Milton Friedman,[6] for from four to twenty billion dollars per year; and to argue that even the larger sum is more than the nation can afford is merely to insist that draftees support the nation by paying, in kind, a tax-rate several times greater than the average paid by civilian taxpayers in money, instead of being compensated for their loss in liberty and added risk. To argue that military service is a duty owed to one's country seems quite beside the point: it is not owed more by a young man than by the old or the middle-aged. And, at a time when a large proportion of enlisted military assignments are in clerical and technical specialties identical with those for which civilians are highly paid, the draft seems merely a form of involuntary servitude.

18   Without a doubt, the Selective Service Act has done more than any other factor not only to exacerbate the conflict between generations, but to make it clear that it is a real conflict of interest. The draft makes those subject to it formally second-class citizens in a way to which no race is subjected any longer. The arrogance and inaccessibility of Selective

[6] Quoted in *Newsweek*, December 19, 1966, p. 100.

Service officials, who are neither elected nor appointed for fixed terms subject to review; the fact that it has been necessary to take court action even to make public the names of draft-board members in some communities; the fact that registrants are specifically denied representation by counsel during their dealings with the Selective Service System and can only appeal to the courts after risking prosecution for the felony of refusing induction—all this is without parallel in the American legal process.

19   But the laws of the land are, after all, what define youth as a discriminated-against class. In fact, it is their discrimination that gives the term "youth" the only operational meaning it has: that of a person who, by reason of age, becomes subject to special constraint and penalties visited upon no other member of the commonwealth—for whom, by reason of age, certain conduct, otherwise lawful, is defined as criminal and to whom special administrative procedures, applicable to no other member of the commonwealth, are applied. The special characteristics of "youth culture" are derived from these disabilities rather than from any inherent age-graded characteristics. "Youth culture" is composed of individuals whose time is pre-empted by compulsory school attendance or the threat of induction into the Armed Service, who, regardless of their skills, cannot get and hold jobs that will pay enough to permit them to marry and build homes, and who are subject to surveillance at home or in school dormitories if they are detected in any form of sexual activity whatever. Youth and prisoners are the only people in America for whom *all* forms of sexual behavior are defined as illicit. It is absurd to scrutinize people who are forced to live under such extraordinary disabilities for psychological explanation of their resistance or bizarre conduct, except insofar as their state of mind can be related to their real situation.[7]

Law Enforcement and Legal Process Applied to Youth

20   In their relationship to the legal structure, youth operate under peculiar disabilities. The educational codes of the several states provide for considerably more restraint even than the compulsory attendance provisions provide—and that provision would be regarded as confiscatory, and hence doubtless unconstitutional, if applied to any member of the commonwealth old enough to be respected as having the right to dispose

---

[7] To be sure, as we become more sophisticated in our conception of mental illness, this becomes more and more clearly true of all forms of mental illness. All states of mind have their psychodynamics; but regardless of the school of psychodynamic thought to which one adheres, the most basic possible definition of mental illness seems to be "a chronic or recurring mental or emotional state which disturbs other people more powerful than the victim"—sometimes, of course, as in the case of certain kinds of paranoid schizophrenics, with good reason.

As a corollary to this point, it seems to follow that the head of a modern, centralized, national state—unlike his poor, royal predecessor—can never go officially mad until his government is overthrown.

of his own time. Soldiers are at least paid *something*. But the code does more than pre-empt the students' time. It is usually interpreted by school authorities as giving them power to set standards of dress and grooming— some of which, like those pertaining to hair length, of a kind that cannot be set aside while the student is not in school. It becomes the basis for indoctrination with the values of a petty, clerical social subclass. Regulations on dress, speech, and conduct in school are justified by this subclass as being necessary because school is supposed to be businesslike; it is where you learn to behave like a businessman. This leaves the young with the alternative of becoming little-league businessmen or juvenile delinquents, for refusal to obey school regulations leads to charges of delinquency—which seems a rather narrow choice among the possibilities of youthful life.

21   But I have written so much more elsewhere [8] about education as a social sanction that it seems inappropriate to devote more space to the functioning of the school as such. I have introduced the topic here simply to point out that the educational code, from the viewpoint of those subject to it, constitutes the most pervasive *legal* constraint on the movements and behavior of youth. It is not, however, from the viewpoint of legal theory, the most fundamental. The juvenile code and the juvenile court system provide even more direct contradictions to the standard of due process afforded adults in American courts.

22   For the juvenile court is, ostensibly, not a criminal court. It is technically a court of chancery before which a respondent is brought as a presumptive ward—not as an adversary, but as a dependent. It is assumed —the language is preserved in the legal documentation used in preparing juvenile court cases—that the authorities intervene *on behalf of the minor*, and with the purpose of setting up, where necessary, a regime designed to correct his wayward tendencies. The court may restrict; it may, as a condition of probation, insist that a respondent submit to a public spanking; it may detain and incarcerate in a reformatory indistinguishable from a prison for a period of years—but it may not punish. It is authorized only to correct.

23   Because action in juvenile court is not, therefore, regarded as an adversary proceeding, the juvenile courts provide few of the legal safeguards of a criminal court. There is considerable public misunderstanding about this, because the effect of recent Supreme Court decisions on the juvenile court process has been widely exaggerated, both by people who endorse and by people who deplore what the Court has done. What it *has* done, in effect, is to require the juvenile court to provide the usual safeguards if its actions are ever to become part of an adversary proceeding

[8] See the books listed in the introduction to this essay.

in a regular criminal court. Since the state may, at its discretion, try as adults rather than as juveniles youngsters over a certain minimum age who are accused of actions that violate the criminal code, and since the more serious offenses are usually committed by older adolescents, it may choose to provide these accused with the safeguards granted adults from the time of arrest rather than impair its chances for subsequent successful prosecution. It is, therefore, becoming usual, for example, to provide counsel for juveniles in serious cases; to exclude, in the event of a subsequent criminal prosecution, statements taken by probation officers or youth-squad members in a legally improper manner; and to permit juvenile respondents to summon and cross-examine witnesses—procedures which have not been part of juvenile court practice in the past.

24   These are improvements, but they leave untouched the much vaster potential for intergenerational conflict afforded by the summary treatment of casual offenders, and, particularly, of those youngsters of whose behavior the law could take no cognizance if they were older; for example, truants, loiterers, runaways, curfew-violaters, and twenty-year-olds who buy beer in a tavern. For such as these, there is no question of compromising future prosecution in a formal court, and their treatment has been affected very little, if at all, by high-court decisions. The law still presumes that its intervention in their lives is beneficial *per se*, and they have few enforceable civil rights with respect to it. If young people are "troublemakers," they are punished for it—that is all. Step out of line, and the police "take you away," as the Buffalo Springfield described it—on the occasion of a Los Angeles police roundup of the youngsters strolling on the Sunset Strip in the autumn of 1968—in the song, "For What It's Worth," that gained them a national reputation among teen-agers.

25   It is quite clear that one's moral judgment of the legal position of youth in American society depends very largely on the degree to which one shares the fundamental assumption on which juvenile proceedings are based: that they are designed to help; that the adults who carry them out will, by and large, have the wisdom and the resources, and the intent to help rather than to punish. Legal authorities have caviled at this assumption for some time. Thus, Paul W. Alexander writes in a paper on "Constitutional Rights in Juvenile Court":

> In the area of the child's constitutional rights the last decade has seen a minor but interesting revolt on the part of some highly distinguished judges. So repellent were some of the juvenile court practices that the judges were moved to repudiate the widely held majority rule that a delinquency hearing in a juvenile court is a civil, not a criminal action. . . . This doctrine appeared so distasteful to a California appellate court that the following language appeared in the opinion: "While the juvenile court law provides that adjudication of a minor to be a ward of

the court should not be deemed to be a conviction of crime, nevertheless, for all practical purposes, this is a legal fiction, presenting a challenge to credulity and doing violence to reason." [9]

Youth Today Have No Respect for the Law

26   The kind of legal structure which youth face would appear to be, of itself, sufficient to explain why young people are often inclined to be skeptical rather than enthusiastic about law and order—and about those of their number who are enthusiasts for law, as student leaders and prominent athletes tend to be. Yet, the hostile relations that develop between youth and law-enforcement agencies are, even so, probably more attributable to the way in which police generally respond to young people than to the oppressive character of the legal system itself—though the two factors are, of course, causally related, because the fact that youth have few rights and many liabilities before the law also makes it possible for law-enforcement agencies to behave more oppressively.

27   With respect to youth, law-enforcement agencies assume the role of enforcers of morals and proper social attitudes, as well as of the law, and—having few rights—there is not much the young can do about it. Police forces, moreover, provide a manpower-pool by "moonlighting," while off duty, as members of private enforcement squads hired to keep young people from getting out of hand, a task which they often try to perform by making themselves as conspicuous as possible in order to keep the young people from starting anything—exactly what police would *not* do in monitoring a group of orderly adults in a public place.

28   My own observations at folk-rock concerts and dances, for example, which are among the best places for learning how young people express themselves and communicate with one another, confirm that surveillance on these occasions is characteristically officious and oppressive. It often expresses a real contempt for the customs of the youngsters, even when these are appropriate to the occasion. Police, clubs in hand, will rush onstage or into the pit at any sign that the performers are about to mingle with the dancers or audience—if a soloist jumps down from the stage, say, or if members of the audience attempt to mount it; or they will have the lights turned up to interrupt a jam session or freakout that has gone on too long, or with too great intensity, for their taste; or insist on ruining a carefully designed and well-equipped light-show by requiring that the house-lights be kept bright. All this is done smirkingly, as if the youngsters at the concert knew that they were "getting out of line" in behaving differently from a philharmonic audience. It should be borne in mind, considering the fiscal basis for rights in our culture, that tickets for the

[9] Included in Margaret K. Rosenheim, ed., *Justice for the Child* (New York: Free Press, 1962), p. 83.

Beach Boys or Jefferson Airplane are now likely to cost more than tickets for a symphony concert, and the youngsters are poorer than symphony subscribers, but they rarely enjoy the same right to listen to their music in their own way, unmolested.

29   The music itself provides some of the best evidence of the response of the "further-out" youngsters to police action, which, indeed, sometimes inflicts on them more serious damage than the annoyance of having a concert ruined. In Watts, San Francisco, and Memphis, the civil disorders associated with each city in recent years were triggered by the slaying of a Negro youth by a police officer. "Pot busts" are directed primarily against young people, among whom the use of marijuana has become something of a moral principle evoked by the destructive hostility of the legal means used to suppress it: thirty students at the State University of New York at Stony Brook, for example, were handcuffed and herded from their dormitories before dawn last winter, before the lenses of television cameras manned by news agencies which the Suffolk County police had thoughtfully notified of the impending raid.[10] Rock artists, speaking to, and to some degree for, youth, respond to the social climate which such incidents, often repeated, have established. I have already cited the Buffalo Springfield's song "For What It's Worth." The Mothers of Invention are even more direct in their new album, *We're Only In It for the Money*, where they represent the typical parent as believing that police brutality is justified toward teen-agers who look "too weird" and make "some noise." [11]

Bringing It All Back Home

30   Finally, exacerbating the confrontations between youth and adults is the fact that the control of youth has largely been entrusted to lower-status elements of the society. Custodial and control functions usually are so entrusted, for those in subjection have even lower status themselves, and do not command the services of the higher grades of personnel that their society affords. Having low status, moreover, prevents their being taken seriously as moral human beings. Society tends to assume that the moral demands made on the criminal, the mad, and the young by their respective wardens are for their own good and to reinforce those demands while limiting the subjects' opportunities for redress to those situations in which the grossest violations of the most fundamental human rights have occurred. The reader's moral evaluation of the conflict that I have described will, therefore, depend very largely, I believe, on the degree to which he shares society's assumption.

[10] *The New York Times*, January 18, 1968.
[11] Copyright by Frank Zappa Music Company, Inc., a subsidiary of Third Story Music, Inc. (BMI).

31   As has surely been obvious, I do not share it. The process by which youth is brought into line in American society is almost wholly destructive of the dignity and creative potential of the young, and the condition of the middle-aged and the old in America seems to me, on the whole, to make this proposition quite plausible. Nevertheless, the violation of the young in the process of socialization fulfills an essential function in making our society cohesive. And curiously—and rather perversely—this function depends on the fact that custody and indoctrination—education is not, after all, a very precise term for it—are lower-status functions.

32   American democracy depends, I believe, on the systematic humiliation of potential elites to keep it going. There is, perhaps, no other way in which an increasingly educated middle-class, whose technical services cannot be spared, can be induced to acquiesce in the political demands of a deracinated and invidious populace, reluctant to accept any measure of social improvement, however generally advantageous, which might bring any segment of the society slightly more benefits than would accrue to it. Teachers, police, and parents in America are jointly in the business of rearing the young to be frightened of the vast majority who have been too scarred and embittered by the losses and compromises which they have endured in the process of becoming respectable to be treated in a way that would enrage them. Anything generous—or perhaps merely civil, like welcoming a Negro family into a previously white community, or letting your neighbor "blow a little grass" in peace—does enrage them, and so severely as to threaten the fabric of society. A conference of recent American leaders associated with a greater measure of generosity toward the deprived—John and Robert Kennedy, Martin Luther King, Jr., and Malcolm X, for a start—might, perhaps, agree, if it could be convened.

33   Many of today's middle-class youth, however—having been spared, by the prevailing affluence, the deprivations that make intimidation more effective in later life—are talking back; and some are even finding support, rather than betrayal, in their elders—the spectacle of older folks helping their radical sons to adjust their identifying armbands during the spring protest at Columbia University is said to have been both moving and fairly common. The protest, in any case, continues and mounts. So does the rage against the young. If the confrontation between the generations does pose, as many portentous civic leaders and upper-case "Educators" fear, a lethal threat to the integrity of the American social system, that threat may perhaps be accepted with graceful irony. Is there, after all, so much to lose? The American social system has never been noted for its integrity. In fact, it would be rather like depriving the Swiss of their surfing.

Questions for Criticism and Discussion

1 Stylistically, would you describe this discourse as restrained, impersonal, calm? If not, how would you describe Friedenberg's style? (Consider his choice of language and analogy particularly.)

2 Does the style of this discourse alienate certain groups or audiences? How does Friedenberg "carve out" the audience he wishes to address?

3 If the discourse alienates significant groups, is this result a rhetorical shortcoming? Could Friedenberg, in fact, have meaningfully addressed most or all of the American public?

4 Discuss this discourse as an example of confrontative rhetoric. In what ways does Friedenberg confront the "old"? The "young"?

5 This discourse hardly conciliates and unifies; it seems clearly to heighten conflict and generate controversy. How do you evaluate this rhetorical intent ethically?

For Further Reading

Philip G. Attbach et al., "Students Protest," The Annals of the American Academy of Political and Social Science, Vol. 395 (May 1971), entire issue.

Paul Goodman, Growing Up Absurd (New York: Vintage Books, 1956).

Ronald D. Laing, The Politics of Experience (New York: Ballantine Books, 1967).

James McEvoy and Abraham Miller, eds., Black Power and Student Rebellion (Belmont, Calif.: Wadsworth Publishing Company, 1969).

Theodore Roszak, The Making of a Counter Culture (Garden City, N.Y.: Doubleday & Company, 1969).

Lionel Rubinoff, The Pornography of Power (New York: Ballantine Books, 1967).

Jerome H. Skolnick, The Politics of Protest (New York: Ballantine Books, 1969).

Douglas J. Stewart, "Disfranchise the Old: The Lesson of California," New Republic, Vol. 163 (August 29, 1970), pp. 20–22.

Eleven

Eliezer Ben Yisrael

This discourse is a document from what might be termed the rhetoric of "radical Israeli protest." If there is a genre that may properly be called "the rhetoric of confrontation," this discourse should surely be included in it. Like the rhetoric of radical Black Protest, this discourse is addressed to at least two different audiences, and despite its blunt attacks it seeks to create some bases for identification even with the audience it criticizes. Of the discourses in this book, it addresses the audience most directly; it is the agonized outcry of Israelis against centuries of oppression and conditions that engage the modern state of Israeli in an apparently endless struggle for survival.

The discourse is both an essay and a speech. It first appeared in The Times of Israel *and was later delivered to the Israeli Knesset (Parliament) after the Six-Day War in June 1967. Like many other impassioned expressions of deep personal feeling, it is both a rhetorical act and a dramatic symbol.*

A Letter
to the World from Jerusalem

1   I am not a creature from another planet, as you seem to believe. I am a Jerusalemite—like yourselves, a man of flesh and blood. I am a citizen of my city, an integral part of my people.

2   I have a few things to get off my chest. Because I am not a diplomat, I do not have to mince words. I do not have to please you, or even persuade you. I owe you nothing. You did not build this city; you do not live in it; you did not defend it when they came to destroy it. And we will be damned if we will let you take it away.

3   There was a Jerusalem before there was a New York. When Berlin, Moscow, London and Paris were miasmal forest and swamp, there was a thriving Jewish community here. It gave something to the world which you nations have rejected ever since you established yourselves—a humane moral code.

4   Here the prophets walked, their words flashing like forked lightning. Here a people who wanted nothing more than to be left alone, fought off waves of heathen, would-be conquerors, bled and died on the battlements, hurled themselves into the flames of their burning Temple rather than surrender; and when finally overwhelmed by sheer numbers and led away into captivity, swore that before they forgot Jerusalem they would see their tongues cleave to their palates, their right arms wither.

5   For two pain-filled millennia, while we were your unwelcome guests, we prayed daily to return to this city. Three times a day we petitioned the Almighty: "Gather us from the four corners of the world, bring us upright to our land; return in mercy to Jerusalem, Thy city, and dwell in it as Thou promised."

6   On every Yom Kippur and Passover we fervently voiced the hope that next year would find us in Jerusalem. Your inquisitions, pogroms, expulsions, the ghettos into which you jammed us, your forced baptisms, your quota systems, your genteel anti-semitism, and the final unspeakable horror, the holocaust (and worse, your terrifying disinterest in it)—all these have not broken us. They may have sapped what little moral strength you still possessed, but they forged us into steel. Do you think that you can break us now, after all we have been through? Do you really believe that after Dachau and Auschwitz we are frightened by your threats of blockades and sanctions? We have been to Hell and back—a Hell of your making. What more could you possibly have in your arsenal that could scare us?

7   I have watched this city bombarded twice by nations calling themselves civilized. In 1948, while you looked on apathetically, I saw women and children blown to smithereens, this after we had agreed to your request to internationalize the city. It was a deadly combination that did the job: British officers, Arab gunners and American-made cannon.

8   And then the savage sacking of the Old City; the willful slaughter, the wanton destruction of every synagogue and religious school; the dese- cration of Jewish cemeteries; the sale by a ghoulish government of tomb- stones for building materials, for poultry runs, army camps—even latrines.

9   And you never said a word.

10   You never breathed the slightest protest when the Jordanians shut off the holiest of our holy places, the Western Wall in violation of the pledges they had made after the war—a war they waged, incidentally, against a decision of the U.N. Not a murmur came from you whenever the legionnaires in their spiked helmets casually opened fire upon our citizens from behind the walls.

11   Your hearts bled when Berlin came under siege. You rushed your airlift "to save the gallant Berliners." But you did not send one ounce of food when Jews starved in besieged Jerusalem. You thundered against the wall which the East Germans ran through the middle of the German capital—but not one peep out of you about that other wall, the one that tore through the heart of Jerusalem.

12   And when the same thing happened 20 years later, and the Arabs un- leashed a savage, unprovoked bombardment of the Holy City again, did any of you do anything? The only time you came to life was when the city was at last re-united. Then you wrung your hands and spoke loftily of "justice" and the need for the "Christian" quality of turning the other cheek.

13   The truth is—and you know it deep inside your gut—you would prefer the city to be destroyed rather than have it governed by Jews. No matter how diplomatically you phrase it, the age-old prejudices seep out of every word.

14   If our return to the city has tied your theology in knots, perhaps you had better re-examine your catechisms. After what we have been through, we are not passively going to accommodate ourselves to the twisted idea that we are to suffer eternal homelessness until we accept your Saviour.

15   For the first time since the year 70 there is now complete religious freedom for all in Jerusalem. For the first time since the Romans put the torch to the Temple everyone has equal rights. (You preferred to have some more equal than others.) We loathe the sword—but it was you who forced us to take it up. We crave peace—but we are not going back to the peace of 1948 as you would like us to.

16   We are home. It has a lovely sound for a nation you have willed to wander over the face of the globe. We are not leaving. We have redeemed the pledge made by our forefathers: Jerusalem is being rebuilt. "Next year"—and the year after, and after, and after, until the end of time—"in Jerusalem!"

Questions for Criticism and Discussion

1   To whom do the pronouns "I" or "we" and "you" refer?

2   Evaluate this discourse as direct confrontation that makes not the slightest move to please or appease but is an example of self-creating and self-identifying "symbolic violence."

3   Do you find this discourse primarily or wholly alienating and confrontative? If so, do you consider references to the desire of all peoples for a homeland, the common humanity of individuals, the familiar Biblical materials, the oppression of a small group, or groups, by much larger and more powerful forces, the need for freedom, the pride and heroism in being victorious although outnumbered *alien* to the Western tradition or *outside* the Judeo–Christian ethic of our society? Explain.

4   In contrast to the previously suggested evaluations and analyses describe this discourse as a dramatic and poetic act. Compare this discourse with Eldridge Cleaver's essay.

For Further Reading

Gerald Astor, "The Agonized American Jews," *Look*, Vol. 35 (April 20, 1970), pp. 17–19.

J. Robert Moskin, "Israeli Youth: The Coming Explosion," *Look*, Vol. 35 (June 15, 1971), pp. 21–26.

Jean-Paul Sartre, *Anti-Semite and Jew*, trans. George J. Becker (New York: Schocken 1948).

Twelve

Emmet John Hughes

Emmet John Hughes teaches at the Eagleton Institute of Politics at Rutgers University. He was an administrative assistant to former President Eisenhower and is the author of The Ordeal of Power.

This essay is a probing analysis of the politics of the sixties and focuses on the political paradoxes of the personalities and policies of that decade. Although the author was associated with a Republican administration, his disfavor is limited to no single party or group. Indeed this essay qualifies for the label "a plague on both your houses." It is no mere diatribe; rather it is a tightly reasoned piece of rhetoric as well as an example of rhetorical criticism, for Hughes uses the rhetorical events of the period as part of the evidence for his conclusions.

The Politics of the Sixties—
From the New Frontier to the New Revolution

Probe the earth and see where your main roots run.—*Henry David Thoreau*

Above all, what this Congress can be remembered for is opening the way to a New American Revolution.—*President Richard Nixon, 1971 State of the Union Address*

If I get around to writing a general history of the recent past, I'm going to call the chapter on the sixties "The Age of Rubbish."—*Professor Richard Hofstadter*

1   Or the whole political season—from the New Frontier through the Great Society and on to the New Revolution—could be called The Age of Outrageous Paradox. The more elaborate insult probably would be more welcome to most makers and movers of the politics of the nineteen-sixties. They relished the taste of ornate verbiage. They sadly lacked any nose for the smell of cant.

2   By whatever name, it was, as decades go, a muddle. The political life of a democratic society, in any age and on any continent, always seems rife with anomalies, of course. But I doubt that there have been many chapters in the story of the American Republic when the incongruous has appeared so stark, the irrational so irresistible and the clearly improbable so eventually certain.

3   This was the time, after all, that simultaneously witnessed two great flights by Americans: to the beckoning stars and from their crumbling cities. This was the period, too, when the nation's chosen leaders, Democratic and Republican alike, concurred that the future of American civilization depended far more urgently on the erasing of communism in Southeast Asia than the erasing of poverty in the United States; and they wagered more than $20-billion a year—year after year—on the soundness of this judgment. Across the nation, the most stirring change of the age, the advance of black Americans toward dignity and opportunity, progressed slowly under the least likely political auspices: it was dramatically encouraged by the first Southern President since the Age of Reconstruction while "the party of Lincoln" fretted, evaded and dawdled. All the while, some 25 million needy Americans, a half on welfare rolls and a half on poverty-level incomes, stayed stoically calm as the children of the relatively more affluent, on campuses from Boston to Berkeley, violently protested *their* suffering and deprivation. Finally the peace-lovers, almost 200 million strong, divided into two armies distinguishable not by confidence in their own virtues but only by their choice of weapons: the older seekers of "peace with honor" principally relied on incantations, helicopters and a little napalm; the younger zealots of "peace and love" usually favored obscenities, bricks and a little vandalism.

4   The general parody of rationality found faithful recording in most of the decade's speeches, resolutions and debates. On the whole, the parody was conducted in a bipartisan spirit, as Republicans and Democrats competed to wrap old policies in new packages and to paste different slogans on the same ideas. Such was the nature of much of the national

debate over Vietnam. From 1962, the Republicans collectively set the
stage for travesty, of course, by abdicating any serious opposition role as
they shunned the expression of any doubts, much less critiques, about the
unfolding American venture in Southeast Asia. By 1964, the Tonkin Gulf
Resolution, supporting further undefined military action, proved that the
Senate, almost unanimously, could behave with the same mindless acquiescence as the G.O.P. By 1966, the public leaders most outraged by the
consequences of that authorization included many of the same Democrats
who had voted it; but by the autumn of the same year, a President no
longer concerned with their counsel was himself in Vietnam, exhorting his
soldiers: "Come home with that coonskin on the wall!" By 1968, in the
snows of New Hampshire, the footprints of the President soon to be leaving the White House crossed the path of the candidate soon to be arriving
there (or so it would later seem). President-to-be Richard Nixon avowed
on nationwide radio: "It is essential that we end this war, and end it
quickly, but . . . in such a way that we win the peace." An attentive ear
would have caught the fact that the Johnsonian and Nixonian exhortations
varied only in verbal style—the first command in the jargon of a Western
evangelist, the second in the fuzzier idiom of an Eastern lawyer. But each
was appealing to a military court for just one verdict. Both men wanted
the coonskin.

5   The most contagious anomaly of these years, however, was the ad-
diction of the decade to self-conscious self-esteem. While the drug habits
of the younger generation alarmed much of the country, little note was
taken of the uninhibited indulgence by elder statesmen in two deadly
hallucinogens of politics: the fancied image of historic greatness and the
revered sound of one's own voice. Thanks to such stimulants, almost all
national matters appeared swollen to sizes never less than vast. A kind
of innocent but indicative keynote might first have been heard in the
ringing Inaugural Address by John F. Kennedy in 1960; it saluted no mere
New Administration, but a whole New Generation. In like spirit, the nation's legislators and leaders in the succeeding years almost never faced
anything so puny as a problem; it had to be a crisis. To despairing critics,
the society was not just gravely distraught and deeply divided; it was
plainly doomed.

6   If an era can be thought to act like a man, the age neatly performed
the old jest about human vanity—it mastered the art of strutting while
sitting down. To bring off the trick, it was necessary only to appraise all
items on the national agenda as not just impressively big but also profoundly *new*. Thus, for the nation's prosperity there were the New Economics; for its security there was the New Foreign Policy cannily directing
the New Diplomacy, and for the general entertainment and excitement of

the electorate there were the New Politics. Eventually, the escalation of rhetoric had to reach a kind of climax. This came with the call to the American people to mobilize for a New American Revolution. And who could issue the command so logically—so aptly for an age of such anomaly —as the era's most resolute antirevolutionary and the nation's 37th President, Richard Milhous Nixon?

7   No man could have closed out all the public speech of the last decade, all its pallid pieties and vivid hyperboles, with so fitting a peroration as the President's State of the Union address to the 92d Congress. Its timing was almost flawless; it missed by just two days the 10th anniversary of the Kennedy inaugural. It stayed faithful to the semantic fashion of the nineteen-sixties, too, sprinkling the adjective "new" as if it were an indispensable mark of punctuation. And showing the sense of both history and humor so typical of both the Administration and the age, the President's chief political counselor, Attorney General John Mitchell, judged the Chief Executive's pronouncement to be "the most important document since they wrote the Constitution"—an opinion whose implied disparagement of that continuingly nettlesome Emancipation Proclamation might have been largely inadvertent.

8   Yet no appreciation of the President's address surpassed his own. Aloft once again on "the lift of a driving dream," he announced——vaguely but vigorously—the end of "a long, dark night of the American spirit." He went on to set forth some substantive matters for legislative action, and the two most important were the sharing of Federal tax revenues with the beleaguered states and cities and the redrawing of the administrative frontiers of the Cabinet departments. Nonetheless, the worth and relevance of even these ideas were made only more difficult to assess by the awesome seriousness with which the President professed to view them. Again and again calling upon the Founding Fathers to anoint his proposals, he stated that their enactment called for no less than the same "vision" and "boldness" as the James Madisons and the James Wilsons had shown in their constitutional labors of 184 years ago. A general assent to all this by the members of the 92d Congress—so the President promised them— would do more than assure their perpetual remembrance for "a record more splendid than any in our history"; it would enlist them in "a revolution as profound, as far-reaching, as exciting" as the Old American Revolution. And to many a wide-eyed Senator and Representative, there appeared to be little left out of such a prospective melodrama other than a vignette of Secretary of Defense Melvin Laird kneeling in the snows of Valley Forge, a glimpse of Senator J. Willian Fulbright cowering in the uniform of Benedict Arnold or a vision of National Security Adviser Henry Kissinger, sashed and sworded, waving his tricorn as he sped off to take the surrender of North Vietnam's armies at some Asian Yorktown.

9   The important incongruities of this study of the State of the Union, however, were more than shows of verbal extravagance. They were matters of basic substance. And two were most striking.

10   First, for all its ardent professing of the new, it pathetically echoed the old. Read as prologue, it could only be remembered as epilogue. For his economic prescriptions, Richard Nixon reached back to the essentially heretical practices of Franklin Roosevelt to discover anew the uses of deficit financing, now rendered orthodox by the euphemism of "a full employment budget"—the spending of Federal funds "as if we were at full employment." For his political definitions, the President described the humanity and the efficiency of local government in language that sounded as though it had been carefully culled from the most forgettable speeches of President Herbert Hoover. For his social solutions, he stayed more modern, going back only five or so years to the early days of the Presidency of Lyndon Johnson and finding there a public discussion of Federal revenue-sharing that now struck him as "historic." The steady flow of such Federal dollars to state and city would long since have started, of course, if Lyndon Johnson and Richard Nixon had not assigned a truly "historic" priority to Washington's revenue-sharing with Saigon.

11   Second, for lighting the path out of the "dark night" of the nineteen-sixties and into the seventies, the President held up the torch of one central doctrine. This was the faith that "local government" has been and must be "closest" and "most responsive" to the people. Such goverment cannot fail, he said, to be "far more intimate" with the citizenry than any "bureaucratic élite in Washington." In short, the time had come for "power" to be shipped out from the national capital and "turned back to the people."

12   The implications of such a homily from such a pulpit had to stun a little. No American President, probably not even Herbert Hoover, had ever stated with such seeming personal conviction that the Federal establishment over which he presided—from an office whose painful pursuit had cost this President some 20 years of fund-raising dinners and soul-searing disappointments—afforded, after all, only the least responsive and sensitive government in all the land. The notion was enough to make some citizens wonder why a politician so patriotic and so neighborly had not spent all his energies striving to become a councilman or a mayor. And it was enough to prod others to consider whether a leadership so self-effacing had intended to call for a New American Revolution or a New American Spiral.

13   The decade deplored by a Richard Hofstadter was not, of course, designed by a Richard Nixon. The President was not its masterful architect but its typical product. And the incongruities of his political life carried back to 1960, when he did something quite alien to his critics' image of him. Privately, he then yielded the office for which he had publicly fought and would fight again.

14   The 1960 Presidential campaign had seen John Kennedy and Richard Nixon duel each other almost to a draw. So narrow a decision—by some 118,000 votes—set political experts of all persuasions to frantic search for the tiny clue to victory. Some thought they found it in the face-to-face debates of the two candidates; the younger man had simply won by the phraser's edge. Others argued a kind of political predestination; it sufficed to look at Richard Nixon's heavy jowls or snore over his heavy platitudes to know, just absolutely know, that this man was a born loser and a natural non-President. And there were those closest to the defeated candidate who were quite certain of a less mystical explanation: that they had been cheated by the voting machines of Cook County, Ill., and the voting blocs of marble from the graveyards of a few counties in Texas. For these last observers, the political moment did not call for automatic congratulating of the winner; it called for absolutely raising hell.

15   There followed a remarkable scene. In a motel not far from Los Angeles, Richard Nixon met with a small group of his closest confidants to consider whether he should charge that he had been cheated of the Presidency. There were none present who doubted this to be the fact. He listened to all, and he overruled them. To one, he explained: "A national argument like this would make American democracy ludicrous to the whole world." To another, he added: "If this were to become a public dispute, it could conceivably carry us all toward the brink of a kind of civil war." A challenge to the election could, indeed, have embittered the nation, and the blame for the stress might have fallen on anyone. But in an era whose ironies were almost altogether melancholy, there appeared something worthy of respect and remembrance in the decision of Richard Nixon to ignore his political counselors and defer his political dreams.

16   Between the renunciation of 1960 and the return of 1968, there surged—or careened—across the national political scene no less than three quite distinct hosts or movements. All of them inevitably proclaimed their essential newness, of course, even as each struck out in a wholly different direction. And each deserves a quick backward glance.

17   The first was the New Frontier of John F. Kennedy. Because its life—his life—would be so sickeningly short, this must remain the hardest to judge of all the larger political thrusts of the sixties. For whatever reason, an impression lingers that its style was considerably grander than its substance. Even this, however, may have been the product less of

artifice than of analysis—the quite cool appraisal of J. F. K. himself. On
the night of his inauguration, I happened to be in the Georgetown home of
his close friend Joseph Alsop when the President startled some dozen
guests by suddenly appearing for a quiet, postmidnight chat. After idle
banter turned toward serious politics, he spoke one conviction categor-
ically: "The country is going to the right, of course. We are on a conservative pendulum, no doubt." (I recall vigorously dissenting.) Shrewdly or
mistakenly, the fact is that the hero of the nation's liberals, at the very
moment that he assumed power, assumed not much at all about the future
of American liberalism. Perhaps from this lack of faith there followed the
apparent lack of zeal, over many, many months on the part of the President and his brother, the Attorney General, in pressing action to assure
the civil rights of black Americans. This lack seemed so clear that one
member of the civil rights commission, Father Theodore Hesburgh, the
president of Notre Dame University, came close to resigning to summon
public attention to what he viewed as the New Frontier's unconcern over
any new frontier for more than 20 million Americans. Some years later,
there ensued one more of the happier ironies of the decade, when Robert
Kennedy, well before his murder, made himself a trusted hero to the same
20 million.

18   The second passionately "new" political movement followed, in
1964, the leadership of another United States Senator of nearly comparable personal appeal and wholly contrary political purpose. Senator Barry
Goldwater of Arizona nostalgically cherished a far older kind of "frontier"; an America of mid–19th-century outposts manned by sheriffs and
marshals who knew how to impose mid–20th-century law and order on
Europe's foreign-aid rustlers or Asia's war-of-liberation highwaymen, so
that the road of history could be kept clear for the stagecoach of American democracy speeding into the future. For millions, however, the promise of the vision was not at all old but wondrously new. Since the Senate
days of Robert A. Taft, they had been waiting for a Presidential election
affording them "a choice, not an echo." They got their wish. And their
party barely survived their spell of joy.

19   And the third host of political pioneers marched in 1968 under the
banner of the New Politics and behind yet another Senator, Eugene Mc-
Carthy of Minnesota. Of the three "insurrections" in the politics of the
sixties, there seems little doubt that this one ignited the most intense zeal
and unselfish devotion. There also seems little doubt that this movement—
true to an age so anomalous—finally showed itself to be the most self-
centered and the most self-defeating. Even as it aroused the nation's
conscientious dissenters and radicals, especially among the young, the
New Politics of Eugene McCarthy had rather little to say ardently and
persuasively about civil rights or cities' dying. Even as it pressed just

one issue—the tragedy of Vietnam—with more singleminded intensity than any other national movement in a modern election, it stayed remarkably cryptic about precisely what it proposed to do to end the tragedy. Soon after it had run its course, it left a host of its disciples wondering what the din had truly meant. Perhaps they would have wondered somewhat earlier, had they known of one revealing episode midway in the 1968 primary campaigns. On this occasion, the Senator from Minnesota met in New York with an important group of editors. They asked for his choice for President, after himself, among all other candidates. He unhesitatingly answered: "Richard Nixon." One can only guess the incredulous look on the faces of his most devoted followers had they been privileged to hear such candor.

20   Through all the decade of politics dominated by these three different sorts of insurgency, there spread a practice for which I find only one reasonably descriptive term: the politics of masturbation. These political exercises were conducted in a spirit that essentially did not care whether they created or communicated or convinced in any fruitful sense; they simply wanted to be heard or felt. Ultimately, they did not much desire to give birth; they aspired only to give pleasure. And this pleasure-seeking, too, could claim a largely bipartisan popularity.

21   Perhaps the American right indulged more obviously, on levels from the national to the municipal. The ascendancy of Barry Goldwater in 1964 provided an instance difficult to match in self-serving political foolishness: a national party deliberately chose a "Southern strategy" to unseat the first President in more than three generations who could himself be called "Southern." At the 1964 Republican convention in San Francisco, the ruling emotions could probably have been called less political than sensual: the revulsion toward Gov. Nelson Rockefeller, the flagellation of the news media and the adulation of a "faithful" Republican in the person of the Senator from Arizona. The prevailing passions of most delegates, moreover, had been heated by their avid reading of such political pornography as "A Choice Not an Echo" or "None Dare Call It Treason." As one despairing liberal Republican Senator grieved to me: "These people don't give a damn about ballots—they want blood." So they proceeded to design their own disaster.

22   As with the Western hero of American conservatism, so it would be with its Eastern oracle, William F. Buckley. A year after Goldwater's humiliation, Buckley entered the lesser but exciting arena of New York City politics. Unambitious personally for City Hall, he was nonetheless confident that his epigrams and epithets could keep so offensively liberal a Republican as John Lindsay from becoming Mayor. The pundit enjoyed the exercise enough to write a whole book about it later. And there occurred in all this but one flaw: his intervention subtracted enough Catholic votes from normally Democratic ranks to seal victory for the Republican he had sought to rout.

23   Still, the American left performed almost as confoundingly. In New York four years later, a campaign by Norman Mailer in the Democratic primary discovered the same delight in self-defeat earlier enjoyed by William Buckley. Mailer's siphoning off of liberal votes from two leading liberal contenders made possible the nomination of Mario Proccacino, the demoralization of New York liberals and the re-election of John Lindsay, who had to begin to marvel at his luck in always being challenged, rather than supported, by the community's more aggressively political intellectuals.

24   On a larger scene and for a longer span, the political measure of much student violence of these last years has to be taken in terms of the same contempt for consequence. Fist or oath or bomb, the resources of the movement have appeared again and again to serve less as weapons than as drugs—the paraphernalia for a "trip," as it were, but in political terms a journey to nowhere. This was the express warning of the radical priest Father Daniel Berrigan, when he wrote the Weatherman band three days before his own arrest last August: "The movement . . . shows how constantly we are seduced by violence, not only as method but as an end in itself." And from all this self-thwarting confusion of angry young citizens there followed, perhaps inexorably, the inner illogic that eventually came to control the McCarthy campaign of 1968. The campaign could not have been more loudly committed to a New Politics militant enough to smash precedents and shake establishments. In immediate terms, it did shake the confidence of President Johnson. But in more fateful terms—by its nationwide sullenness toward the Democratic candidacy of Hubert Humphrey, by its encouragement of liberal apathy in such key states as California—it no less surely helped to bring about the final arrival at the White House of Richard Nixon.

25   Since the 1968 campaign closed the circle on the Presidential politics of the decade, it might be expected to afford its own study in irony. It did, indeed. Most briefly stated, the incongruity of the election may be seen in three dimensions: political, psychological and personal.

26   In political terms, the result for Richard Nixon could be called a victory only with some serious abuse of the word. More accurately, it amounted to an almost incredibly narrow avoiding of an almost unbelievable defeat. Perhaps no myth of partisan politics was so religiously recited throughout the sixties as the fable of the sagacity of Mr. Nixon, the awesomely canny politician. He endured three grinding campaigns in this decade, and his progress in all three, from start to end, was consistently backward. He began his 1960 campaign with a substantial 6 per cent lead in the opinion polls over John Kennedy—and he lost it. He began his 1962 campaign for the Governorship of California with a 16 per per cent lead—and he lost it. He began his 1968 campaign with the same lead of 16 per cent recorded in August—and he barely missed losing it. This kind of accomplishment in reverse can be properly appreciated only in the context of the historically extraordinary erosion in Democratic strength that had taken place after the equally extraordinary Democratic triumph of 1964, when Lyndon Johnson had won 61.3 per cent of the vote. A study of the voting swings since 1892 shows that the percentage change between 1964 and 1968 was exceeded only twice, by the swings from Wilson to Harding and from Hoover to Roosevelt. The collapse of Democratic power in 1968, in other words, had no precedent since the collapse of Republican strength in 1932; in both cases, the abrupt decline in support for the incumbent Administration exceeded 18 per cent. Yet in all such swings since 1892 there was no gain so small for the winning party as the mere 4.9 per cent recorded by the G.O.P. in 1968. As one scholar has said of the Nixon victory: "Only a political upheaval of near-catacylsmic proportions could have created the conditions in which his election was possible at all." *

27   In psychological terms, the "conditions" contriving this result suggest a special irony. By the judgment of almost all veteran watchers of political omens, the fate of the Johnson Administration was decreed by one political fault: its loss of credibility as a decisive number of citizens came to feel that it was a government of double-talking and double-dealing. A citizenry so alienated had to rebel. But the curiosity of future historians surely will be stirred to wonder how the disenchanted then turned for leadership to one man whose whole political life had been shadowed (fairly or falsely) by one indictment above all: his lack of credibility.

28   In personal terms, a kind of mystery about the man persisted through this victory of the candidate. It was perhaps most crisply, if unintentionally, stated by Kevin P. Phillips, the author of "The Emerging Republican Majority," who served in 1968 as a special assistant to the campaign manager, Attorney-General-to-be John Mitchell. To cite Mr. Phillips's later appraisal of the campaign: "It was a catastrophe—millions of dollars spent by Madison Avenue lightweights who converted certain victory into near defeat. The soap salesmen drained all of the issues out of

* Walter Dean Burnham, "Election 1968, The Abortive Landslide," in *Trans-Action*, December 1968.

the campaign that would have won it big . . . Nixon knew his campaign stunk. He wanted to be himself, and he knew he should have fought the campaign on the issues Middle America was ready for . . ." Such an opinion from so friendly a source raises more questions than it answers, of course. Why did not the man on his way to the White House act on what he "knew"? Could "soap salesmen" also be blamed for the defeats of 1960 and 1962? And if the President-in-the-making was not his own self, whose was he?

29   From an election decided by such anomalies, there could follow only an Administration of seemingly interminable ambivalence. This it has been. A Republican President—who probably has repeated more often than any living politician the hoary aphorism that the Government must balance its budget so that all American families can balance their budgets —has needed only two years in office to proclaim his new Keynesian faith in unbalanced budgets. A President with a mind trained in law and sensitive to the political role of the Supreme Court, Richard Nixon has managed to have his first two nominees to the Court spurned by the Senate. A President so impressed with the quality and importance of his new Cabinet that he introduced all his nominees to the people on national television, he has excelled almost any predecessor in the White House in treating the Cabinet as a kind of hopelessly vestigial organ of government. Addressing himself to the trials and problems of black Americans, he could issue in March, 1970, a command of some 10,000 words for school desegregation in the South; but nine months later he could avow on nationwide television that he would, in effect, do only what the law compelled to encourage desegregation of housing. Taking the occasion of his inauguration in 1969 to appeal to the people for a general lowering of voices, he made his own intervention in the 1970 campaign the most tasteless display in recent memory of Presidential intolerance and stridence.

30   To explain this disconcerting public performance, there have been varying, if not satisfying, theories over the years. Probably this President, through 20 years of American politics, has had no apologist so loyal and persuasive as Secretary of State William Rogers. And during the Eisenhower Presidency, I recall his explaining: "The trouble with Dick— and I keep telling him this—is not just that he sees both sides to every question, like a good lawyer. The trouble is that he appears in public— without meaning to—confessing that he does." It would be hard to make a more compassionate or subtle excuse for irresolution.

31   A more complex apologia was spoken in December, 1970, by Daniel Patrick Moynihan in his tribute to the President on leaving the White House to return to university life. He hailed the "profoundly important" leadership of Richard Nixon, while regretting that the President's "initial thrusts were rarely followed up with a sustained . . . second and third order of advocacy." Consequently, he said, "the impression was allowed to arise," with regard to White House proposals like the Family Assistance Plan, that "the President really wasn't behind them." The accolade—or exoneration—carried an odd echo: Mr. Moynihan on the Nixon Presidency sounded precisely like Mr. Phillips on the Nixon campaign. The most obvious question to follow was: Who "allowed" the "impression" of Presidential uninterest to "arise"? The more important question was: Did the candidate of 1968 who could not be himself now preside over an Administration in 1971 that could not know itself?

32   A search for any answer has to return to the official definition of his Presidency that Richard Nixon gave in the form of his State of the Union address in January. And here it may suffice to take a quick look at one of the message's central propositions, the reliance on local government.

33   The President's avowed faith in government removed as far as possible from Washington, and hence made "closest" to the people, both decreed and exalted Mr. Nixon's plan for Federal revenue-sharing. While the technical merits of the fiscal formula invited legitimate debate, the political fallacies of the inspiring doctrine, as stated, are flagrant enough to need but brief noting. There were three most pertinent: (1) The often clumsy centralization of powers and programs on the Federal level—far from proving the superior quality of local governments—has followed from a long history of the abdication or incompetence of government at lower-than-national levels. (2) By any comparison of national and local governments, it is the national authority that receives the more intense critical public scrutiny, while the Federal Government has also been for generations incomparably more dedicated to concern for individual freedoms and civil rights. (3) In all the American Federal structure, there are no regimes to match local governments in venality and corruption, nor political authorities with boundaries more archaic and absurd than the frontiers of most states. None of these facts, of course, is the least novel or obscure. The one remarkable fact is that few politicians in the nation are more wholly aware of them than President Nixon.

34   As for the President's proposal of nothing less than "a complete reform of the Federal Government itself," he here pointed to a path incredibly simple: "I propose that we reduce the present twelve Cabinet departments to eight." To be sure, a "complete reform" of the Federal establishment "to match our structure to our purposes," as Mr. Nixon urged, could refresh the whole nation's faith in its leadership. This kind of reform would have to deal with a number of grievous problems, perhaps most urgently with these: the reasonable restraint of Presidential caprice in foreign policy and military commitment, the freeing of the legislative branch from the shackles of seniority and filibuster and the restoration of the Cabinet to a level of effective responsibility.

35   The singular distinction of the President's call for reform was that it was "complete" in only one sense: it avoided totally the mention of any one of these issues. So doing, the oration called to mind the rhetoric of Warren Harding: "not heroism but healing, not nostrums, but normalcy . . ." And at that early date, the lasting meaning of such speech and thought was definitively described by William Gibbs McAdoo as "an army of pompous phrases moving over the landscape in search of an idea."

36   The Army that has moved longest and most painfully over the political landscape of the sixties has not been made of words, of course, but of men. Their terrain has been Indochina. Their search, equally unavailing, has been for a purpose whose attainment could possibly justify their presence and repay their sacrifice. And their grim pursuit has been proof that over nearly a decade the national leadership could learn, amend, repent, enlighten and progress as absurdly little in foreign policy as in national policy.

37   The political knack of the time—for confusing paralysis with progress—may be nowhere more obvious than here. In 1961, a serious sort of precedent was set by the naming of a special Presidential adviser to reside, with ample staff and authority, in the White House as the Chief Executive's immediate and personal counselor on foreign policy. He was a man of talent, intelligence and persuasiveness. He came from a distinguished academic background—Harvard University. Sincerely and strongly, he believed that his own confidence and skill could impose a new kind of order on the often haphazard ways of American diplomacy. On the immediate Washington scene, he impressed diplomats and journalists alike with his articulate renderings of current events; there was almost nothing done or said by the Administration for which he could not offer an intriguing explanation or a beguiling excuse. As for the global scene, he felt no timidity about the deployment of American power in any arena where it might bring the enhancement of American prestige. As for the specific arena of Southeast Asia, he believed firmly in the necessity for American intervention, the vulnerability of Communist forces and the reality of a democratic future. In 1961, the name of this Presidential assistant to John Kennedy was, of course, McGeorge Bundy. In 1971, this Presidential assistant, now serving Richard Nixon, had become Henry Kissinger. Aside from this change of name, all had stayed constant: the same teacher from the same campus was in the same office applying the same doctrine, dedicating it to the same ends and defending it with the same arguments.

38   A study of the intellectual and political odyssey of Henry Kissinger through the sixties may make the general incongruity more vivid. During the whole decade, as well as in earlier years, Dr. Kissinger's principal employer in politics was Governor Rockefeller, who has always summed up his foreign policy views toward Communism generally and Vietnam particularly with a candor rare for the times: "I'm simply a hardliner." It was Dr. Kissinger who consistently inspired and frequently authored the Governor's public speeches in this vein—including those pronouncements during the 1964 Republican primaries arguing flatly that there could be no substitute for victory over the Vietcong. During the same years, however, the professor from Harvard quite often joined the White House councils of President Kennedy. Under the Johnson Administration, he did even more, undertaking official missions both to Vietnam and Europe and reporting all intelligence gleaned to Washington's policy-makers. It was in these years, too, that he somehow persuaded such Democratic critics of official policy as Averell Harriman that, in the former New York Governor's words, "Henry was as much a dove as I."

39   With the approach of the 1968 campaign, the threads of Dr. Kissinger's beliefs and associations ramified considerably as the political scene became more tangled. On his return to Cambridge from his official missions abroad, he sought out those academic colleagues known for their closeness to Senator Robert Kennedy, generously briefing them for the Senator's benefit; as one of them has later recalled, "he gave at least the clear impression of believing Bobby the best qualified candidate for the Presidency." Meanwhile, he continued regularly to counsel Nelson Rockefeller not only on world affairs but also on national politics urging his candidacy with special insistence on the grounds that the New York Governor quite possibly was "the only leader who could, in the final analysis, keep a lightweight like Bobby Kennedy out of the White House." When the Governor's campaign was carried to the Republican convention in Miami, Dr. Kissinger, vigorously representing Rockefeller's foreign policy views before the appropriate platform committee, voiced only scorn for those put forth in the name of Richard Nixon. Indeed, he had long since distinguished himself among all Rockefeller advisers as the one most pithy and scathing in his personal contempt for the Republican nominee. In one nicely concise and relatively temperate comment on Mr. Nixon's nomination, he observed: "The man is, of course, a disaster. Now the Republican Party is a disaster. Fortunately, he can't be elected—or the whole country would be a disaster area." And the question may fairly be asked: could so idiosyncratic an itinerary through the politics of the sixties come to any logical end except in the White House as the chief architect of Richard Nixon's world strategy?

40   As with Washington strategists in war and peace, so, too, with a great many of the capital's pundits and prophets; the accompanying rhythms of their commentaries have tended to change as imperceptibly as policies have changed. The case of the Alsop brothers, the veteran columnists Joseph and Stewart, may suffice to illustrate. In the Camelot of the Kennedys at the start of the sixties, no clairvoyant in the realm enjoyed greater favor with the President and Mr. Bundy than Joseph Alsop; in the Middletown of Richard Nixon, the same official favor has touched both brothers, who respond with equal appreciation of the policies of the President and Dr. Kissinger. Along the way, the journalistic accents and fortunes of the two brothers have varied slightly, of course. By the middle of the Johnson Presidency, the armies of North Vietnam had so inconsiderately refused to panic before Joseph Alsop's repeated threats of imminent American triumph—and even the American armies had so often disobeyed his military theories—that threats and theories alike became something of a journalistic jest. By the middle of the Nixon Presidency, however, the slack was taken up by the rather newly militant writings of Stewart Alsop. Few if any Washington correspondents have been led by Dr. Kissinger more frequently or more gladly into that room in the West Wing of the White House on whose door those less favored have fancied seeing the stern sign: KEEP OUT—ADMISSION ONLY TO THE ABSOLUTELY ANONYMOUS AUTHORITATIVE SOURCE AND HIS STUDENTS.

41   From that room few men emerge unaffected. The recent commentaries on Indochina by Mr. Alsop so attest. These have included apologies for Administration policy in terms of analogies often almost breathtakingly inappropriate. One of these recently challenged the "selectivity" of Democratic critics who deplored "the horrors of war" in Vietnam as "obscene" while failing to find anything "obscene" in the air force of Israel, which had "used their American planes" to inflict thousands of Egyptian casualties before the cease-fire in the Middle East. If a theoretical analogy itself can be called "obscene," this last would qualify. Precisely by its decrying "selectivity," of course, it argued that the "horrors" of war may not be variously judged in terms of the purposes of a people or the policies of a nation; a corpse is a corpse is a corpse; and all causes for which men suffer death, therefore, must really be pretty much the same, obscene or clean.

42   There follows from this a fairly critical point about the intellectual life of Washington. If the author of these improbable analogies were an innocent in journalism or a lackey of Government, the gist of them would never be worth noting. Instead, of course, he is an experienced and respected commentator as well as a perceptive and compassionate man. So the hidden commentary in such writings must apply to the atmospheric hazards of uninterrupted life in this political factory town whose one industry is Government. As in almost all such towns, the thickest gases causing the densest pollution generally belch out from the tallest official chimneys. And there are nearly none who can avoid inhaling some of them.

43   Into this political air, the exponents of the Nixon–Kissinger Asian strategy tried, over at least the last year, to float a half-new kind of quasi rationale for the continuing military semipresence in Vietnam. An explanation specially calculated to impress moderately liberal observers, it has been soothingly confided by the White House's Absolutely Anonymous Authority in roughly these terms: *"You* know and *I* know that the President wants to withdraw from Vietnam as fast as he can. How fast should this be? It is a pace that must not provoke a wild outcry from the radical right—all the professional patriots bewailing another sellout to Communism and yelling the gospel of neo-isolation. Who would want to plunge the nation into that kind of crypto-Fascist mood? So (don't you see?) he must move in your direction—but *slowly."*

44   To some skeptics, this sort of talk might dismayingly insinuate that just as President Lyndon Johnson thought he might sneak into Vietnam without potential critics quite noticing at all, President Richard Nixon imagines he can sneak out.

45   Moreover, this strategy by subterfuge raises a couple of harsh questions. Beneath the surface of its assurances, does there not appear an almost terrible crudity in the contention that a lower American death rate in Vietnam, for an indefinite while, is a sacrifice well worth making to deceive and to assuage America's radical right? Does not this official doctrine deliver over American soldiers to be held not as captives in Communist jails but as hostages in the hands of American fanatics? Does this not come close to putting national policy into the stinging language of Mylai, where killing amounts only to prudent "wasting" and a few more casualties add up to "no big deal"? Finally, by what imaginable irony could Richard Nixon, whose entire political life has rung with his cries against all "appeasement" of national enemies abroad, let himself be committed, at such cost, to appeasement of potential enemies at home?

46   A larger mystery still—and a kind of distillate of all the politics of evasion of the sixties—has been described by the full trajectory of Richard Nixon's views on Vietnam. These stayed clear and predictable through the middle years of the decade, with Mr. Nixon frequently visiting Vietnam and calling for a faster and larger American military buildup. On one trip to Saigon, he urged an expeditionary force of more than 500,000 men with an insistence plainly implying that such action, promptly taken, promised victory. By 1968, the Nixon formula suddenly became much less explicit. He still hailed the conflict as nothing less than "a cause fundamental to man's hope," and he deplored the "gradualism" that had kept American military involvement too slow and small. But he hastened on from these generalities, with not much explanation, to his pledge to "end" the war "quickly" and also "win the peace." Shortly thereafter, he declared for himself a "moratorium" suspending all discussion of Vietnam—a dispensation scarcely ever interrupted through primary and campaign. Thus, by 1969, he could be said to have traveled all the way to the White House in a political sort of sealed train, silently waving to the nation's crowds from behind debate-proof glass. Once installed as President, he proceeded with reasonable dispatch to press forward programs called deescalation and Vietnamization, so that two years later he had brought American strength in Vietnam down to the level that five years earlier he had denounced as woefully inadequate to fight "a cause" so "fundamental."

47   What is striking in this political performance is no mere question of the candidate's or the President's consistency or sincerity; with some reason, it may be assumed that he felt equally sincere at all times. What is remarkable is that—faithfully following his own military and political maps through the years—he was able, in effect, to point to the strategic mountain, urge its swift scaling, storm to its summit and march straight down its farther side without breaking stride and without feeling at all pressed to account for any possible change of mind about the merit of the whole costly climb. In substance and in speech alike, he thus successfully managed to record the most elaborate and elusive *non sequitur* in modern American foreign policy.

48   A politician capable of executing such a tour de force might be forgiven the presumption behind the President's second report to Congress on "the State of the World." The report's 65,000 words on "Building for Peace" scarcely bothered to pretend to add anything noticeable to general sum of American knowledge. Inevitably, the President's words congratulated his Administration for designing "a new foreign policy for a new era." The rhetoric about Vietnam, however, was cautious if not slightly nervous. He acknowledged "little progress toward a negotiated peace"; he foresaw "some hard choices" ahead on the battlefield, and he qualified all the hopes of "Vietnamization" by stating that the program "cannot, except over a long period, end the war altogether." Distinctly vague about the future of Laos and Cambodia, he merely remarked that "we believe that the two Governments can survive"—an affirmation that stayed as far as possible from the central question of any American action possibly necessary if such faith proved in error. In short, all the 65,000 words expounding "the new foreign policy" were unblemished by a single proposition that might not have been written some 15 years previously by the author of SEATO, John Foster Dulles.

49   A kind of postscript from Henry Kissinger proved a bit more revealing of official thought. In a televised interview, he observed that "all the tough decisions" by any President are "very close . . . on the basis of maybe a 55–45 balance." But he went on to assert: "Once you've made the decision, you are committed to it or you are stuck with it 100 per cent." This conveys a notion of foreign policy that would surely have stunned such figures in Western history as Metternich, much admired by Dr. Kissinger, or de Gaulle, much respected by Mr. Nixon. If the French leader had been inhibited by so binding a rule of international life, the French tragedy in Algeria would even now be lasting as long as the American tragedy in Indochina. If the Soviet leaders since World War II had been inspired by such an understanding of "commitment," they long since would have been reigning in Iran, occupying West Berlin and stockpiling nuclear missiles in Cuba.

50   Yet the phrase itself sticks. For the nation indeed has stayed "stuck with" a long and venerable array of myths and shibboleths, taboos and fantasies—snarling national purpose and wrenching national policy. Of all such myths, perhaps none guarantees larger grief than the lethal legend that America—alone of all great powers in all ages—has been destined never to know a defeat or yield an arena, commit a great blunder or confess a great wrong. And the propagating of legends of this spirit must be as wicked as the teaching of a son by his father that the sublime mark of manhood is never to cry.

51   We have had occasions during the sixties to learn anew that instant history can be a snare and prophetic history a fraud; but it is hard to resist the reckless guess that some future study of the collective leadership of the Nixon Presidency must appear under the title of "Profiles in Complacence." As its principal figures have beheld each other and their works, in any case, they have seemed almost to flush with pleasure. It has been thus whenever Attorney General Mitchell has publicly appraised Richard Nixon. "He was programed and made to be President," Mr. Mitchell recently exulted on national television. "Since he has been in office, he has always kept his cool. I've never really seen him angry at anything." This is the kind of official self-congratulation that can be almost embarrassingly self-revealing. The technology of the times supposedly serves to "program" computers and machines, not candidates or Presidents; and there have

been few popular doubts more haunting to Richard Nixon over the years
than the fear (reasonable or wrong) that he was altogether too much of a
computer, a human calculating machine able to do no more than add
ballots and divide opponents. As for a "cool" lack of "anger," this was, of
course, precisely what chilled millions of citizens when they beheld a
White House wholly incapable of indignation over such outrages in 1970
as the National Guard killings at Kent State or a South Carolina white
mob's assault on school buses filled with black children. In all the litany
of human qualities ever cited as desirable for Presidential leadership, I
know of no longing for a want of passion.

52   The Richard Nixon who grew to power through this age—so fittingly
to preside, at last, over its politics—has excited almost endless analysis
and even psychoanalysis. I distrust such studies, hostile or amiable; it is
hard enough to know one's friend or neighbor, much less one's President.
Usually, it is also challenging enough to dissect a President's nostrums
without pretending to diagnose his neuroses. And this said, there may be
perhaps only two paradoxes about this 37th President worth noting for
some wiser future weighing.

53   The first is a matter central to his whole political career. Of the
hundreds who have closely watched or worked with him for much more
than a decade, there possibly is not one who has not described him as a
"lonely" man. Also, there probably is none in the same ranks who would
not name as his decisive political patron President Eisenhower. And thus
do the masks and cosmetics of national politics sometimes, almost un-
believably, deceive. The fact is that no one in public life may have done
more to seal Richard Nixon's sense of personal isolation than Dwight
Eisenhower. For the General–President acted as a political father to his
official successor with roughly the enthusiasm that most men show in
situations of wholly unplanned paternity.

54   The record here, though not public, has been unmistakable to those
knowing both men through the years. In 1952 the tension and alienation
began with Eisenhower exasperating Nixon by his slow acceptance of
Nixon's televised account of his controversial political fund. In 1956, the
President was trying to nudge the Vice President off the Republican ticket,
solicitously urging him to acquire "administrative experience" in some
such office as Secretary of Defense, while explaining more softly to others
that "Dick's just not Presidential timber." In 1960, the retiring Republican
President earned the silent rage of the future Republican President by his
casual confession at a Washington news conference that he would need
some time to remember a substantial contribution by Richard Nixon to
any major national decision of the Eisenhower Administration. In the

ensuing Presidential campaign, Nixon clearly resolved to stand stoically alone, beyond the embracing shadow of Eisenhower. Quite possibly, this determination more than all else assured his defeat. A fortnight before the election, Eisenhower, offended by the candidate's failure to plead for all possible help, responded to one Republican leader with the icy lament: "He just seems like a loser to me. I look at those slumping shoulders and those drooping eyes, and I can tell you he'd never get a promotion in any army of mine."

55   Such an experience in high politics could drive almost any man into a sort of steely privacy. For this particular man, the refuge has been a room full of yellow legal pads and gray political possibilities, a place where he may follow his own thoughts, hide his own hurts, draft his own speeches, frame his own decisions and imagine his own mandates. In personal terms, all of this adds up to something easily understandable. In political terms, however, it amounts to a sum of qualities that totals not so much a President as a man in the Presidency. By force of this distinction, the great role itself becomes not "I" but "mine."

56   And this points straight to the other major paradox probably worth pondering by future historians: the abiding nature—the ruling temper— of the Nixon Presidency. Its sovereign spirit appears to be one that neither wholly feels, wholly enjoys nor wholly understands sovereignty itself. A distinguished Washington journalist who has closely watched the life of the White House through all the sixties recently depicted this spirit thus:

> We all have seen for years the inner tensions and the outer contradictions of this man—the professional politician and the emotional hermit, the reasoning lawyer in private who becomes the inflaming orator in public. Again and again, we have seen his startling swings from reticence to militance and from near-statesmanship to super-partisanship. Now, the result is the kind of Government that de Gaulle ascribed to the French Fourth Republic—the sort of leadership that is "perpetually oscillating between melodrama and mediocrity." Why should it be so? It was no idle sneer when Lyndon Johnson called Richard Nixon "a chronic campaigner." This is the serious truth. The longing of his political life has really not been to govern but to campaign. The "lift" of his "driving dream" has been to win, not to lead. But having won, he finds that the very meaning of victory—the Presidency itself—eludes him. And the race that meant everything is now, alas, over.

57   This may not be exactly so, but it must strike exceedingly close to the political truth, for it describes a Presidency true to its times. Such a Presidency does more than capture—it almost celebrates—the political age, all the reaction on the right preached purely for the pleasure of its preachers, all the insurrection on the left never shying from the fight and never looking toward the future. As citizens of one temper came to practice national violence as an end in itself, there could be no more fitting response from citizens of a different mind than enjoyment of a national campaign as an end in itself. And what sort of sovereignty could finally crown all politics of the time so rightly as a Government not eager to govern and a leadership not ready to lead?

58   All this cannot, I fully believe, long serve or suffice. It cannot suffice for the Presidency. And it cannot serve the people.

59   The first American President was a man of immense common sense and quite uncommon insight but not much famed for concise aphorisms. Yet he wrote one rarely remembered sentence stating a law of popular leadership with a precision that has never been surpassed. "The truth is," Washington said, "the people must *feel* before they will *see*." The simple statement measures the problem of his 36th successor: how can the sight of the people be clarified—their support aroused and their energies enlisted—by a leadership that itself feels nothing in particular?

60   As for the related problem before the people . . .

61   "Probe the earth and see where your main roots run." The advice of Thoreau for a man is just as sound for a nation.

62   The political roots in question run far beneath the surface of all the politics of facile maneuver and easy answer. They mark values, not evasions. They trace firm beginnings, not fancied endings. And the purpose of their searching out is to learn, not to hide.

63   This is the kind of hard labor that any avowedly and seriously free people has to do for itself. It cannot be vicariously performed by politicians, professors, self-appointed prophets or even nationally elected Presidents. A people that does not too much mind being fooled some of the time will get, and perhaps deserve, a longer and falser charade than it ever imagined.

64   The heart of the matter has nothing to do, in short, with New politics or New economics or New diplomacy. It has only to do with concerns and convictions very, very old. It is, ultimately, a matter of whether any people or any nation can be self-governing unless it is also self-perceiving. It is a matter, quite simply, of whether a people wants to know itself badly enough to find itself and go on to be itself.

65   The roots are there.

Questions for Criticism and Discussion

1 Apply the methodologies of the three systems of criticism to this discourse. What elements of the discourse does each highlight? What does the application of the three systems reveal about the complexity of this essay?

2 This discourse relies heavily upon stylistic elements in achieving its effects. However, it also presents evidence and careful reasoning. On what grounds could you defend a critique that placed major emphasis on one or the other of these dimensions?

3 This essay contains a strong ethical indictment of the politics, the rhetoric, and the criticism that have characterized the decade of the sixties. Taking the author on his own terms, review the various approaches to the ethical criterion discussed in chapter 3 and apply them to this discourse.

4 Discuss how this essay influences your attitude toward the Nixon address and the critique of it found in chapter 4. In what ways is Hughes' essay a rhetorical criticism?

5 Compare and contrast Northrop Frye's concept of "bastard speech" as the "voice of the ego" used in the critique of the Agnew addresses in chapter 6 with Hughes' discussion of the politics of masturbation. Discuss these concepts in relation to confrontative rhetoric and consider the circumstances under which they might be used to indict such rhetoric.

6 Read Richard Nixon's 1971 State of the Union address and develop a more detailed critique of it along the lines suggested by Hughes.

7 In light of the concepts of credibility, *ethos*, and the *persona*, discuss how this essay serves to create an identity for the author. Does this rhetorical act meet the criteria for the preservation of "selfhood" developed by Thomas Olbricht (see chapter 1)?

8 Hughes uses the rhetoric of the sixties as an index of the quality of the politics of the decade. In what sense is this a dramatistic approach to criticism? Defend or reject the thesis that Hughes uses the dramatistic system of criticism. Consider the nature of the criteria used for evaluation, the rhetorical techniques by which the essay develops, and the qualities of feeling, passion, and self-perception to which the author appeals.

9 As "a plague on both your houses" statement, is this discourse weakened or strengthened? Is the condemnation too inclusive, the satire too biting to be effective? In the conclusion when Hughes addresses the general public, is there a sense in which he ends in confrontation? Accusation? Insistence on the assumption of responsibility?

For Further Reading

Lewis Chester, Godfrey Hodgson, and Bruce Page, *An American Melodrama: The Presidential Campaign of 1968* (New York: The Viking Press, 1969).

Joe McGinniss, *The Selling of the President 1968* (New York: Trident Press, 1969).

Hans J. Morgenthau, *Truth and Power: Essays of a Decade, 1960–1970* (New York: Frederick A. Praeger, 1970).

Peter Schrag, *Out of Place in America: Essays for the End of an Age* (New York: Random House, 1971).

Neil Sheehan, Hedrick Smith, E. W. Kenworthy, and Fox Butterfield, *The Pentagon Papers* as published by the *New York Times* (New York: Bantam Books, 1971).

Theodore H. White, *The Making of the President 1960* (New York: Atheneum Publishers, 1961).

Theodore H. White, *The Making of the President 1964* (New York: Atheneum Publishers, 1965).

Theodore H. White, *The Making of the President 1968* (New York: Atheneum Publishers, 1969).

Index